FROM RAILWAY TO FREEWAY

Exemplifying the style and grace of California's motor stage manufacturing in the 1920s, this El Dorado poses for a builder's photo. This Motor Transit Co. product was typical of the side-door stages of that bygone era. *California Historical Society*

INTERURBANS SPECIAL 90

FROM RAILWAY TO FREEWAY

Pacific Electric and the Motor Coach

by Eli Bail

INTERURBAN PRESS • GLENDALE, CALIFORNIA • 1984

FRONT COVER PAINTING

Artist Larry Fisher picked the one location in Southern California where the stage could be set to dramatize the evolution of public transportation from the electric railway to the freeway. It is the crossing of the Pacific Electric's Los Angeles–Long Beach rail line over the newly completed Long Beach Freeway, circa 1956. Metropolitan Coach Lines has taken over both rail and bus service, but the TDH-5103 coach still wears PE's silver-and-red livery. At the time, there was no motor coach freeway service on this particular stretch, but the artist has taken a bit of license and—who knows?—there might have been a non-revenue movement at this exact moment!

FRONT ENDSHEET

In the years just prior to World War II, Wilshire Blvd. was a less hectic thoroughfare. The big May Co. store at the corner of Fairfax Ave. is under construction, and the Los Angeles Motor Coach Co. offers service on both arteries. The double-decker on Wilshire is 726, a 1926 Fageol owned by co-parent Los Angeles Railway, and it is heading toward downtown Los Angeles. Crossing Wilshire southbound on Fairfax is 1931 Yellow Coach 3103, owned by LAMC's other parent, Pacific Electric. The year is 1939. In the mid-1980s the long-sought Wilshire Subway would make a curve here from Wilshire to Fairfax, with a planned station right under the still-existing May Co. store *Whittington Studio*

REAR ENDSHEET

The far-flung Pacific Electric system is shown on a 1949 map. Several major rail passenger lines were still operating, but the bulk of the system was served by buses. *Interurban Press*

FROM RAILWAY TO FREEWAY

Library of Congress Cataloguing in Publication Data

Bail, Eli, 1937—
From railway to freeway.

(Interurbans special ; 90)
Includes index.
1. Bus lines—California, Southern—History. I. Title. II. Series.
HE5633.C2B34 1984 388.3'22'097949 84-705
ISBN 0-916374-61-0

Published by Interurban Press
P. O. Box 6444 • Glendale, California 91205

FIRST PRINTING: Spring 1984

To Phyllis, Sam and Elise

CONTENTS

ACKNOWLEDGEMENTS

THIS VOLUME is the culmination of years of my own research; however, during that time it has benefited from contributions by many others. It therefore becomes very important at the outset to acknowledge their help. This book had its genesis in a series of articles which first appeared in *Motor Coach Age* magazine. The key factor in their creation was the guidance provided by MCA editor Albert Meier; without his patience, encouragement and incredibly fine maps, there could have been no book.

The writing of the magazine stories as well as this book, were spurred by the founder of Interurban Press—Ira Swett. His dedication to recording the history of the Pacific Electric, and other electric railways, was contagious and it was Ira's impetus that started the long hours of research and analysis which led to this volume. His recognition of the fact that PE's passengers rode on rubber tires as well as steel wheels, since early days, was heartening. It was amazing to find that he was equally fascinated with the history of PE's early competitor, the Motor Transit Company.

Relatively factual historical accounts are available for two of California's "big three" early passenger stage lines—Pickwick Stages and California Stages, but, reflected in later days only by the "Motor Transit Lines" legend on some Pacific Electric buses, Motor Transit's origins remained relatively obscure. The origins of Pacific Electric's own bus operations were similarly clouded. From a start as a misunderstood stepchild, PE's motor coach operations grew until they fell heir to the entire empire.

The story of Pacific Electric's bus operations originally appeared serially in *Motor Coach Age* magazine—the beginnings in the San Bernardino story (June 1974) and continuing more recently, Part 1 (1917–1936) in February 1978; Part 2 (1936–1942) July 1978; Part 3 (1942–1953) September 1978; and the concluding installment covering Metropolitan Coach lines in November 1978. Only the more important aspects of the story could be dealt with in the magazine articles and a significant amount of new material is presented here.

The primary pieces of the Motor Transit history also appeared previously in *Motor Coach Age*—Pickwick Stages (October 1972); Mountain Auto Line (June 1974); Motor Transit Co. (February 1975); and San Diego Part 1 (September 1975). In the wake of this coverage, new photographs and more information have come to light and new insights into the history of Motor Transit continued to emerge.

The history of Los Angeles Motor Coach, a partnership of PE and the Los Angeles Railway, was also previously published in *Motor Coach Age* (March 1976). The last piece, on Asbury Rapid Transit, a longtime competitor of PE and LARy, eventually acquired by Metropolitan Coach Lines, appeared in August–September 1980.

While preparing the original magazine articles, it became apparent that the histories had as many facets as the original sources. *Motor Coach Age* is a monthly publication of the Motor Bus Society and materials from the library and photograph collection of the Society were the genesis of this book. Particular thanks must be extended to John Hoschek, Librarian (and sometime President) of the Motor Bus Society, for diligently searching out this source material. Perusal of Regulatory Commission cases and decisions, company records from the collection of Interurbans as well as private sources, and interviews with former employees and observers of the transit scene all provided grist for the mill. Material from trade journals and house organs also provided a contemporary view. Assembling the information and placing it in perspective became a chore of some magnitude and, as new information became available, portions of the story once thought completed received new dimensions. It is hoped that the picture is now reasonably complete.

Besides opening the resources of the Interurbans collection, Ira contributed a basic part of this story through his recollections and his personal photographs. It is also important to acknowledge the help of those others who contributed to its content since their contribution of photographs and research materials as well as insights into key events, were invaluable. Without the support of those listed below, the record could not have been reconstructed:

Bob Ayer
Frank Barnes
Bob Burrowes
Jay Castillo
Al Copeland
Joe Corbin
Dave Garcia
Jim Gibson
the late Max Green
Andrew Harrison
Floyd Hayhurst
John Hoschek
Gary Korutz
the late Lazear Israel
Albert Meier
E. R. Mohr
Bill Moore
Delorez Nariman
Victor Plukas
Mac Sebree
Jerry Squier
the late Ira Swett
Tom Van Degrift
Ed Vandeventer
Jim Walker

ELI BAIL
ALMADEN VALLEY, CALIFORNIA

INTRODUCTION

The last effort made by Pacific Electric to upgrade its passenger rail service occurred in 1946, when a number of large passenger cars formerly operated on Southern Pacific San Francisco Bay area rail lines were refurbished for Southern Division passenger service out of Main Street Station. In that year car 317 was posed in the 7th Street surface yard alongside of White 2034. But the freeways were already on the drawing boards, and it would not take long for the torch to be passed from the 317 to the 2034 and a long line of rubber-tired successors. *Author's Collection*

THE HISTORY of urban bus transportation, today's most common form of public transit, spans only some 60-odd years. During this time, significant changes have been made in the travel habits of most city dwellers. First, horsecars and then the electric railways, played the dominant role in the urban transit picture. Not until the 1880s, when the tinkerers of the industrial belt turned their attention to the horseless carriage powered by the internal-combustion engine, did the country witness the first stirrings of an alternative to tracked transportation.

Both hobbyists and entrepreneurs quickly recognized the potential of adapting the internal combustion engine for commercial use. As early as 1905 gasoline engines propelled occasional limousines and touring cars carrying passengers and baggage between railroad stations and resorts and hotels.

Yet, only individuals with a certain pioneering spirit and inventiveness could expect to participate in the development of commercial motor vehicles from the yet to be proven automobile.

First, buses as such did not exist and wagon-makers recently turned truck-body builders had yet new demands placed upon them by pioneer bus entrepreneurs. They themselves had frequently entered the field via auto or truck dealerships. Parts, sometimes nearly impossible to secure from manufacturers, had to be forged by local blacksmiths. Unimproved roads rapidly chewed up tires, which were rarely interchangeable between vehicles of different makes and models, and tire recapping and rebuilding proved to be a major expense in operating commercial motor vehicles. Spurred by World War I, the industry prospered and came of age as standardization and familiarity made automotive engineering a less mysterious art.

While the word jitney brings to mind a Model T Ford careening down the road with passengers clinging to its side, the term was applied equally to full-sized and even double-deck buses. The common denominator was that the vehicles were owner-operated, unregulated and, at first, totally undisciplined. Urban short-haul lines were the first to be hurt, but within a few months after the start of the new craze in Los Angeles during 1914 it spread to other cities prompting Charles N. Black, vice-president of the United Railroads of San Francisco, to make the following observation:

> ". . . if the jitney-bus is a real advance in transportation service, existing street and interurban railways will have to be discarded, but unless it can perform all the functions of an electric car as efficiently and as economically, it will unquestionably fail."

What Black did not acknowledge was that serious bus operators would be hurt just as much by this unregulated competition. This problem was, however, recognized by Richard W. Meade, then president of the pioneer Fifth Avenue Coach Company, who reacted in the following manner:

> "The danger in the situation is that the [jitney] busmen, the city authorities and all others concerned, are apparently plunging ahead without giving much thought to the consequences. The surface cars in these cities are subject to rigid regulation on the part of the city and state commissions, they pay heavy sums into city and state treasuries in the way of taxes and license fees, and as responsible corporate bodies they can be held to account for their claims. . . ."

The wisdom of regulation was soon recognized and most cities passed "jitney ordinances" within a few years. Some municipalities, however, chose to promote this competition in answer to the railroad, utility and real estate interests which had so far monopolized local transportation.

Particularly in California, where population and commerce expanded more quickly than steel rails could follow, bus lines were extended to meet transportation needs. The high initial investment required to extend the rail lines stopped expansion of the interurban system by 1915 and the bus operators eagerly filled the gap.

In these early years, fares and schedules were determined casually by whatever the traffic would bear. State governments realized, however, that the traveling public would be better served if the free-wheeling aspect of the industry were regulated.

As a result, on May 1, 1917, California passed the Motor Carrier Act which declared that the Railroad Commission would regulate motor carriers in addition to the state's other utilities. While existing companies were granted "grandfather rights" to continue operation, the first function of the Railroad Commission seemed to many bus operators to be to protect the competitive posture of the Southern Pacific Railroad and its subsidiaries. Although rail interests vigorously opposed applications for new or extended bus service after 1917, the motor stage business grew rapidly and the men and machines that constituted its most important ingredients worked hard to keep pace.

Against this counterpoint were played the roles of the Pacific Electric Railway and its competitors. The game was always interesting despite the fact that the strategy sometimes left little to the imagination. The winner was not always evident but at times the traveling public was clearly the loser. The Railroad (later Public Utilities) Commission slowly increased the span and depth of its control until the depression of the 1920s when its reins started to loosen. The Commission, as arbiter, tried to assure that the rules of the game were followed, but in fact it occasionally played a joker of its own, causing some interesting events to occur. As the story unfolds, it will become clear that decisions were driven by economics rather than emotions, but it is left for the reader to decide which factors most influenced the end result.

CHAPTER ONE

PACIFIC ELECTRIC • 1917-1930

Jitneys and feeder lines; the great experiment

An idea of the appeal that Southern California had for so many in the 1920s may be had from this view in Westwood. Faced with the requirement of having to operate a different sort of service, the Pacific Electric Railway turned to a different type of bus for its Castellamare line. This so-called "boulevard" route, operated at a premium fare, rated deluxe equipment—in this case, the low-headroom Yellow Coach Type Y parlor bus. One is seen here on a palm-lined stretch of Beverly (later Sunset) Blvd. headed for the Pacific shore. *SCRTD Collection*

THE PACIFIC ELECTRIC RAILWAY was formed in 1901 and was reorganized in 1911 as a subsidiary of the Southern Pacific to merge four electric interurban railroads in the Los Angeles area and to formally separate these from the purely local streetcar lines within Los Angeles, which were operated by the Los Angeles Railway. PE's rail lines were grouped into four operating districts: *Western* to Hollywood, the San Fernando Valley and the beaches; *Southern,* to Long Beach, San Pedro, Newport Beach and Santa Ana; *Northern,* to Pasadena, the San Gabriel Valley and San Bernardino; and *Eastern,* comprising local lines in San Bernardino, Redlands and Riverside.

When unregulated jitney buses appeared in Los Angeles in July 1914, they took more passengers from LARy local lines than from PE. An independent attempt to offer double-deck bus service on a route that was directly competitive with PE's busy Venice Short Line was unsuccessful. By 1916, however, it was estimated that the railway was losing at least $30,000 a month to independent bus competition, particularly in Pasadena, Long Beach and Santa Monica. Efforts to persuade city governments to institute regulatory measures were foiled by the popularity of the independent buses, but after a few years of sometimes unreliable jitney service, some cities were ready for a more stable bus service, and PE was ready to offer it.

PE did not hesitate to experiment with the introduction of trial bus services when it appeared that they might provide increased patronage for the interurban rail system or protect it from independent competition. When such services did not provide the anticipated return, they were dropped. During the first 10 years of its bus operation, PE started more than 50 bus lines and discontinued more than

Frank Fageol, an innovative automobile builder, constructed 17 tractor-trailer sightseeing vehicles for the Panama-Pacific Exposition of 1915. Obviously impressed with the performance of these novel conveyances, the Southern Pacific ordered four similar units for its subsidiaries: Pacific Electric, Fresno Traction and the Peninsular Railway. The first unit was built in 1916 and was followed by three more during the next year. The first so-called "flexible bus" used a Case automobile as the tractor and on the radiator, the new company's name—for ease of pronunciation—was spelled "Fadgl." The passenger semi-trailer reportedly was built by PE in its Torrance Shops. Here is the Peninsular unit going through its road testing just prior to its delivery to San Jose. *SCRTD Collection*

20 of them. While some, it is true, were intended as only short-term services because of track renewal programs or other emergencies, most were genuine attempts to establish permanent routes. In this regard, PE took every advantage of the flexibility of bus operation.

Expansion of feeder bus service was one of Pacific Electric's main activities during the 1920s, when the population of Southern California was undergoing a rapid increase. Incorporation of bus lines into existing tariffs gave an advantage which independent operators could not match, because transfers to car lines were permitted. At the same time the interurban rail network was being improved through the purchase of 210 new cars and construction of the downtown Los Angeles subway terminal.

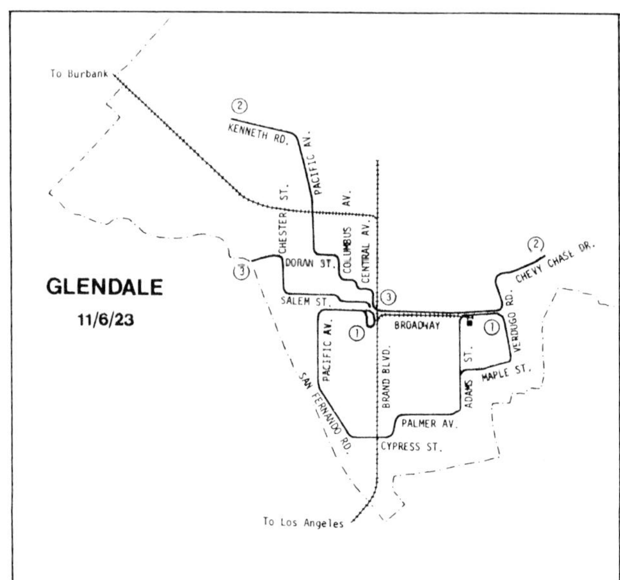

This was the Glendale feeder bus system in 1923. Route 1 dated to December 7, 1921, and routes 2 and 3 were added on November 6, 1923. The Pacific Electric rail line from Los Angeles is shown running up Brand Blvd. with branches east on Broadway and west to Burbank. *A. E. Meier*

Unfortunately the anticipated growth of rail passenger traffic never came about, owing to the low density of residential development and the early swing to automobile travel.

San Bernardino and Redlands. The first PE venture in motor bus transportation began in 1917, when the 6.6-mile Highland Transportation Line of H.H. Eastwood was purchased to supplement a local car line between San Bernardino, Highland and Patton. The two lines followed different routes, which were, in some places, nearly a mile apart. Interchangeable tickets were sold on a mileage basis. The first bus used was a PE-designed tractor-trailer similar to those delivered to the Fresno Traction Co. and the Peninsular Railway, also SP properties. The Fageol unit was powered by a Case automobile engine. Later three Reos were used to operate a two-hour average headway. By 1926, the bus line was carrying three times the load of the car line.

The next bus line was in Redlands, 10 miles east of San Bernardino, where a route was started on September 1, 1921, to supplement the local trolley lines. The line served a part of town which included the University of Redlands and which had been without any local transportation; its operation eliminated the necessity of building a mile of new track. Initial service over the 1.7-mile line was run every 30 minutes using a Moreland bus. The fare was 10 cents, or seven rides for 50 cents, with free transfers between streetcars and buses. In its first six months the bus line carried an average 7,850 passengers per month.

Because a California state corporation tax of 5 ¼ percent was levied on the gross income of all railroads, Pacific Electric placed its new bus lines under the banner of the subsidiary Pacific Electric Land Co. In this manner PE could continue to compete with independent bus operators on an equivalent financial basis.

Glendale. Two Reo Speed Wagons started feeder service over a 3 ½-mile route in Glendale on December 7, 1921, when that city just to the north of Los Angeles had a popu-

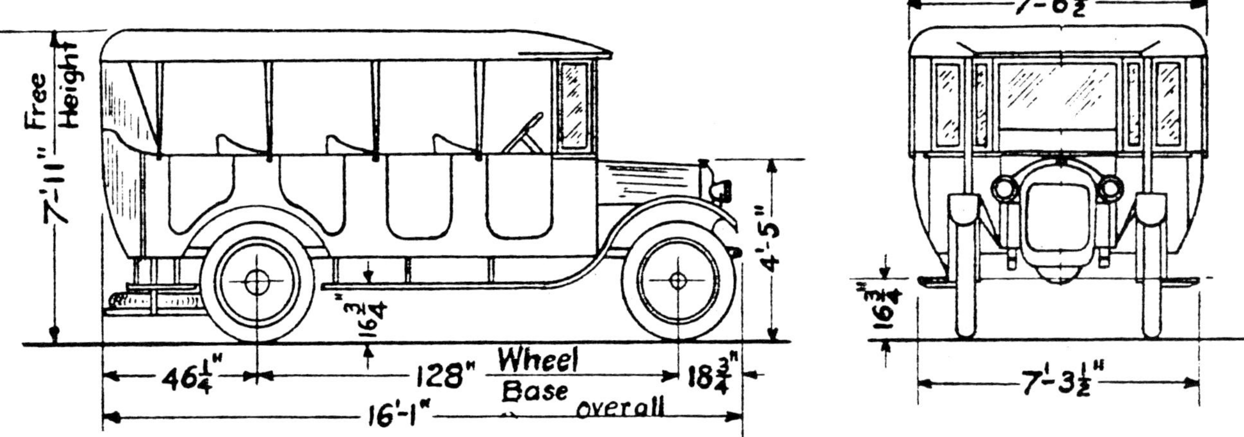

Pacific Electric's early buses reflected the range of its operations—from open tourers used on the remote Eastern District lines to small closed buses for the urban feeder and shuttle routes. These surviving diagrams show examples of both types of equipment constructed on Reo Speed Wagon chassis of the early 1920s. Note that bumpers were still an item for the future. Developed for use in a light truck, early builders found the Speed Wagon chassis with its 4-cylinder L-head engine ideal for small buses. When demand shifted to larger, more sophisticated vehicles, the underpowered Reo was left behind. The closed Pacific Motor Bodies design of coaches 16 and 17 (below) was also used in a smaller version on Los Angeles Railway Reos.

Interurban Press

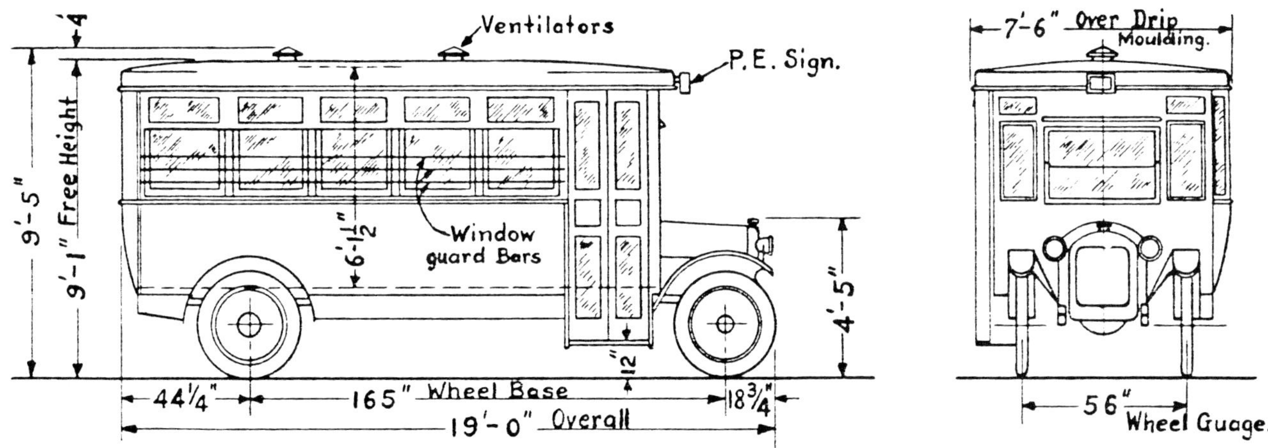

lation of about 20,000. The bus line connected two outlying sections with the interurban line to Los Angeles at Brand Blvd. and Cypress. Thirty-minute service was provided at a 6-cent fare. Five months after the line was started it was carrying 9,650 passengers per month, and it was soon extended at both ends.

Two more Glendale local lines were started on November 6, 1923. Glendale bus service now totaled 10½ route miles, and all lines were routed through the center of the business district at Broadway and Brand. When not in use, buses shared a storage yard at Broadway and Chevy Chase Drive with interurban cars. By 1927, further extensions had increased route mileage to 15½, and the base equipment consisted of seven Whites. Growing with a fast-growing city, the Glendale local operation was considered successsful and became a model for further efforts.

Santa Ana. PE's fourth feeder bus system was in Santa Ana, a city of 18,000 people located in Orange County, 35 miles southeast of Los Angeles. Here a 10-year franchise was purchased from the city for $1,000 in February 1922. Service was started on August 1 over three routes, each

The PE bought two Reo model F Speed Wagon chassis with 22-passenger Crown Motor Carriage Co. bodies to start its Glendale local service in 1921. Number 8 poses for this view resplendent in its livery of PE red with gold lettering and pin stripes. The hardwood-framed body was finished with sheet-metal side panels and had glass drop-sash windows, a feature not perpetuated on future bus orders. The interior features included imitation leather seats and electric dome lights, niceties that were included in later equipment purchases.

Crown Coach

Above: Posed at 6th and Los Angeles streets behind the Pacific Electric building, bus 19 was the model for 69 similar Whites placed in service during 1923. The destination sign suggests a plan for an Alhambra local line that never materialized. Early PE buses bore the logo of the Pacific Electric Land Co.—an artifice used to avoid a state tax on railroads and thus gain equality with other bus operators. *White*

Left: New Whites were used to start two new lines in Glendale during 1923. Bus 25 on Line 2 is inbound from Chevy Chase Drive on Broadway at Maryland Ave. in 1925. *Magna Collection*

with a 30-minute headway. A garage was opened, and the initial fleet consisted of Reos, Morelands and a White.

As in Glendale, the only previous local transportation in Santa Ana was provided by PE interurbans, a principal route from Los Angeles running through the city from west to east along 4th Street and less important lines operating north to Orange and south to Huntington Beach. Santa Ana service was never as well patronized as that of cities closer in.

Service was increased and fares lowered in October of 1926 in an attempt to increase patronage, but to no avail. The routes were cut back and rearranged in 1928 and by 1929, PE was ready to sell out or give up service entirely. After an abortive attempt to sell the lines to one R.F. Rountree, PE abandoned its Santa Ana local lines in September of 1929. The city would, however, be without transit service for only one day as will shortly be seen.

Alhambra. Established cities bordering Los Angeles and linked to its central business district by Pacific Electric rail lines were among the first to benefit from the wave of migration into Southern California that characterized the 1920s. To the east of Los Angeles is Alhambra, a city of 12,000 people when PE inaugurated three local bus lines on February 19, 1923. Each line was operated every half hour, and each connected an outlying district with interurban cars on Main Street. All buses ran along Main Street to the center of Alhambra's commercial activity at Garfield Avenue. A 6-cent fare was charged with free transfers offered between buses and cars within the city limits.

A north-south bus line along Garfield Avenue from South Pasadena through Alhambra to Monterey Park was started by PE in June 1923. The Alhambra–Monterey Park portion was acquired from Thurlo T. Davis, who had operated since 1921 as Alhambra Auto Taxi, and was combined with new rights between Alhambra and South Pasadena. The 4½-mile bus route provided connections with PE rail lines at four different places.

Pasadena. It took a municipal election to put PE into the bus business in Pasadena. In 1922 the railway was faced with $750,000 worth of track renewal expenses, independent buses paralleling the local car lines, and insufficient traffic to support both modes of transportation. The company was ready to expend the renewal funds in exchange for an exclusive franchise, but the city felt that the public would not stand for removal of the competing bus lines.

After protracted negotiations had yielded no solution, the city called an election on a bond issue to finance a municipal bus system. The Chamber of Commerce and one newspaper backed the bond issue, while the other leading newspaper and an independent association of businessmen backed PE's plan for a combined rail and bus system. The bond issue was defeated on December 5, 1922, by a narrow margin, and negotiations between the city and Pacific Electric were reopened.

As a result, PE ordered 81 White model 50 bus chassis on February 16, 1923—reported by the trade press to be the largest bus purchase yet made by any company. Much was made of the railway's plan to manufacture the bus bodies in its newly completed Torrance Shops. Apparently based on the design of sample bus 19, they strongly resembled buses being built locally by the Motor Transit Company in size and appearance. Remaining records indicate that only 62 bodies were built up at Torrance with the remainder having been produced elsewhere—perhaps by Motor Transit itself. The Torrance-built bodies were installed on later buses of the series and can be physically distinguished by their lack of a beltrail.

An aspect of this venture that was not well publicized

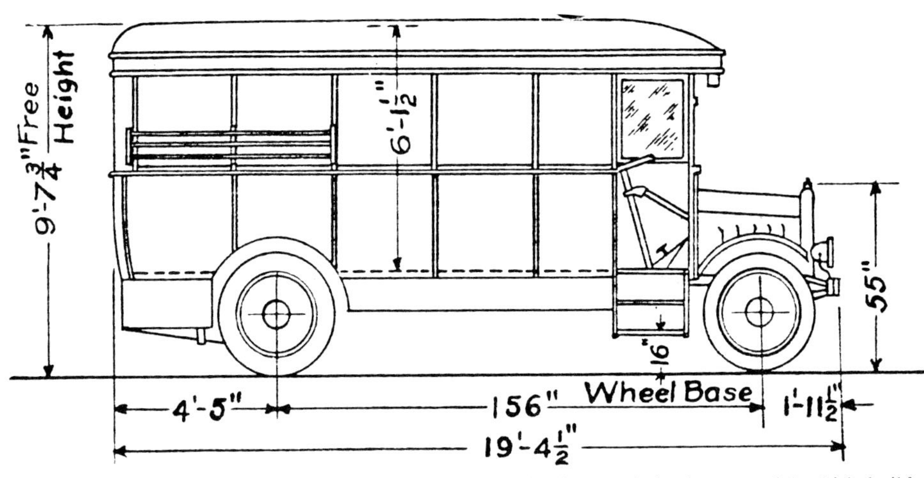

Some of PE's early bus equipment was provided by Moreland, an early local commercial vehicle builder. Burbank-built 1½ and 2-ton stock truck chassis powered by 4-cylinder Continental engines were the basis for these buses; they were used to expand service in Glendale and to start the feeder bus system in Santa Ana. An interesting feature of many California buses of this era was the identification light over the center of the windshield. It illuminated the initials of the operator and was usually of a distinctive color. In this case the "PE sign light" was green. Moreland buses like these (but larger) were a favorite of some of the stronger driver associations like the ARG Bus Company (Los Angeles–San Bernardino) and B&H Transportation (Long Beach) which competed with the PE in the early 1920s. *Interurban Press*

was that 12 of the Whites were assembled for the Los Angeles Railway (its 400 series) and two were sold to the Pacific Palisade Co. Whites from the fleets of both PE and LARy were used to help start the service of the jointly owned Los Angeles Motor Bus Co. in August 1923.

The first of the PE Whites went into service on the local lines in Glendale, Santa Ana and Alhambra, but 48 of them were assigned to the newly built Pasadena garage at Broadway (now Arroyo Parkway) and Bellevue. Five local car lines were discontinued, five independent bus lines were replaced, and the Pasadena local system as it was developed during the period May to July 1923 consisted of nine bus routes lettered A to I and four remaining car lines, through-routed as Lincoln–East Colorado and North Fair Oaks–North Lake.

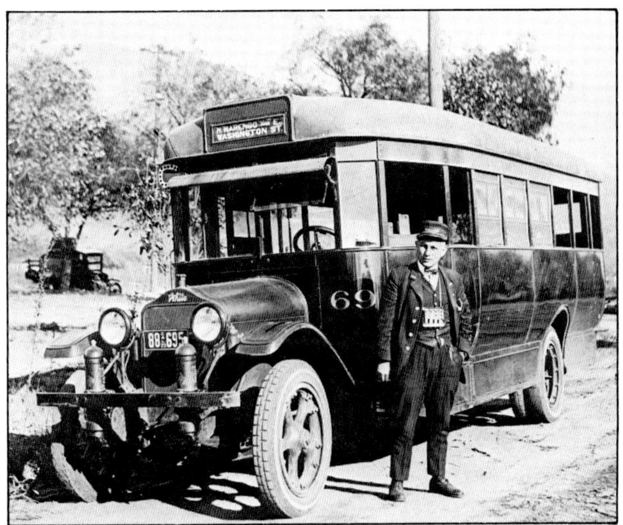

Operator and vehicle take a break at Tierra Alta Drive, the outer end of the East Washington line in Pasadena in 1923. Operation to this point, just outside the city limits, thrust PE into a jurisdictional controversy with the state Railroad Commission. *Security Pacific National Bank*

At least 11 buses were acquired from the independent operators at the time of the Pasadena takeover but they did not last very long in PE service (if they were used at all). The closed body from one of the Pasadena Reos was used to replace the open body of one of PE's own early Reos in 1924.

Not included in the Pasadena local system as it was formally designated was the Avenue 64 line. It connected the Annandale terminus of the Avenue 64 branch of the South Pasadena interurban with the western end of the Arroyo Seco local car line, soon replaced by the West California Street bus. In earlier years there had been a plan to extend the Avenue 64 car line across this short gap, but the cost of bridging the arroyo for relatively few passengers could not be justified. Another Pasadena line that was not considered to be part of the local system was the Flintridge route, a scenic eight-mile line leased in December 1923 from the Flintridge Motor Coach Co. The line had been started by a real estate developer and the terms of the lease were such that the promoter paid PE for any losses incurred by its operation.

Early Changes in Pasadena. The local fare in Pasadena at the outset of PE bus service was 6 cents, with 10 tickets sold for 50 cents. Transfers were free, allowing a single-fare ride anywhere within city limits. PE's capture of Pasadena cost $500,000, and it soon became apparent that the investment would not earn an adequate return. Operating results were not encouraging, as Pasadena had more transit lines and more service than it could support.

In June 1925, hearings were held in Pasadena on the company's request to increase local fares to 7 cents. During the hearings it was discovered that extension of the East Washington line to Tierra Alta, a short distance beyond the city limits, had made the entire Pasadena system subject to California Railroad Commission regulation, but that PE had never applied for a certificate. The commission held that it could not legally rule on the fare increase,

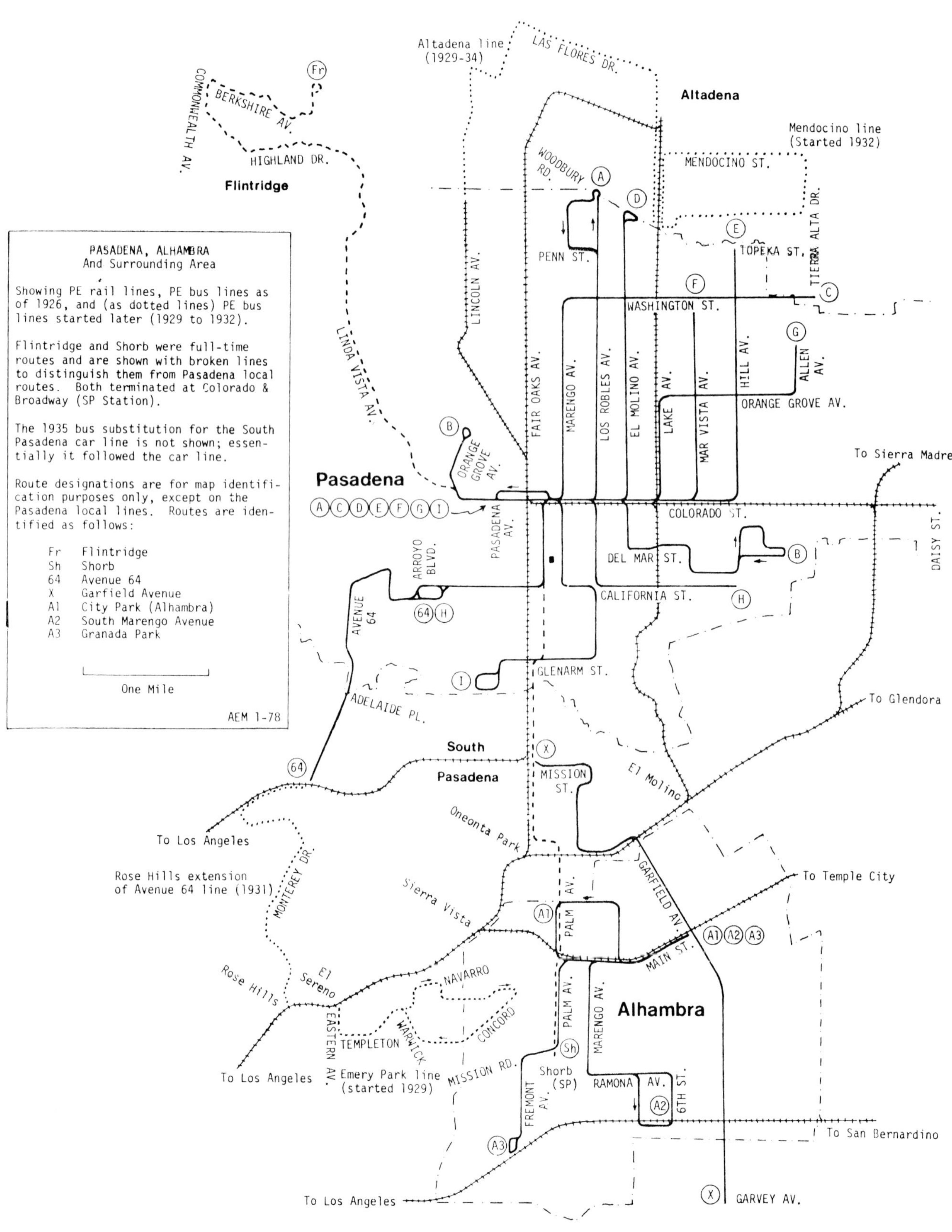

By 1926, Pacific Electric had a comprehensive network of local routes in Pasadena including two through-routed car lines and many bus lines.
A. E. Meier

Pasadena buses lined up and ready to go: by 1927, 58 buses were headquartered in Pasadena to serve the PE local lines as well as the feeder routes in the adjacent territory. The majority were 1923 Whites like these. *SCRTD Collection*

and the legitimacy of the whole system was called into question.

Despite objections from PE and counsel for the city, the Railroad Commission held firm, and on May 7, 1926, PE formally filed for a certificate of convenience and necessity. Hearings were held in June, and both the certificate and the fare increase were granted. No changes were made to the routes at that time, but one-zone fares went from 6 to 7 cents, two-zone fares from 10 to 12 cents and tickets from 10 to 8 for 50 cents.

By 1927, the Pasadena buses were carrying 530,000 passengers per year over 34 miles of route. On September 5 of that year, through routings were revised and service reapportioned; population had increased by 20,000 since PE buses had appeared in Pasadena. Fifty buses were in use at that time to serve the 11 purely local lines, and another eight were needed for other lines in the area.

Local Competition. There were two municipalities within PE's service area where its efforts to defeat local competition were not successful. These were the coastal cities of Long Beach and Santa Monica, and independent bus service operated in both cities until eventual municipal takeover. In Long Beach, jitneys were competing with PE's local streetcars by 1914. In December of that year, the Long Beach Transportation Co. was formed to operate two bus lines at a 5-cent fare, while PE's local fare was 6 cents. It was not until 1923 that the competition was restricted from duplicating the streetcar routes. By that time, two independent companies operated 77 buses, and their fare was still 5 cents.

In February 1924, PE offered to invest $1.5 million in the Long Beach local system, in return for a 35-year exclusive franchise covering a rearranged rail network and eight bus lines. As in Pasadena, PE buses would have replaced those of the independent operators as well as the weaker car lines. Nothing came of this proposal except a short-lived Redondo Avenue–Recreation Park bus line, which was given up on July 1. In 1927, Pacific Electric once again offered to operate a citywide transportation system in Long Beach. The new proposal was based on a 7-cent fare. Once again the independent competitors prevailed when Lang Motor Bus Co. was given a 30-month permit at a 6-cent fare.

Lang immediately made an offer to buy out the largest local operator, B&H Transportation Co. The partnership of Betts and Haskell, which also built its own buses, was the successor to Long Beach Transportation Co. A third operator of Long Beach local lines was the West Side Transit Co., which also ran an interurban bus line from Long Beach to Western and Manchester in Los Angeles. In 1930, Lang was awarded a 10-year franchise, effectively putting an end to any PE hope of gaining control of urban transit in Long Beach.

PE's problems in Santa Monica actually began in 1912 when the Los Angeles interurban fare was set at 2 cents higher than the fare to rival Long Beach. Thus began a long battle by the City of Santa Monica and its civic organizations to rectify the fare inequity. In 1914, the rate

Top: One of the first Whites assigned to the new Pasadena local lines, 27, carries the logo of the Pacific Electric Land Co. During this period the Land company was resurrected to operate the bus lines allowing PE to avoid paying the extra taxes then required on railway-owned buses. The disparity was soon equalized allowing the Land company to be dissolved and the buses returned to PE ownership.

Above: Fageol combo 217 performed train connection duties on the Pasadena-Shorb line from its inception in 1924 until it was replaced in 1940, surely a testimonial to the ruggedness of the Oakland-built products. This classic pose is at SP's Shorb station in Alhambra.

Right: PE's first Fageol Safety Coach is seen here in service on the Pico line. The loads did not last, particularly after Santa Monica started its Municipal Bus Line which provided a one-seat ride into the city. *Dave Garcia Collection*

What the PE Did to Your Bus Line

PACIFIC ELECTRIC won a clear-cut victory over one jitney operator with the demise of competing bus service over Venice Blvd. in December of 1924. The jitneys ran from Venice Circle to Motor Ave. in Culver City in direct competition with the rail-operated Venice Short Line. The service was operated by the Community- Merchants Bus Line organized by Ralph Carrasco, a well-known transportation entrepreneur in the beach cities. He also ran several local routes in the area which reached back into the hinterlands of Venice and his operation was commonly referred to as the "Backwoods Bus Line."

PE's complaints against Carrasco had little effect when Venice was an independent town, but its incorporation into the city of Los Angeles put the jitneys under the jurisdiction of the Bureau of Public Utilities and Transportation. Finding that the line was operating without benefit of any authority, the BPU&T upheld the PE complaint and shortly put an end to the trunk route of the Backwoods Bus Line. Carrasco continued his other routes for some years, finally selling out to Bay Cities Transit in 1930.

Reo Speed Wagons were commonly used by early jitney operators and the development of locally built bodies for these chassis is well illustrated by this series of 1924 photos.

Above right: A center-entrance body with perimeter seating, typical of those built by Porter-Brown in the early 1920s. They were of open wood construction with high steps, pantasote curtains and no doors.

Next we find a more sophisticated body complete with spare tire and turn signal, but still without windows. Both photos were snapped at Venice Circle; the bench and shelter provided for waiting passengers can be seen in the second photo.

The third view, snapped along Venice Blvd., shows a much more substantial machine, the body design no doubt influenced by the Birney Safety Car. Glass windows, ventilators and a drop step are significant advances in passenger amenities.

Finally, we see the jitney operators lament on public view in Venice. Five Reos and two smaller buses (on Ford Model TT chassis) stand idle to illustrate the end of jitney competition on Venice Blvd.
All: Dave Garcia Collection

This view of Pomona's City Transit 54 was retouched by Mack for publicity purposes. The vehicle consists of a standard 25-passenger Mack body on the classic Model AB "low bus" chassis, nearly 3,700 of which were delivered between 1924 and 1931. It was, perhaps, the longest production run and largest volume of any bus model and was used with minor variations from coast to coast.
California Historical Society

battle was carried to the Railroad Commission, but in June of that year, PE entered into another conflict as jitneys started running on Santa Monica Blvd. in competition with its interurbans. By October, the route had been extended along the beach to Venice and the jitneymen had banded together to form an association. PE won the rate battle but was never to recover from the jitney war.

Some 100 jitneys were running on the Venice–Santa Monica–Sawtelle route in 1915 and by the end of the year the jitney association bragged that it was carrying 90 percent of the local traffic. Well they might as PE President Paul Shoup wrote to the Chamber of Commerce decrying the decline in revenue despite PE's quarter-million-dollar investment, and threatening the abandonment of local streetcar service in the city. In August of 1921, the jitney association incorporated as Bay Cities Transit Co. with 18 vehicles and a strong will to survive.

In response to an offer of a citywide franchise in August of 1922, PE offered a combination of local trolley and bus lines at a 6-cent fare. Bay Cities offered a 5-cent fare but no improvement of its rundown equipment or the casual conduct of its employees. Neither proposal was accepted, and the city, after revising its requirements, again solicited bids at the end of the year. PE continued to lobby for a 6-cent fare which it considered minimal and hinted that the local car line on Third St. would be abandoned if it lost the franchise. BCT meanwhile wrestled with the new franchise requirements regarding the condition of equipment and the wearing of uniforms by drivers.

Bids were formally opened in February of 1923 and after another round of haggling in which the city fathers' dislike of PE and its 6-cent fare prevailed, the franchise was awarded to Bay Cities. It required five lines including the Santa Monica Blvd. and Wilshire Blvd. lines already being run by BCT. PE's rejection in Santa Monica culminated 10 years of frustration due to ignored pleas for lower fares and better service as well as outright hostility due to the not very subtle arm-twisting employed at the local political level. PE considered Santa Monica as a captive interurban market and treated it accordingly. Later events would cause this approach to be questioned. The Third St. line continued to run until declining passenger counts caused it to be discontinued in December of 1929.

Pomona. Quite a different situation obtained in Pomona, where PE concluded that continuation of local service was a hopeless proposition even if buses could be substituted for streetcars. The Pomona city fathers resisted the railway's attempt to abandon, since a 50-year franchise had been awarded to PE in 1910. The company's method of gracefully discontinuing its five local lines took the form of inducing a local operator to provide replacement bus service.

Accordingly, City Transit, Inc., was organized in August 1924. The largest investor was Joseph K. Hawkins, and the other principals were J.H. McKee and W.E. Dean. In September, Hawkins purchased the Orange Belt Bus Line, which ran from Pomona to nearby LaVerne and San Dimas. The seller was W.H. Neher, and with the purchase came his two Reo stages, one of which was soon destroyed in a fire.

City Transit replaced the rail service on October 1 using five new Mack AB buses (three 25-passenger and two 29-passenger). A sixth new bus, a Lang-bodied Mack parlor car, was placed in service on the San Dimas route. Two years later, Hawkins sold that line to the Motor Transit Co.

Other Early Bus Lines. In April 1923, three months after PE's abandonment of a shuttle car line, bus service was substituted between the Beverly Hills station and Coldwater Canyon. This was the first bus line in the Western District and was based at Sherman (West Hollywood) carhouse, as were those which joined it in later years. The line ran as a shuttle until it was absorbed into the Wilshire–Sunset route in June 1925.

Pacific Electric inaugurated a bus line serving the new Los Angeles Union Stockyards and other industries in Maywood on June 1, 1923. Applications by three other pros-

This unusual photo of Cahuenga Pass in the late 1920s shows no fewer than three buses. In the foreground one of the Pickwick Stages Cherokee-class, buffet-parlor cars climbs the hill to the San Fernando Valley and eventually to San Francisco. In one of the most unusual bus designs ever produced, the driver sat isolated in an upper level cupola with most of the passengers in a separate elevated compartment behind. Coming down the hill is a more prosaic Pickwick coach behind a tow car and just beyond, a Pacific Electric Fageol returns from the Valley on the Ventura Blvd. line. Tracks of PE's San Fernando Valley interurban line can be seen across the arroyo. Today, a 10-lane freeway slices through the area, flanked on both sides by high-rise buildings. *Automobile Club of Southern California*

pective operators had been denied. The new route connected with PE rail lines at 20th Street (on the Long Beach line) and at Maywood (on the Whittier branch), as well as with LARy cars at 26th and Santa Fe in Vernon. The battle over the right to operate the Maywood route suggests that its potential was regarded as considerable; in fact, it ran for only about four years.

The longest PE bus line so far was a 19-mile route from Hollywood through the Cahuenga Pass and out Ventura Blvd. to Girard (now Woodland Hills), using two Whites and instituted on October 10, 1923. This line was the direct result of sporadic attempts by an independent operator to start a route from Hollywood to Van Nuys, both points being served by PE cars. The proposed independent route lay far enough from the rail line that it would have been approved by the Railroad Commission if PE had chosen not to operate its own bus line. Diversion of passengers from the rail line was avoided by terminating the new bus route in a rural area far from the car tracks, resulting in unprofitable operation for several years.

February 1, 1924, brought the bus lines back under the Pacific Electric Railway flag, when amendment of the corporation tax law allowed all PE Land Co. rights along with the buses to be reacquired by the parent company.

During this month new feeder lines were started in Lamanda Park, Whittier, Bellflower, San Gabriel and Wilmar. Of these, only a portion of the Lamanda Park–Michillinda line would endure. This line, along with the Whittier loop routes, was started on February 1. It provided a connection between the East Colorado trolley line

Three Garfords were acquired with PE's purchase of the Compton Transportation Co. These were powered by the Buda 4-cylinder YBU, considered a strong engine for the time. While commonly found east of the Rockies, Ohio-built Garford chassis were rare in the west. It is shown in service on the Long Beach-Huntington Park line.
Dave Garcia Collection

of the Pasadena system at Daisy St. and the Michillinda station of the Monrovia–Glendora interurban on Huntington Drive.

The Whittier lines took the form of two loops passing the interurban station on Philadelphia St. Service was offered at half-hour intervals staggered such that one bus could cover both routes. Patronage was not great and the lines were discontinued on October 1, 1925. Another feeder was started on February 9 connecting the Clearwater station of the Santa Ana interurban at Ocean Ave. and State St. with Somerset Ave. and Center St. in Bellflower.

Two similar but longer lines were started on February 16 connecting the Temple City interurban at the San Gabriel Mission with the Covina–San Bernardino interurban. Both routes started at Mission Drive and Junipero St. The Wilmar–New Ave. line connected with the Covina line in Wilmar looping southbound on Del Mar Ave. and returning northbound on New Ave. The Rosemead–San Gabriel line ran to the Rosemead station via Broadway and Rosemead Ave. southbound and returning northbound via San Gabriel Blvd. All three lines were discontinued on July 1, 1924, only to be reinstated the next year and finally discontinued in the spring of 1927.

Whittier Bus Service. PE's decision to abandon the Whittier loop lines caught the interest of Carl Eckles, a local resident and former operator of a stage line in the High Sierras. Inspection of PE's operating results convinced him that the lines could be made to pay by cutting operating hours and using more economical equipment. On this basis he convinced the Whittier City Council to award him the franchise.

After his request for a loan to make a down payment on a bus was refused by a local banker, he seized on a novel subscription financing scheme to enable him to start service. He sold 20 local merchants advertising space on his timetable as well as $25 worth of free rides to use as premiums. When the $500 down payment had been accumulated, Eckles picked up his vehicle and the Whittier Bus Service took over the lines the day after PE quit. By doing the books of a local garage owner at night in return for maintenance on his bus, Eckles managed to complete his first year of operation without missing a run.

He soon was offered the opportunity to pick up a school transportation contract and this time he had no problem getting financing for new buses. In 1929 he read that PE was ready to give up service in Santa Ana and, based on his experience in Whittier, the City Council awarded him the franchise there. His new Santa Ana Bus Service survived the depression and Eckles continued to run both small operations through the Thirties.

The 16-mile Huntington Park–Long Beach route was acquired by PE on April 10, 1924, from the Compton Transportation Co. along with several buses. This line had been started by the partnership of Compton and McReynolds in 1919. Incorporation took place in 1920, and a second line from Long Beach to Venice via Compton was started in 1921. This line was retained for a time after sale of the Huntington Park line.

The purchase by PE blocked further independent bus competition in the important Long Beach Blvd. corridor where 30 modern steel cars provided frequent electric interurban service to and from Los Angeles. The demand for local transportation was shown by the assignment of four 29-passenger Fageols to the line as of 1927, operating on headways of 30 to 45 minutes and transporting 25,000 passengers per month.

A power shortage caused by dry weather provided PE

with a reason to replace several marginal rail lines with buses during 1924. Rail service between Pasadena and Shorb (Alhambra), subsidized by the SP, was abandoned and replaced by a shorter bus line, on which some trips were run by a combo specially rebuilt for the route. Rail lines converted during July included San Dimas, part of San Antonio Heights, West Olive Avenue (Redlands), Smiley Heights (Redlands) and Western and Franklin (Hollywood), and the remainder of the San Antonio Heights line (from Upland to La Cima) was replaced by buses in October. Trolleys returned to Western and Franklin and to the Redlands routes in 1925, but the others continued as bus lines. A line on Lankershim Blvd. in North Hollywood was started on July 8, 1924, between Magnolia Blvd. and San Fernando Rd.

Pico Blvd. In December 1923 the Railroad Commission held hearings to determine who would operate buses on Pico Blvd., the last major artery to have been completed (in 1918) between Los Angeles and Santa Monica. Based on the Commission's belief that streetcar service would eventually be required along the route, rights were awarded to Pacific Electric, with the decision requiring PE to stipulate that the rail line would be built when traffic warranted it.

The decision was protested by the City of Santa Monica on the grounds that the Commission had created a transit monopoly for PE and that Bay Cities Transit Co. offered a lower fare. The Commission denied the protest and pointed out that Bay Cities could not finance the new buses that would be required to start the line. Pacific Electric inaugurated service with 29-passenger Fageols on August 4, 1924; the line stretched for 11 miles between Santa Monica and Vineyard, junction point of the two principal PE rail routes to the beaches. In November of 1925 service was reduced from a headway of 45 minutes to hourly, and shuttle service which had been operated on 104th Ave. between Sawtelle and Reo Blvd. was abandoned.

By 1927, a 20-minute rush-hour headway was maintained between Vineyard and Westwood, with through trips to Santa Monica still operating hourly. Thoroughly dissatisfied with the service and the fare, the City of Santa Monica started running its own buses over the same route at a lower fare in April 1928, and in the face of that competition, PE abandoned its service on September 22. Patronage had dropped from a peak of over 40,000 in March of 1928 to less than 18,000 in July. This was the origin of the Santa Monica Municipal Bus Lines, one of the most successful of California's early publicly owned transit systems.

Western District Lines. A 1.7-mile feeder route from Hollywood Blvd. and Vine Street to the newly developed Hollywoodland district was started in December 1924. Another short line on Hyperion Ave. and Glendale Blvd. in the Silver Lake district was inaugurated in the spring of the following year in order to link the Hollywood rail lines at Sanborn Junction with the Glendale–Burbank line at Edendale. After being temporarily discontinued, it was reestablished and extended on November 15, 1926. It ran as a PE route for seven years before being transferred to Los

Major routes such as Pico Blvd. and Long Beach–Huntington Park were served in the 1920s by 29-passenger Fageols of the 200 series, one of which is seen here employed in promoting the John Ford movie, "The Iron Horse." *Security Pacific National Bank*

Angeles Motor Coach Co., which rearranged the line as a means of forestalling efforts by an independent group to establish bus service between Los Angeles and Glendale via Silver Lake.

In June 1925 the short Coldwater Canyon feeder route was discontinued as such and superceded by a new 7-mile U-shaped bus line known as Wilshire–Sunset. Beginning at Fairfax Avenue, this route ran west along Wilshire Blvd. to Canon Drive, then northwest past PE's Beverly Hills station and along Beverly Drive to the Beverly Hills Hotel, where it turned eastward via Sunset Blvd. to Gardner Junction. Beverly Hills was being developed at that time, and the new bus route met an immediate need. It provided transportation into the area from rail connections at Beverly Hills and Gardner, and from LARy's Wilshire Blvd. bus line at Fairfax Avenue (which was to become a Los Angeles Motor Coach route upon its extension to Beverly Hills in 1928). A 20-minute headway was offered using four 16-passenger Morelands (one a spare).

Compton Transportation Co.'s second route, Long Beach–Compton–Venice, was acquired in 1925, and the Long Beach–Compton leg was discontinued in favor of a connection with the Long Beach interurban in 1927. The remaining portion of the line lasted another year.

The Lankershim line was extended to Burbank via Magnolia Ave. on July 1, 1925, replacing the service of real estate promoter Earl White. Hourly service was offered over the 11-mile route until it was sold to brothers John and Clarence Auld on August 22, 1926.

The 10-Year Mark. As of January 1927, Pacific Electric was operating 122 buses on its own lines and owned 43 more which were in Los Angeles Motor Bus service. There were 32 PE routes, covering 200 route miles carrying an average of 820,000 passengers a month. The lightest lines were served by 16-passenger Morelands, the intermediate group used the 1923 Whites, and the heaviest lines required 200-series Fageols. Almost half the fleet was garaged in Pasadena, with other service and storage areas being at Santa Ana, Glendale, and the San Bernardino,

SEEING LOS ANGELES

Motor Tours

Inc.

"See America First"

Los Angeles Pasadena

City, Hollywood and Beverly Hills

Hollywood, Beverly Hills and Beaches

Movie Studio—Mt. Lowe

Riverside and Orange Empire

San Diego and Tia Juana

Santa Barbara, Del Monte and San Francisco

MAIN OFFICES AND STARTING POINTS

AUDITORIUM HOTEL, 507 West 5th Street, Telephone MU tual 7711
CLARK HOTEL LOBBY, 426 South Hill Street, VA ndike 6770
HOTEL MAYFAIR, 7th St. at Hartford & Stewart Sts., FI tzroy 4161

Author's Collection

Wicker Chairs and a Gray Line Lecturer

JUST AS Pacific Electric was quick to adopt the notion of putting on feeder bus lines to enhance its interurban system, it extended the same philosophy to its premier sightseeing attraction—Mount Lowe. In this case, a new tour was instituted in combination with the Gray Line, starting in Los Angeles and stopping at a movie studio before the passengers transferred to PE cars for a ride up the mountain.

Gray Line headquarters was at the Clark Hotel on Hill St. in downtown Los Angeles. From here, tours left for Pasadena, Hollywood, Beverly Hills and the beaches ($2-$4); to Riverside and the Orange Empire ($6); and to San Diego and Tijuana ($12 for two days, meals and lodging not included). All service was provided with smart looking gray Pierce-Arrow parlor cars sporting the distinctive blue trim and Gray Line diamond insignia. They were outfitted with individual wicker chairs, the last row facing rearward over the railroad-style observation car railing. Each car had its own lecturer, complete with microphone, to explain the points of interest along the tour route.

Sightseeing by bus was already an accepted and popular pastime in the mid-1920s. In Los Angeles, as in 24 other cities in the U.S. and Canada (as well as Honolulu and London), the Gray Line offered lectured tours. Descriptive literature advised tourists to "use the Gray all the way" and was careful to point out that the Gray Line was in the business of selling only sightseeing service and had "no connection with real estate, stock or other promoting schemes."

The new combination tour stopped at the Paramount Ranch and the First National Studio before traveling through Glendale and Flintridge to reach the Pasadena carhouse. There, passengers transferred to Mount Lowe interurbans for the next leg of their trip. Tourists were treated to lunch at the Mount Lowe Tavern after which they could return at 2:00 or 4:40 p.m. On weekends, an additional evening trip was offered which provided a view of the valley lights on the downward ride. The fare for the day's excursion was $4.50.

Right: Gray Line's Pierce-Arrow parlor cars were fitted with handsome Buffalo bodies, manufactured (as were the chassis), in that upstate New York city. Here, two cars pause to allow their touring passengers to admire a stately Flintridge mansion.

Opposite, above: Pacific Electric's Pasadena carhouse provides a background for touring passengers to board an interurban for continuation of their trip to Mount Lowe. The Pierce-Arrow and the wooden interurban are examples of classic transportation vehicle design.

Both: Dave Garcia Collection

THE GRAYLINE
1115

Prospective home buyers board a real estate promoter's bus in Hollywoodland in 1926. They are transferring from a PE 150-175 series Moreland, the type of bus used on the lightest lines and having only 16 seats. Today, SCRTD's line 217 terminates at this very spot, and the California Mission-style house in the background is unchanged.
Joe Corbin

Pomona, Sherman and Long Beach carhouses. Overhaul, painting and heavy maintenance were handled at the Torrance Shops.

Pacific Electric had concentrated during the first 10 years of bus operations almost entirely upon the provision of supplementary feeder service, getting involved in trunk lines as a reaction to real or potential independent bus competition. The regulatory posture of the Railroad Commission was an important factor and had been established quite early in the era of its jurisdiction over motor bus service: the first carrier to operate between two points had preemptive rights, unless it could be shown that service was below required standards.

Diversion of traffic by rival Motor Transit Co. along the Whittier and San Bernardino corridors provided ample evidence of the damaging effects of a well-run bus service upon the rail lines. These routes had been secured to Motor Transit by the "grandfather" clause in the 1917 legislation granting bus regulatory authority to the Railroad Commission, and having learned its lesson, PE zealously challenged any new applications for through bus routes in its territory. The railway always won, with the proviso that it institute equivalent service to that proposed by the would-be competitor. Thus PE was drawn into the operation of trunk lines, if not precisely against its will, then at least without aggressively seeking such routes.

Castellamare. One of PE's most interesting bus lines had its start in November 1926 as a feeder route between the Beverly Hills station and the posh Bel Air residential district. A 16-passenger Moreland provided half-hourly service in peak periods and hourly service during the rest of the day. In 1927 the 3½-mile line was extended from Beverly Hills to Los Angeles and from Bel Air to the Pacific Ocean to become PE's first limited-stop bus route.

An application for such a route had been made by Francis I. Brunner, who operated a bus line in the Malibu Mountains that eventually passed to Santa Monica Municipal Bus Lines. The rights had actually been awarded to Brunner by the Railroad Commission, but PE acquired them before he could start his service. In a marked departure from its previous practice, PE bought five type Y Yellow Coaches and lettered the beltrails especially for this line, which started at Pershing Square and ran nonstop out Beverly Blvd. to Beverly Hills, thence via the isolated outer portion of Sunset Blvd. (still called Beverly Blvd. then) through Bel Air and Brentwood to the Pacific shore at Castellamare.

PE advertised the Castellamare route as "America's greatest boulevard trip," and perhaps it was the most economical at a dollar for the scenic 47-mile round-trip ride. Attractions listed in the promotional brochure included "homes of famous moving picture stars," the Wilshire Country Club, Beverly Hills Hotel, UCLA (under construction), the Botanical Gardens and the Will Rogers Ranch.

Laguna Beach Short Line. Edward Logsden and Norman Robotham, doing business as Laguna Beach Shortline Automobile Stage Co., were certificated to operate along the coast road from Balboa to the Santa Fe station at Serra on June 12, 1924, and extended service to San Juan Capistrano via Roscoe Road in 1925. Logsden transferred his interest to E.W. Conkey in February 1926, and

To start the 23-mile Beverly Blvd. route from Los Angeles to Castellamare Beach in 1927 (the first trunk bus line on the system), PE turned to Yellow Coach for five Type Y's and followed Yellow's advice by painting them in a distinguished pearl gray with a brown roof and the traditional PE red belt stripe.
Gerald L. Squier

ROSTER OF BUSES

Pacific Electric Railway
(1917–1930 only)

Numbers	Make	Model	Seats	Built	Notes
(?)	Fageol	—	17	1917	Tractor-trailer using modified Case auto; SP subsidiaries had four, PE at least one
5	Reo	F	16	1920	Open stage body replaced in 1924
6	Reo	F	19	1920	Porter Brown Auto Body Co. body
7	Moreland	21-B	19	1921	
8-9	Reo	F	22	1921	Crown Motor Carriage Co. bodies
11-15	Moreland	EX	19	1922	
16-17	Reo	F	17	1923	Pacific Motor Bodies Co. bodies
19	White	50	25	1923	
20-88	White	50	25	1923	PE bodies
100-108	Reo	?	16	?	(1923) Pasadena jitney operators
111-112	?	?	?	?	(1923) Pasadena jitney operators
150-175	Moreland	RC	16	1923	
200-205	Fageol	—	29	1923	
206-216	Fageol	—	29	1924	
1	Garford	51-D	30	1923	(1924) Compton Transp. Co.
2-3	Garford	51-D	32	1923	(1924) Compton Transp. Co.
4	Moreland	AC	25	1924	(1924) Compton Transp. Co.
300-304	Yellow	Y-U-316	29	1927	
217	Fageol	—	15	1928	Combo
218-219	Fageol	—	19	1928	Combo
400-409	Twin	40	40	1929	
110-112	Moreland	AC	25	1923	(1929) ?

Typical of California stage operators at the time, Pacific Coast Motor Coach Co. used sedan-style Whites with luggage compartments built on to the rear. One is seen northbound at Laguna Beach, circa 1926. *California Historical Society*

Conkey and Robotham formed Pacific Coast Motor Coach Co. to operate the route. Package express rights were granted in October 1926, and the roster then consisted of two 16-passenger buses (one Reo and one Moreland) and a 1922 Stevens touring car.

Through traffic arrangements made in November 1926 offered a new way to travel between Long Beach and San Diego. The first leg was by PE interurban car from Long Beach to Newport Beach, where passengers transferred to Pacific Coast Motor Coach buses as far as San Juan Capistrano. There they boarded Santa Fe trains for San Diego. The number of through passengers over this route was small, but more than 10,000 people transferred between PE cars and the connecting buses at Newport Beach during 1927, attesting to the attractiveness of the "Laguna Beach Short Line" as a means of getting to the Orange County beaches.

A Railroad Commission survey made during the summer of 1927 described the Pacific Coast Motor Coach Company as follows:

"The coaches of this company park alongside the Pacific Electric tracks at Newport Beach, passengers transferring having only approximately 8 feet to walk from one conveyance to the other. The schedules are arranged so that the average wait outbound from Los Angeles if trains are on time is 14 minutes, and inbound to Los Angeles the average wait is 18 minutes. The summer schedule for 1927 reduces this time to 6 and 14 minutes respectively.

"Traffic arrangements with Pacific Electric Rly. provide that the cars of either company wait for their connections, and since May 1925 when this became effective there has never been a single case of either coach or train missing connections. Practically the entire town of Laguna Beach lies within 3 blocks of the route followed by the coaches of this company. Through ticketing arrangements are in effect with both Pacific Electric Rly. and Southern Pacific Railroad.

"The route followed lies close to the shore line, and has very few intersections and no railroad crossings between Newport Beach and Laguna Beach. At the stops en route this company has provided seats for the convenience of its passengers."

Upon completion of paving work on the new Seashore Highway (bypassing Dana Point) in 1928, Pacific Coast Motor Coach applied to operate south along the new road to Serra, where the Seashore Highway joined the older Coast Highway. At the north end, it was proposed to extend service 20 miles along the new road to Long Beach. PE did not object to this extension, because the beach access would be preserved for its Los Angeles passengers, while the small number of travelers originating in Long Beach would be spared the inconvenience of the transfer.

The application was approved with the provision that

PE operated the Pacific Coast Motor Coach route during 1929 and assigned new Fageols to the route. Taken in Long Beach, this picture shows that they were painted like the Yellows.
Gerald L. Squier

new buses be obtained to replace two aging 21-passenger Whites which then comprised the Pacific Coast Motor Coach fleet. Presumably unable to finance the purchase, the small company sold out to Pacific Electric in December 1928, though it continued in existence as a subsidiary. Three older PE buses were assigned to the line, including two Morelands, an AC converted to a combo and a smaller RC converted to a baggage bus.

In January 1929, two new Fageol combos were placed in service, and the baggage bus was replaced by a larger converted Reo. Local rights were secured between Long Beach and Newport Beach through a trade with Motor Transit, which had previously been restricted to protect PE between Huntington Beach and Seal Beach. The parties agreed that neither would be harmed by open-door operation in this lightly traveled corridor.

The long-distance bus operators were interested in this corridor as well. As the Coast Highway was extended northward, it became an attractive route prospect for Pickwick Stages and for the Southern Pacific Motor Transport Co., but a dispute over which would serve the route was cut short during 1929 by formation of the Pacific Greyhound system as eventual successor to both. Pacific Coast Motor Coach rights between Long Beach and San Juan Capistrano passed to Pickwick in January 1930.

Ontario, Wingfoot and Emery Park. When buses replaced streetcars on the Ontario–Upland line in October of 1928, the reason, perhaps unique for the time, was indicative of PE's approach to the business of transportation. The City of Ontario had recently placed a 10-mph speed restriction on the streetcars. PE's analysis showed that a one-man bus operating at normal schedule speeds would certainly be more economical than the two two-man cars required because of the speed restriction. While the City protested, the Railroad Commission agreed with the company, and the change was made.

In March 1929, PE started a new bus line from Wingfoot station, terminus of a Southern District freight spur, to the Ford plant in Long Beach. The route paralleled the interurban main line and provided direct service to a number of industries including Goodyear, Firestone and Samson Tire plants and the Pan-American Petroleum Co. When the depression reduced employment in these factories, the line was discontinued. Another Long Beach improvement was replacement of the old American Avenue carhouse, which stood on prime real estate, with modern rail facilities at Fairbanks yard, including a separate bus garage.

In response to local agitation for public transportation in an isolated area on the Los Angeles–Alhambra boundary, the Emery Park bus line was instituted on July 15, 1929. The 5-mile route connected with the Northern District's rail service at Huntington Drive and Eastern Ave. (El Sereno station) and prevented invasion of the territory by an independent operator.

Pacific Electric's first large buses arrived during September 1929 in the form of 10 Model 40 Twin Coaches. They were to provide PE bus patrons a level of comfort never experienced except on the premium-fare parlor coaches of the Castellamare line. Deep leather seats, wide aisles and low steps were features which proved popular with passengers. Six of the new buses replaced 29-passenger Fageols on the Long Beach–Huntington Park line and the other four similarly upgraded the Ventura Blvd.–Girard line.

The Road to Ocean Park. When Pacific Electric bus service was started between Hollywood and Santa Monica on November 20, 1929, it was as the result of a chain of events that began three years earlier. In 1926, T.C. Gillespie had been authorized to start operation of the Studio Stage Line linking major motion picture studios in Universal City, Hollywood and Culver City. His request for local rights between Hollywood and Culver City was opposed by LARy in the name of Los Angeles Motor Bus, but the

Seven years old and still going strong, a PE-bodied White holds down the Ontario–Upland line in 1930. Note the wooden batting which holds the fraying canvas roof together. *Magna Collection*

rights were granted anyway. Encouraged by the decision, Gillespie applied for local rights on the Hollywood–Ocean Park (Santa Monica) segment of the Pasadena–Ocean Park Stage Line, which he also owned.

It became apparent at public hearings that patrons would support bus service as an alternative to PE's wooden interurban cars, and in December 1928 the Railroad Commission denied the Pasadena–Ocean Park Stage Line's application provided that PE would devise a plan for bus service between Hollywood and the beach. The company was in no rush to start a line that could only divert rail traffic, and so the plan was prepared in an extremely methodical manner.

The opening of the UCLA campus in Westwood brought the situation to a head. PE started serving the university from Hollywood under temporary authority on September 23, 1929, and soon Bay Cities Transit Co. was operating a similar service from Sawtelle. Meanwhile, an application had been filed for a 2-mile extension of the Santa Monica–Soldiers Home line of Bay Cities. Pacific Electric promptly applied for the long-awaited Hollywood–Ocean Park bus line, to operate from Hollywood and Vermont via Hollywood Blvd., Highland Ave., Santa Monica Blvd., Sunset Blvd., UCLA and Wilshire Blvd. Local rights beyond Federal Ave. were not requested in deference to the existing Bay Cities route. The line was soon approved and inaugurated.

The new Hollywood–Ocean Park route duplicated the Hollywoodland–Beverly Hills bus line along Hollywood Blvd. between Vine and Highland and on Sunset Blvd. between Holloway Drive and the Beverly Hills Hotel. (Hollywoodland–Beverly Hills was the former Wilshire–Sunset route, revised in 1928 to operate between Hollywoodland and the Beverly Hills Station.) These two routes were consolidated on December 1, 1930, to offer through service between Hollywoodland to Ocean Park via the University, or to Beverly Hills.

Tripper service was maintained over the original University route to and from Hollywood and Vermont during hours of heavy student travel, and a shuttle service was instituted between Hollywood and Highland and Sunset and Holloway via Highland Ave. and Santa Monica Blvd. In 1931 the shuttle was eliminated and the regular route was diverted over Crescent Heights Blvd. and Holloway Drive in its place; the Sunset Blvd. routing was restored in 1937.

Operation of PE buses through to Ocean Park continued until July 7, 1932, when that branch of the line was cut back to Wilshire and Westwood and replaced by a further extension of the Los Angeles Motor Coach Wilshire Blvd. line. Providing through bus service between downtown Los Angeles and Santa Monica, this became a popular route, with express service being inaugurated in 1934 and limited service in 1936. With later minor revisions the Hollywood–Beverly Hills line continued to operate until conversion of the Hollywood Blvd. service from streetcars to buses in 1954.

The Torrance Shops turned out only one more bus body after the original 1923 order. This bus was not for revenue service, but there were some similarities. Once again a White chassis was selected and again the bus had no windows or heater. This time, however, there were no passenger complaints; its purpose was to transfer vacationers between the San Bernardino rail station and the PE camp, obviating the need for using rival Motor Transit's mountain buses. *Dave Garcia Collection*

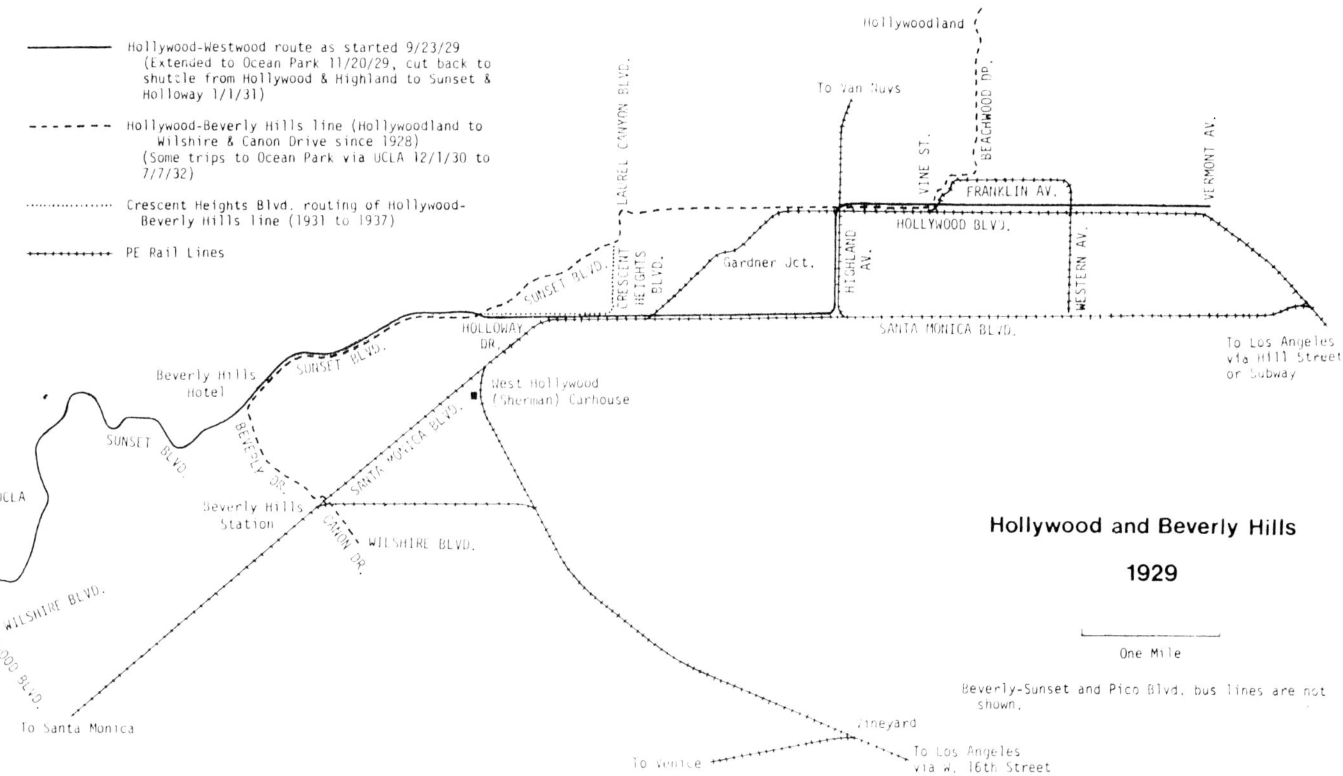

Various feeder bus routes tying in with the trunk rail lines were tried out in the Hollywood-West Hollywood-Beverly Hills sector over the years; this was the position in 1929. *Motor Coach Age*

Type Y 304 is snapped on the beach at the end of its run. Note the destination and route spelled out on the beltrail, a common notion in the twenties when buses were dedicated to a specific route. *Dave Garcia Collection*

The Fageol brothers left American Car & Foundry in 1927 to produce a revolutionary dual-engined, 40-passenger, heavy-duty transit coach. The new bus was dubbed the "Twin Coach" and the name stuck even though later (and smaller) designs had only a single engine. Almost 1,200 model 40s were produced between 1927 and 1934; PE received its 10 in September of 1929. The new buses had 15 more seats than PE's Whites but were only five feet longer. Powered by two 6-cylinder Hercules engines, they featured spacious interiors with mostly forward-facing seats; longitudinal benches were installed over the wheel wells and the amidships engine compartments. The buses were put into service on PE's heaviest lines (Long Beach–Huntington Park and Ventura Blvd.) and were used extensively for charter movements. They ran on into the late 1930s when they were converted to non-revenue use. *Both: Joe Corbin*

CHAPTER TWO

MOTOR TRANSIT • 1914-1930

The El Dorado System; from the mountains to the sea

A noteworthy example of the coach builder's art, 500 was a 1925 product of the Market Street Shops. Built before Motor Transit settled on the El Dorado shield as a trademark, this 20-passenger stage carries O.R. Fuller's initials enclosed in an arrowhead on its distinctively shaped White radiator shell. *Security Pacific National Bank*

FEW NEW RAIL LINES were built by the Pacific Electric Railway after its formation through merger in 1911, its predecessor companies having completed a decade of furious construction activity. By that time in Southern California, highways rather than rail lines were beginning to trigger residential and commercial development. PE opened its San Bernardino rail line in July 1914 with great fanfare, but the existence of a good paved road nearby permitted organized bus competition to begin only three months later.

The railway was never threatened on many major routes that did not have convenient parallel roads, but one bus company that developed from early independent motor stage lines grew by the late 1920s to be a formidable competitor, particularly on the San Bernardino, Riverside and Whittier routes.

This was the Motor Transit Co. of O.R. Fuller, operating from a terminal building at 5th and Los Angeles Streets in downtown Los Angeles (at time of writing still there but used for other purposes) and building its own buses in well-equipped shops. The Railroad Commission, which first required the filing of tariffs by bus operators as early as 1917, was inclined to encourage Motor Transit's acquisition ventures just as it supported PE against smaller independents.

The familiar legend MOTOR TRANSIT LINES appeared on buses of the Pacific Electric Railway throughout the 1940s and early 1950s. This might lead a casual observer to conclude that the suburban bus operation of earlier times known as Motor Transit Co. started as another Southern Pacific subsidiary. Nothing could be further from the truth; Motor Transit's origin may be traced to the very beginning of California's motor stage industry, and at its height the system reached from San Diego to Bakersfield and from Long Beach to Lancaster. In fact, by 1920 Motor Transit was the largest auto stage passenger carrier in the state of California.

Not until 1926, fairly late in the course of its development, was the company transformed into a purely suburban operator and thus thrust into direct competition with the Pacific Electric on routes to the east and southeast of Los Angeles. The history of Motor Transit is in some respects similar to that of the PE—its major competitor (and eventual owner). Both grew through the merger and amalgamation of independent predecessor companies. The chief difference was that the PE rail system was already unified when Motor Transit was building its bus system between 1916 and 1920.

During most of that time, too, the motor stage industry in the state was already being regulated by the California Railroad Commission. As elsewhere, all carriers operating and filing tariffs as of the date on which regulation became effective were vested with "grandfather rights." In this case the date was May 1, 1917, and the basic route structure of the future Motor Transit system was in existence at that time, though not all of it was as yet operated by Motor Transit's immediate predecessor.

By 1917, in fact, much of California was laced with motor stage routes. Antagonism between bus and rail interests was high, stemming from the recent days of unregulated bus competition. It has been said that during the early years of motor carrier regulation the function of the Railroad Commission seems to have been to protect the competitive posture of the Southern Pacific and its subsidiaries, one of which was PE. Applications for new or extended bus service were vigorously opposed by rail interests, yet the motor stage business grew so rapidly that the men and machines that constituted its most important ingredients could barely keep pace.

The topography of Southern California caused the development of north-south routes along the valleys emptying into the Los Angeles basin, and necessitated some difficult hill climbing to leave the basin by crossing the mountains. The growth of settlements along these routes was a natural consequence of their increased use, and the roads were rapidly developed into an outstanding system of paved highways. This trend led to an unusually high per capita motor vehicle registration figure—already one vehicle for every 4½ people in 1922. This environment also fostered the early development of the bus industry.

O.R. Fuller. The driving force behind the Motor Transit Co. was its founder and owner, Oliver R. Fuller. When Southern California's rapid growth required a flexible transportation mode suitable for areas and levels of service known to be uneconomical for railroad expansion, Fuller controlled the resources to provide a potential solution. He was then president of the White Auto Co., the Los Angeles outlet for White Trucks and Stephenson autos, in which position he had ample opportunity to assess the viability of the motor transport business. When, in 1913, he sold two trucks to a purchaser who could not make them pay, he reluctantly took them over and started a trucking company. He was determined to make the venture profitable, and he shortly proved that it could be run successfully.

When the opportunity presented itself to purchase a passenger stage line in the same way, he did so, naming it White Bus Line and leasing new White buses to it from White Auto Co. It is to Fuller's credit that he believed strongly enough in his new enterprise to go on to found the Motor Carrier Association of California in 1918 and so to help unite the growing industry in the far west.

White Bus Line was formed on December 1, 1916, to buy out the PE Stage Line (no relation to the railway), a partnership, operating between Los Angeles and Anaheim via Whittier and Fullerton (28 miles). The purchase included seven White and four Buick autos. Competing with the White Bus Line in the territory was the Valley Stage Line ("Short Line") of F.P. Ogden and Francis Wilson, which reached Anaheim via Norwalk and Buena Park. Soon there was also through service from Los Angeles to San Diego over both routes, operated by E.S. Good's A.R.G. Bus Co.

At Anaheim, passengers of the White and Valley lines could transfer to the Crown Stage Line of A.B. Watson to continue their trips to Orange and Santa Ana. Joint rates from Los Angeles through to Santa Ana were authorized in 1917. White Bus Line scheduled 28 round trips a day over its route to Anaheim in 1919, and half again as many buses were actually run, in order to protect the schedules and to accommodate overloads. The Railroad Commission frowned on standees, and the style of bus then in use would not have permitted standing in any case.

The popularity of the bus service, core of what was later called Motor Transit's Southern Division, was understandable when compared to the competitive Whittier car line of PE. A more direct routing favored the buses by allowing comparable travel times to and from Whittier (45 minutes), while the fare over that part of the route was 30 cents compared to PE's 41 cents. The bus service was much closer to intermediate population centers than the car line. The crowds came and stayed, so that the doubling of busy schedules became a characteristic of the heavier routes.

White Bus Line's earning power with increasing population and traffic led Fuller to seek expansion opportunities once he had spent a few years getting used to life as a bus operator.

San Diego Service. Sharp competition from Pickwick Stages on its San Diego route and from Fuller himself on the San Bernardino line (of the Eastern Division, to be described below) brought financial difficulties to A.R.G.

Few suburban bus operations encountered traffic conditions like these as early as 1924. The view looks to the east on Whittier Blvd. in Montebello and shows a 25-passenger Avery-bodied White. *Title Insurance & Trust Co.*

Bus Co. by 1919. The San Diego line was leased to Fuller in February 1920 and was operated thereafter by White Bus Line. South of Santa Ana the route was a scenic one along the Pacific shore, with stops at San Juan Capistrano, Oceanside, Del Mar, and La Jolla. Limited stops were made along the two routes between Los Angeles and Santa Ana.

On December 20, 1920, Fuller acquired and leased to Motor Transit the rights to a third routing between Los Angeles and San Diego via Santa Ana, this one operating due south to Long Beach and then east to Santa Ana; no local passengers could be carried between Los Angeles and Long Beach to protect the busy PE rail line between those points. Motor Transit operated its new route jointly with Thomas and H.H. Morgan's United Stages. There were six trips a day between San Diego and Long Beach, four of which continued on to Los Angeles, compared with 10 Motor Transit runs per day via Anaheim. Late in 1921 Fuller purchased the United Stages' rights and became sole owner of the route via Long Beach.

With Fuller operating the former A.R.G. routes to and through Santa Ana—seat of Orange County and an important commercial center—A.B. Watson sought to stay competitive over the Anaheim–Santa Ana segment by purchasing Valley Stage Line. On March 1, 1920, he combined Valley's Los Angeles–Anaheim route with existing Crown Stages' rights to form a through line from Los Angeles to Santa Ana. Needless to say, joint ticketing arrangements between Motor Transit and Crown Stages were soon given up. Motor Transit scheduled 32 daily round trips to Santa Ana in the fall of 1920, with 22 additional round trips to Whittier and 15 scheduled extra sections to Montebello.

Liberty Stage Line. The Liberty Stage Line was started by M.C. Rutherford in August 1918 to operate between Los Angeles and Downey (11 miles). In March 1920, Rutherford sold out to Mrs. H.A. Varro, who extended the line successively to the County Poor Farm, Norwalk, and the Norwalk State Hospital. The equipment consisted of 14- and 18-passenger Reo Speed Wagons. On April 16, 1921, Liberty's 19 miles of route were added to Motor Transit's Southern Division for a purchase price of $7,500. The branch between Downey, Norwalk, and the state hospital was soon discontinued.

A separate Liberty route between Pasadena and Long Beach, intersecting the lines of Motor Transit's Eastern Division at El Monte, had been acquired in October 1920 from the partnership of Horn and Painter. At the time of purchase of the Los Angeles route, Fuller was not interested in the north-south connector, which was sold instead to E.B. and H.L. Dillingham in September 1921.

Crown Fights Back. The battle was not over, for Watson complained to the Railroad Commission that Fuller could not legally run local buses to Anaheim over former White Bus Line rights and then carry the passengers onward to Santa Ana over ex-A.R.G. authority because A.R.G. had not specified local service in its 1917 "grandfather" tariff. The Commission agreed with Watson, and the ruling was upheld by the California Supreme Court.

Motor Transit recovered local rights between Anaheim and Santa Ana by application in 1924, but was still unable to carry through passengers between Santa Ana and Los Angeles. These rights were awarded as part of a decision on

Left: A Liberty Stage Line Speed Wagon sits in the service station at 6th and Los Angeles streets behind PE's Main Street Station. This location, across the street from the future site of the Pickwick Stages (later Greyhound) depot, was also a common site for PE's own equipment photos until it was razed to make way for the new SCRTD depot. *Motor Bus Society*

Below: The Union Stage Depot at 5th and Los Angeles streets as it appeared in 1920. White Bus Line (soon to become Motor Transit Co.) and Pickwick Stages were the largest of several carriers to use the station at that time. *Southwest Railway Library*

Motor Transit's effort to retaliate by blocking the lease of the "Short Line" to Pickwick by Crown stages; Pickwick Stages was already Motor Transit's chief competitor for San Diego traffic.

The Commission set aside the allegation that Crown's operation of the combined Valley and Crown rights was illegal, because both carriers had always operated local service, and simultaneously approved Crown's application to combine the rights and to lease the line to Pickwick. By November 1924, Pickwick was running 29 trips a day on this line to Santa Ana as well as its 10 trips to San Diego.

While supposedly prohibited from operating local service from Santa Ana to Los Angeles, Motor Transit never really made this apparent to its passengers. In fact, a company map which appeared in a Santa Ana newspaper during April 1924 advertised 14 trips a day to Los Angeles and intermediate points. When the ad was brought to the attention of the Railroad Commission by Crown Stages, an explanation was requested from Motor Transit. Motor Transit, after careful investigation, promised the Commission to correct the oversight—a commitment probably not fulfilled with great haste.

Meanwhile, Motor Transit had extended its San Diego–Long Beach service to San Pedro Harbor in the fall of 1923. A new San Diego depot was opened in February 1924, the tenth to be owned and operated by Motor Transit, at a cost of $150,000. The new depot fronted on First Street, with vehicle entrances to the loading docks from E Street and to the adjacent garage from Front and E Streets. La Jolla Stage Line and Willis Sightseeing Tours shared the facility, Motor Transit moving over from the Union Depot which had been shared with its rival Pickwick.

Motor Transit at its greatest extent as a long-distance operator. In 1924, the system extended from San Diego to Lancaster and Bakersfield in addition to covering Los Angeles, Orange, Riverside and San Bernardino counties.

Author's Collection

The name "La Jolla Stage Line" was used from 1913 to 1917 and again from 1924 to 1927. This view of one of the line's Motor Transit-bodied Whites on a charter was taken during the later period. *P. A. Copeland*

On February 21, 1921, a partnership under the name of the Wilson L.R. Patterson Passenger Stage started a bus line from San Diego east to Encanto, Lemon Grove and Spring Valley. The route followed in general the rails of the San Diego & Arizona Railroad Lakeside Branch to Lemon Grove and served a rural area that was just starting to develop. The route was bought on April 5, 1924, and became Motor Transit's only local line in San Diego. The downtown terminal was naturally changed to the Motor Transit depot at 1st and E.

La Jolla Line. In June 1915, the La Jolla Stage Line commenced operation between downtown San Diego and the suburban community of La Jolla. Sixteen-passenger Franklins were used, primarily for sightseeing purposes, but the line nevertheless offered competition to the steam and motor trains of the Los Angeles & San Diego Beach Railway. In May 1916, the road between San Diego and La Jolla was paved, allowing a considerable improvement in running time for the stage line and bettering its competitive position.

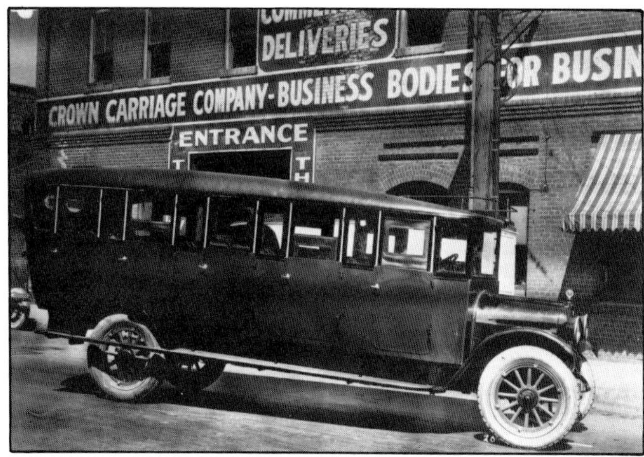

The Crown Stage Line of A.B. Watson took its name from the fact that the bodies on its Reo Speed Wagon chassis were supplied by the Crown Carriage Co. Watson soon turned to larger Fageols for his first line equipment. *Crown Coach*

Another stage line, called the La Jolla Scenic Stage, started operating over a similar route in May 1917. Four round trips a day were operated, two less than the six run by the Stage Line, and seven-passenger cars were used. In October 1917 the two lines were merged and started operating as the La Jolla route of the A.R.G. Stage Co. Service was pared to seven round trips a day. Later in the same month another route was started to the Army's new Camp Kearny, replacing service formally operated by United Stages. This new route was short-lived, however, as early in November United Stages resumed service to the camp and the A.R.G. line ended.

In January 1919 the Los Angeles & San Diego Beach Railway was abandoned and the stage company, now A.R.G. Bus Co., Inc., increased service to 15 trips a day. The La Jolla line remained independent when Motor Transit took over A.R.G.'s through Los Angeles–San Diego service in 1920 but the San Diego terminal was moved from a street-corner stand at 5th and C Streets into the new Motor Transit terminal at 1st and E in 1924, and in October of that year the old name of La Jolla Stage Line was resumed.

Eastern Division. The first bus line later to become part of Motor Transit's Eastern Division was started by Truston Clark in October 1914 and ran from Los Angeles to Pomona, Ontario, and San Bernardino (67 miles). A short feeder line was also operated between Pomona and Chino. By the spring of 1915, A.R.G. Bus Co. was offering competition between Los Angeles and Ontario, and by 1917 this company had extended its bus service to Riverside and to San Bernardino and Redlands.

O.R. Fuller bought out Truston Clark on October 29, 1917, and continued operation of the lines without change. With the purchase he acquired four ¾-ton Menominee trucks with passenger bodies, six Signal buses, and a Seldon automobile. Condition of the equipment was such

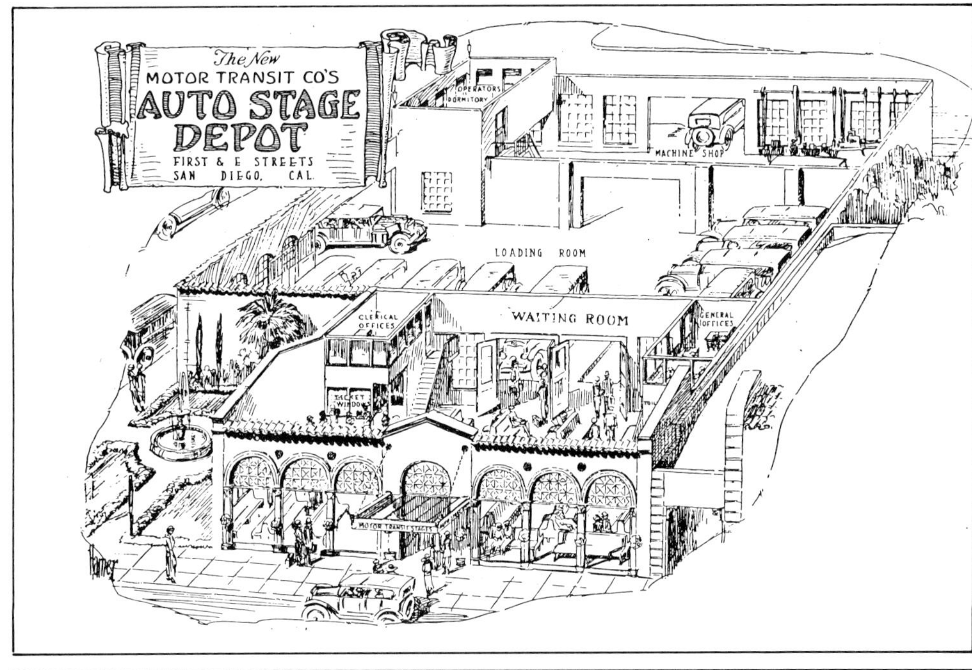

Motor Transit built an elaborate and pleasant depot in San Diego in 1923. The diagram details the indoor "loading room" and machine shop. Coach 500 is shown in front of the new depot. Motor Transit built five of these luxurious stages, still with side doors and no center aisle.
Both: Motor Bus Society

that Fuller immediately added three leased Whites in order to maintain the service. Over the protests of A.R.G., the Railroad Commission subsequently approved the sale to Fuller.

One of the witnesses at the hearing was Franklin D. Howell, chief engineer of the Los Angeles Board of Public Utilities. He was to become even more familiar to the Commission after 1919 as vice president of White Bus Line. Howell was the operating head of White Bus Line and Motor Transit Co. from then on.

The former Clark routes after purchase by Fuller averaged 14,000 passengers per month against A.R.G.'s 10,000 and this plus pressure on its San Diego line from Pickwick Stages forced A.R.G. into trusteeship in 1919. The Moreland Motor Truck Co., A.R.G.'s principal creditor, foreclosed on its equipment obligations and had A.R.G.'s general manager Will R. Forker appointed as trustee.

Forker continued to operate the San Bernardino and Riverside routes under the name of Orange Belt Line until the summer of 1920, when their sale to O.R. Fuller took place. Including 31 Moreland "trucks with passenger stage bodies," the property cost Fuller $150,000 in common shares of his new Motor Transit Co., organized on April

Motor Transit 61 sports a 21-passenger Avery body on a White light truck chassis. This is the type of bus first used by White Bus Lines and its successor on the early suburban and interurban lines. The comely passenger is about to embark on a trip along the Eastern Division main line, helped aboard by none other than O.R. Fuller. *Motor Bus Society*

14, 1920, to succeed White Bus Line. With the purchase came terminal properties in Ontario and at 6th and Los Angeles Streets in downtown Los Angeles.

A new route was started in the spring of 1920 between Riverside and the State Agricultural Experiment Station (now the University of California at Riverside), but it was not successful and was sold in 1922. Consolidation of the former Clark and A.R.G. services was soon accomplished so that in 1921, Motor Transit was operating 26 daily round trips to Redlands and 30 to Riverside. Eight additional trips turned at Ontario and one at San Bernardino; 15 round trips daily served the Pomona–Chino shuttle.

The Chino line was extended to meet the main line again at Ontario in July 1921 and was extended from Chino to Corona in 1922. An alternate mainline route from Ontario to San Bernardino through Bloomington and Colton was authorized in August 1921, but never had much service.

San Jacinto Mountains. In November 1922, Motor Transit reached the San Jacinto Mountain resorts south and east of Riverside by purchasing the rights of G & W Stage Line for $10,000. Rights over the 91 miles of route from Los Angeles via Huntington Drive and Foothill Blvd. to Upland, San Bernardino, Alessandro, Perris, Hemet, and San Jacinto to Gilman's Relief Hot Springs and Soboba Hot Springs had been acquired by G & W in February 1920 from Golden State Auto Tours Corp., a sightseeing and tour operator.

With the Railroad Commission decision authorizing the Motor Transit purchase came two restrictions: no local service was authorized, with pickup points restricted to Pasadena and towns east of Upland, and through-routing with existing Motor Transit lines was not permitted. These provisions protected the operations of J.H. Lord (doing business as Pasadena–Pomona Stage Line) and the Pacific Electric. A request to extend the ex-A.R.G. Riverside line to Redlands via Highgrove and Loma Linda was denied in 1923, but establishment of a separate local line from Riverside to Loma Linda over part of the same route was approved.

Mountain Division. As early as 1918, the eye of O.R. Fuller had turned toward the San Bernardino Mountain resorts. In that year he applied for rights from San Bernardino and Redlands to resort points, but the application was denied because Mountain Auto Line was providing adequate service. This rebuff did not deter Fuller, though his goal took him two years to reach.

The San Bernardino Mountain Auto Stage was started in 1912 by Kirke Phillips, who combined appropriate parts from a Ford auto and a 1½-ton truck into a vehicle suitable for carrying freight from San Bernardino along Rim-of-the-World Drive to the mountain community of Crestline, 14 miles away and one mile up. Mountain residents ordered their groceries and hardware in the morning and had their merchandise that same evening. Brothers Max and Perry Green joined the venture in 1913 and took it over when Phillips died.

Passengers began to be carried as an accommodation; the automotive pioneers who braved the mountain roads of that period soon found out that their vehicles and their driving skills left something to be desired. The Green brothers mercifully picked them up and carried them among the freight. Bolt-on seats were then added behind the driver to provide rudimentary comfort for the passengers, and charter parties were soon riding majestically through Waterman Canyon at three miles an hour, en

Above: Bus 64 waits at the Redlands depot in September 1921 to begin its 3-hour, 20-minute trip to Los Angeles. The building served Motor Transit and the Pacific Electric until 1936.
Redlands Daily Facts

Left: A 21-passenger White makes a publicity appearance at the San Bernardino Orange Show. The placard advertises "half hour service" between San Bernardino and Los Angeles while urging the public to "travel by Motor Stage."
SCRTD Collection

route to the Los Angeles City Vacation Camp at Seeley Flat.

In 1915, the service of Win and Ernie Shea was acquired and the line was extended 45 miles to Little Bear (now Arrowhead) and Big Bear Lakes. The Shea Brothers had run a seasonal service, primarily for fishing parties, but the Greens extended their regular freight and passenger runs into the new area. During these years, weekend excursions and resort trips became popular and made up an ever-increasing share of the Mountain Auto Line's business.

By 1918, the Greens had also bought out the operation of Harry Beal, who had been operating a Packard touring car from Redlands out Mill Creek Canyon to Mountain Home, Knight's Camp, and Big Bear Valley. In the next year, rights were granted for an alternate route via Highlands, City Creek Canyon, and Fredalba.

On March 18, 1920, the Commission authorized Max and Perry Green and Mrs. Nettie Phillips to transfer the

Both the combo and the tourer were built up on White light truck chassis. It took constant attention from the drivers and from self-taught master mechanic Perry Green to keep the primitive machines running. The narrow San Bernardino Mountain roads chewed up tires, the grades tore up transmissions and rear ends, and the extremes of summer heat and winter cold accentuated the rigors of mile-high operation.
Both: Motor Bus Society

Mountain Auto Line to Fuller. Max Green became passenger traffic manager of Motor Transit.

Dr. J.N. Baylis, owner of Pinecrest Resort, is credited with suggesting the name Rim-of-the-World Drive for the route to Crestline because of its particularly fine view. Max and Perry Green incorporated the name into their "grandfather rights" tariff and since it was applied to the entire area, it secured the hold of the Mountain Auto Line against all competitors. Tour publicity and outdoor advertising picked up the theme by advertising "101 miles on the Rim-of-the-World."

Mountain Auto Line service was a part of the local scene as illustrated by the reminiscences of Bill Moore, editor of the *Redlands Daily Facts,* in his column, "With a Grain of Salt."

> "I well remember this early mountain auto line. My father, who had come to Redlands in 1897, had for years been enamored of Bluff Lake and Big Bear Lake. About the time Fuller took over Mountain, Dad decided to take the family for a short vacation in Big Bear.
>
> "We boarded the 'stage', as it was called, at the Motor Transit station located on Citrus Avenue just east of Redlands Federal Savings & Loan.
>
> "It was a cumbersome White 11-passenger stage with about four rows of seats. A canvas top kept the sun out. I was seated alongside the driver, and the rest of the family was in the rows of seats and Dad in the very back.
>
> "As we were proceeding up Mentone Boulevard, just above the town of Mentone, a car in front of the stage decided to make a sudden left turn into a side street. The bus driver swerved to avoid a collision and the top-heavy stage overturned. It pinned Dad down, and it was some time before the stage could be jacked up to extricate him. He was taken to the old Redlands hospital at the corner of Nordina and Clark. Fortunately he was not seriously injured, but the accident cancelled our trip to Big Bear.
>
> "Some time later I recall riding a stage to Forest Home. The engines were not cooled with circulating systems of the variety now used and we would stop along the way to let the engine cool off so that it could pull up the steep grade."

The Mountain Auto Line (whose name was retained because of its separate tariff) brought a new vertical dimension to the operations of Motor Transit Co. The mile-high altitudes and rough, narrow roads that routinely climbed at grades of 8 to 18 percent proved a challenge to the movement of passengers and freight. Snow often closed the southern approaches to the mountains during the

Mountain Auto Line 3, a White tourer, loads at Forest Home before returning down the mountain to Redlands, circa 1917.
Motor Bus Society

Below: On a sunny day in November of 1920, half of the Mountain Auto Line fleet was photographed at San Bernardino waiting for the Pacific Electric train from Los Angeles. These Whites had removable seats so that freight could be hauled. *White*

Shown leaving the Pine Knot post office on the south shore of Big Bear Lake is 233, a 14-passenger stage on a White chassis. Its riders are about to enjoy a scenic trip to Lake Arrowhead along Rim-of-the-World Drive.
Motor Bus Society

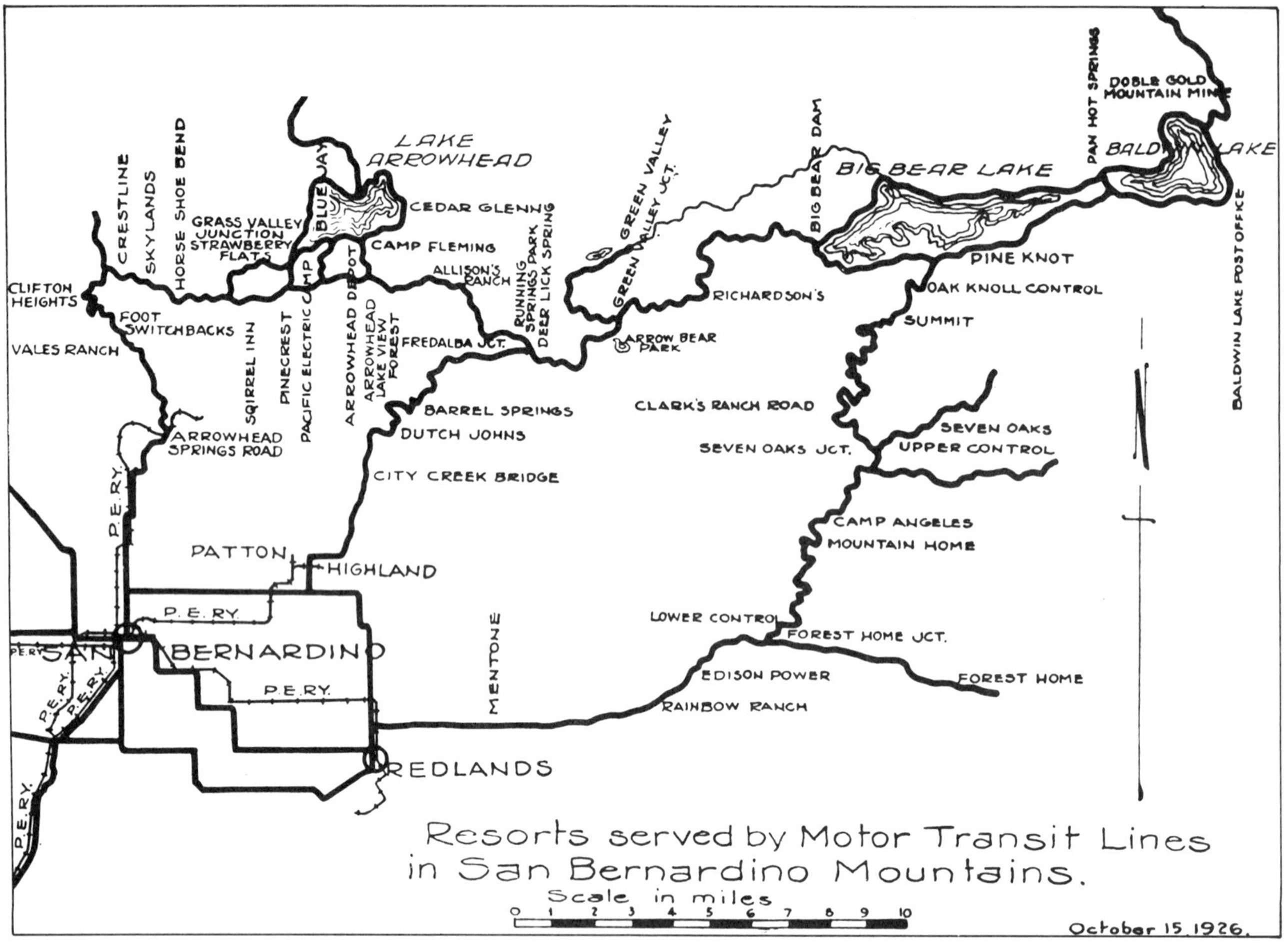

Resorts served by Motor Transit Lines in San Bernardino Mountains.

Scale in miles

October 15 1926.

This 1926 map illustrates the extent of service offered to the San Bernardino Mountain resort area. Circle trips were advertised to induce a vacationer to ascend by one route and, at the end of his stay, descend by another. By far the most interesting was the easterly route via Camp Angeles. Stations at Lower Control, Upper Control and Oak Knoll Control regulated traffic on this stretch of winding single-lane road by means of a baton system. *Author's Collection*

Whether for publicity or purely due to the innovativeness of its owners, Motor Transit published a joint tariff with Big Bear Airlines in September of 1924. The ubiquitous White poses here with an airliner of the day. *California Historical Society*

Mountain resort business provided an important source of revenue for Motor Transit until cars and drivers became good enough to brave the mountain roads. Special trips and cut rates were featured during the summer to lure vacationers to the mountains. In the years before the automobile became the mainstay of California life, Motor Transit never seemed to have quite enough equipment during the summer months. These two photos show both ends of the line—the San Bernardino station (right) featuring a sheltered driveway for passenger loading and a plug for the "Rim of the World Drive" and the Big Bear Lake depot hosting three 200-series stages. *Motor Bus Society; California Historical Society*

winter, permitting access only by way of a circuitous desert route through Victorville.

The primary difficulty was in finding a vehicle able to perform the difficult tasks of the Mountain Division; another was to find drivers and agents able to cope successfully with the terrain, the weather, the roads, and the traveling public. The inherited ¾-ton Whites, most of them built in 1917, were unreliable and caused the San Bernardino Chamber of Commerce to support an application for competitive service, but by the end of the 1921 season, Motor Transit had begun to place in operation a series of 11-passenger White stages modified from ¾-ton chassis but having rear ends taken from 2-ton chassis. These proved adequate and set the pattern for future Mountain Auto Line equipment.

The economics of the mountain operation were also troublesome. Due to seasonal changes in the type of traffic handled, it was impractical to use stages without cargo space except in the summer months. Since all Mountain Division vehicles were geared for operation on the excessive grades, they were equally useless for flat running, so they sat idle all winter.

The mountain lines were further plagued by local tour operators using their own automobiles and charging cut rates. Motor Transit complained about these pirates, but to no avail, as the Railroad Commission as yet had no jurisdiction over trips that returned to the point of origin. It was not until 1927 that single-terminal tour and sightseeing bus service was regulated in California.

Northern Division. The lines comprising Motor Transit's Northern Division were acquired in 1920. Antelope Valley Transportation Co.'s "Blue Line Stage" was purchased in February; this service started at the Rosslyn Hotel in Los Angeles and ran via Mint Canyon or Boquet Canyon to Palmdale and Lancaster (70 miles). In October, the El Dorado Stage Line from Los Angeles to Bakersfield and Taft (125 miles) was acquired for $105,000 worth of Motor Transit stock. With the sale came eleven 8-passenger and six 11-passenger Packards and one 8-passenger White.

The El Dorado Stage Line had its beginning on February

One of the 17 Packard stages acquired from the El Dorado Stage Line with the Bakersfield route. The cars, which were originally named after famous California places and personages, were prosaically numbered by Motor Transit into its first 400 series.
California Historical Society

15, 1917, when it started operating two trips a day between Bakersfield, Taft, and Los Angeles. El Dorado advertised itself as a deluxe service using only the finest equipment chauffered by courteous, uniformed, carefully trained drivers. Its Packard tourers were not numbered but named after men and places of early California: *Bret Harte, Mark Twain, Yuba Bill, Roaring Camp, Poker Dick,* and *Peter Lebec* were some.

The ride to Bakersfield followed the Ridge Route over the backbone of the Castaic Mountains. This highway, when completed, was regarded as one of the outstanding accomplishments of western road construction, and a major purpose was to bring the output of Kern County's numerous oil fields down to the coast. The road rose to a mile above sea level by traversing 1,100 turns within 29 miles; some 50 miles of twisting 10 percent grades afforded an ever-changing panorama with a variety of scenic views.

After acquisition by Motor Transit, service consisted of six round trips a day to Bakersfield and two to Taft. In August 1923, joint service was authorized with the Kern County Transportation Co. and Boyd & Mattly Stages over the cross-country route connecting Taft with Bakersfield. In October, Motor Transit was permitted to buy Cooley Stage Line (Taft–Maricopa), and a significant event was the initiation of joint fares over these routes with California Transit Co., the largest stage operator in the central part of the state.

Valley Route. The Northern Division of Motor Transit between Los Angeles and Bakersfield was the first leg of an

The equipment used on the Valley route varied with ownership but offered a consistent high class of service and comfort. A comparison of cars used in the pool operation (left and opposite) shows Motor Transit and California Transit Whites—both with home-built bodies—and a Valley Transit Fageol, the only stock vehicle of the three.
All: California Historical Society

130
130

Here is the panoramic view seen by a Bakersfield-bound passenger in 1920 on the Grapevine 25 miles north of Sandberg's Log Cabin. These final few miles of the Ridge Route were representative of the finest accomplishments of Western road construction of the era. Postcard view of the bus was taken at the Log Cabin, a favorite meal stop on the 5¾-hour trip between Los Angeles and Bakersfield. Traces of the old Ridge Route are visible today from Interstate Highway 5.

SCRTD Collection; Motor Bus Society

SEE CALIFORNIA IN COMFORT VIA

Motor Transit Co.

STAGE LINES

TICKETS AND RESERVATIONS MADE THRU CLERK OR HEAD PORTER

Heated Stages for Comfort
Dual Tires for Safety

SAN DIEGO

Beautiful 5-hour drive along the Coast.
12 schedules daily. Connections to Tiajuana.

SAN FRANCISCO

16½ hours over the scenic "Ridge Route."
4 thru schedules daily. 4 more leisurely schedules.

BAKERSFIELD AND TAFT

Over the famous Ridge Route.
8 schedules daily to Bakersfield. 2 schedules daily to Taft.

"RIM OF THE WORLD"

101-Mile drive thru San Bernardino Mountains, serving all Mountain Resorts.

Always Specify

"Motor Transit" Stages

UNION STAGE DEPOT
5th and Los Angeles Streets.
Phone Pico 3850.

Author's Collection

inland route to San Francisco via the San Joaquin Valley. The second leg, from Bakersfield to Merced, was operated by Valley Transit Co., incorporated in 1920 to succeed the partnership of Walling and Alexander. California Transit Co. then ran the northern leg from Merced into Oakland.

Three through schedules a day were operating over the Valley Route by 1923: the "Coyote" ran to San Francisco with stops at Bakersfield, Merced, and Oakland; the "Senator" to Sacramento stopping at Bakersfield, Merced, and Stockton; and the "San Joaquin Limited" (later renamed the "Valley Flyer") to Fresno and valley points stopping only at Bakersfield. A pool of buses from the three operators was used to maintain the through schedules.

A fourth through schedule was inaugurated with some fanfare on January 1, 1924. Advertising read, "The Sun Maid Limited—Thru in a Night," and with the cooperation of the Sun-Maid Raisin Growers Association a small box of their product was distributed to each passenger passing through the raisin-producing district of the San Joaquin Valley. The one-way fare to San Francisco at that time was $12.85, and a round-trip ticket cost $20.50. The through cars arrived in San Francisco 16½ to 17 hours after leaving Los Angeles. The competition, in the form of Pickwick Stages, scheduled its Coast Route trips in 16 hours.

The Packard Stage Line was a competing carrier between Los Angeles and Bakersfield, but its route was circuitous and ran through the Antelope Valley and Mojave. Lease of this operation by Pickwick Stages was the first step in an effort to put together a competitive inland route to the north to complement its established coastal route. A second step was taken when certain local rights centering on Fresno were acquired. Further efforts in this direction were blocked when Valley Transit was sold to California Transit in 1925.

Fares and Rights. A zone fare system, established in 1920, was the basis for Motor Transit tariffs thereafter. One-way fares at that time were 2½ cents per mile, with a minimum fare of 10 cents and zone breaks about every 2 miles. Round-trip tickets were priced at 85 percent of twice the one-way fare. Ten-ride tickets were offered at a 30

Buy your ticket to Los Angeles at the California Transit Co. Depot, 55 Fifth Street, San Francisco. (Lankershim Hotel). Get on the stage, which ferries across to Oakland, and you are on your way over the foothills into the pleasant fertile San Joaquin Valley. On through Modesto, Turlock to Merced.

From here the Valley Transit Company stages carry you forward through Fresno, through the San Joaquin Valley to Bakersfield! Thence to the oilfields, over the Tejon Pass by the "Ridge Road" on the Motor Transit Company stages, dropping down to Los Angeles on the other side of the mountains.

The trip takes 15 hours 45 minutes on the limiteds. (Stopover privileges at Merced, Fresno and Bakersfield).

Travel by stage over the great mountain scenic highway and enjoy your trip, whether on business or pleasure.

One-way rates from Oakland to:

Manteca	$2.30
Modesto	2.90
Turlock	3.35
Livingston	3.65
Merced	4.15
Livermore	1.15
Stockton	2.50
Sacramento	4.15
Vallejo	.90

Location of Stage Depots and Phone Numbers:

SAN FRANCISCO 55 Fifth St.	Douglas 632	BAKERSFIELD 19th and N Sts.	1781
LOS ANGELES Fifth and Los Angeles Sts.	Metro. 3850	SACRAMENTO 5th and I Sts.	974
SAN DIEGO 918 First St.	Main 783	STOCKTON 27 S. Hunter St.	479
FRESNO Jay and Mono Sts.	4484	OAKLAND 366 Fourteenth St.	Oakland 80

CALIFORNIA TRANSIT CO.

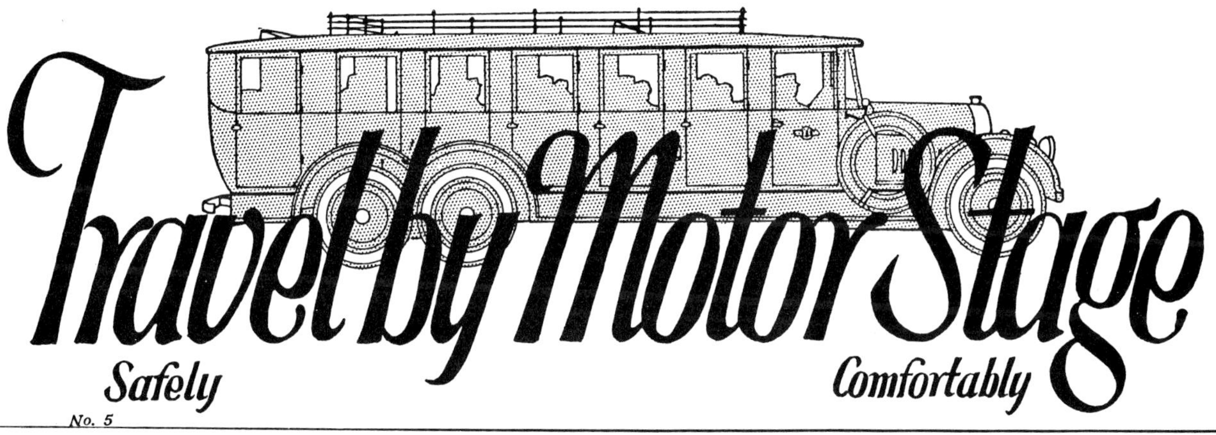

No. 5

In 1924 the California Transit Co. devised a series of newspaper advertisements to dramatize the advantages of bus travel. Here are two examples in a choice art moderne motif. *Author's Collection*

Over MOUNTAINS *a mile high!*

The "Ridge Road", over which we route you, climbs the high divide between Los Angeles and the San Joaquin Valley. Views on both sides through the gardens, vineyards, orchards and dairies.

A grand scenic route—fine motor stage equipment. The stages glide along like private limousines, smoothly, comfortably and safely over the paved highways.

Travel over the "Ridge"—breathe in the mountain air. Arrange your trip so as to get the scenery,—the stages leave at convenient times.

One-way rates from Oakland to:	
Manteca	$2.30
Modesto	2.90
Turlock	3.35
Livingston	3.65
Merced	4.15
Livermore	1.15
Stockton	2.50
Sacramento	4.15
Vallejo	.90

Location of Stage Depots and Phone Numbers:

Depot	Phone	Depot	Phone
SAN FRANCISCO 55 Fifth St.	Douglas 632	BAKERSFIELD 19th and N Sts.	1781
LOS ANGELES Fifth and Los Angeles Sts.	Metro. 3850	SACRAMENTO 5th and I Sts.	974
SAN DIEGO 918 First St.	Main 783	STOCKTON 27 S. Hunter St.	479
FRESNO Jay and Mono Sts.	4484	OAKLAND 366 Fourteenth St.	Oakland 80

CALIFORNIA TRANSIT CO.

The Anaheim depot was on Lemon St. in 1927; stage 255 pauses briefly to make a station stop on its way to Santa Ana. *Motor Bus Society*

percent discount, and 30-ride tickets were sold at a 40 percent discount.

The focal point of the operation after the era of casual curbside loading had ended was the Union Stage Depot at 5th and Los Angeles Streets, on the eastern edge of the central business district of Los Angeles. When the depot opened in 1919, it increased the number of passengers carried by as much as 20 percent on some lines of its eight participating companies.

Motor Transit and Pickwick Stages were the largest users of the depot, which had been built by O.R. Fuller, and they also leased the mezzanine office space. Motor Transit also occupied a maintenance area adjacent to the building for servicing buses between scheduled runs (270 a day by 1922). As these two companies grew by mergers, more and more trips in and out of the city were concentrated at the same terminal.

On April 22, 1924, the Railroad Commission handed down its decision on a year-old Motor Transit appeal for definition of its operating rights and their consolidation into one unified system. No doubt the application arose from the confusion over the former A.R.G. San Diego line, which had only just been settled, and not entirely to Motor Transit's satisfaction.

The decision did provide a new certificate, but consolidation of all the operating rights into a unified system was denied and operation by divisions was formally instituted. This effectively prevented any through-routing or merging of lines. The recently acquired G&W route into the San Jacinto Mountains was specifically singled out for separate operation.

Second, a 40-pound limit was placed on express packages, and finally, local rights on the Northern Division between Los Angeles and Saugus, never authorized, were formally denied, and stops at San Fernando and Newhall were accordingly eliminated.

The same decision also formalized certain operated routings in the San Bernardino Mountains. Another alternate winter route was authorized over a new highway to Lake Arrowhead via Hesperia, and additional routes were approved around Arrowhead and Big Bear Lakes and from Lake Arrowhead to the Last Ranch.

Equipment. Early California stage operators—and Motor Transit was no exception—began service with touring cars. The most successful entrepreneurs preferred heavy cars such as Pierce-Arrow, Packard, and Cadillac. To meet local requirements, many modifications began to be

Bound for Santa Ana, 404 leaves the Fullerton depot with a second section waiting to pull out behind it. The 400s were the first Motor Transit buses with home-built chassis as well as bodies; many White parts were used in their manufacture. *Bob Burrowes*

A Motor Transit charter party of the mid-1920s poses for a group photo. The style of bus bodies seen here was first used on the White chassis of the 80 series and later on the Buda-engined Motor Transit chassis of the 400 series. *California Historical Society*

incorporated, and in some instances the cars were barely recognizable by the time they were placed in service.

Operators of purely local routes, where speed and comfort were less in demand, started with light truck chassis, Reo, White, and Moreland being among the popular makes, and had locally built wooden-framed bodies with open sides fitted to them after the style of the stretched-out touring cars used on the long-distance services.

White Bus Line began in 1916 with ¾-ton White truck chassis. Open-sided 21- and 25-passenger bodies were used for local service, and these vehicles along with similar ones acquired from other operators were numbered from 1 up. Stages of the touring-car type, acquired from other companies, were put into the 100 series, with Whites of that type purchased new or used after 1919 going into the 200s. Constant modifications produced great diversity, especially after Motor Transit occupied its four-story headquarters and shop building at Market and San Pedro Streets about 1921.

Service-tailored equipment could be assembled by fitting specially built bodies to standard truck chassis, stock chassis could be altered to accommodate standard bodies, or vehicles could be assembled from any combination of modified or built-up components and assemblies. Motor Transit was to exercise all these options. The initial manufacturing efforts produced streetcar-type bodies for White Model 50 truck chassis.

As requirements grew, chassis were spliced and lengthened to increase capacity from 21 to 25 passengers. Construction became more substantial as evidenced by the addition of rear-end pipe bumpers, metal wheels and oversized brakes.

Older buses were also continually modified and updated. Starting with the substitution of dual rear wheels (once a practical mounting method which allowed changing of tires was devised), operating equipment was modified as the need arose and the economy proven. For instance, tests were made to show that the dual wheels actually increased stability and decreased tire wear before they were incorporated on the fleet. In later years buses were completely rebodied as well as having their spoked wheels replaced by solid and air springs added to alleviate the traditional bouncy ride.

Side-door stages were also produced starting very early in Motor Transit's building days. These grew by lengthening stock White tourers to 11,- 14- and 18-passenger machines. The later and larger models were often based on White light truck chassis and some were fitted with heavy duty rear ends and compound transmissions for Ridge Route and Mountain Division service.

White trucks and combos taken over with Mountain Auto Line in 1920 became Motor Transit's 300 series, and Packard cars acquired with El Dorado Stage Lines were put into the 400s. Whites with home-built or Avery bodies

The Los Angeles Union Stage Depot is seen here after a facelift that moved the main entrance to the corner of 5th and Los Angeles streets. The interior view was taken during its first decade of service; modeled after a railroad terminal, it was—in 1922—the busiest bus depot west of the Mississippi, serving some 270 runs daily. *Both: Motor Bus Society*

ROSTER OF BUSES

Motor Transit Co.
(1918–1925 only)
Incomplete

Numbers	Make	Body Type	Seats	Built	Notes
36-37	White	Bus	25	1918	New bodies, 1921
38-46	White	Bus	21	1919	38-40, 42, 44; new 25-pass. bodies, 1921
47-49	White	Bus	21	1920	
50, 52	White	Bus	25	1917	New bodies, 1922
51, 53	White	Side-door	18	1917	New bodies, 1921
54-55	White	Bus	21	1916	New bodies, 1920-21
56	White	Bus	21	1917	New bodies, 1920-21
57	White	Bus	21	1919	New bodies, 1920-21
58-76	White	Bus	21	1920	
77-79	White	Bus	21	1921	
80	White	Bus	25	1922	
81-85	White	Bus	25	1923	
86-102	White	Bus	25	1924	
200-201	White	Side-door	11	1914	201 New 14-pass. body, 1921
202-203	White	Side-door	11	1920	202 New 14-pass. body
204	White	Side-door	11	1912	New body, 1921
205-207	White	Side-door	11	1920	
208	White	Side-door	14	1912	New body, 1921
209	White	Side-door	11	1920	
210-211	White	Side-door	11	1914	New bodies, 1921
212	White	Side-door	14	1912	New body, 1921
213-216	White	Side-door	11	1915-16	New bodies, 1921
217-218	White	Side-door	14	1914	New body, 1921
219	White	Side-door	11	1914	New body, 1922
220-222	White	Side-door	11	1916-18	New bodies, 1922
223-224	White	Side-door	18	1922	
225	White	Side-door	14	1912	New body
226	White	Side-door	11	1915	New body, 1922
227	White	Side-door	18	1923	
228	White	Side-door	14	1922	
229-231	White	Side-door	18	1923	
232-233	White	Side-door	14	1923	
234-235	White	Side-door	6	1923-24	Combos
236	White	Side-door	11	1923	
237	White	Side-door	?	?	
238-241	White	Side-door	18	1923	
242	White	Side-door	?	?	
243	White	Side door	6	1923	Combo
244	White	Side-door	14	1912	New body
245	White	Side-door	14	1912	New body
246-247	White	Side-door	18	1924	
248-249	White	Side-door	?	?	
250	White	Side-door	14	1921	New body
251-254	White	Side-door	11	1917	New bodies, 1921
255-258	White	Side-door	18	1924	
301-303	White	Side-door	11	1917	(1920) Mountain Auto Line; compounds, new bodies
304	White	Side-door	11	1916	(1920) MAL; compound
305	White	Side-door	11	1917	(1920) MAL; compound, new body, 1921
306	White	Side-door	11	1918	(1920) MAL; compound, new body, 1919
307-312	White	Side-door	11	1916-17	(1920) MAL; compounds, new bodies, 1922
325-326	White	Side-door	18	1920-21	Combo
401-407	Packard	Side-door	11	1917	(1920) El Dorado Stage Line; new bodies, 1920
450-460	Packard	Side-door	8	1917	(1920) El Dorado Stage Line; new bodies, 1920-21

Introduced on long-distance service, the 550 spent its days after 1926 running in limited service to mountain resorts. It and its sister, 551, had a center aisle and only one door. *Security Pacific National Bank*

Left: A Fageol "Safety Bus" in service on the Los Angeles–Santa Ana "short line." When Crown Stages leased the former Valley Stage Line route to Pickwick Stages early in 1924, its older Reos were sent along as part of the transaction. Watson kept the newer and larger Fageols. *Fageol*

continued to be added to the 1-up series for local lines and the 200s for long-distance service until 1924, when purchase and modification of stock chassis was dropped in favor of building complete buses from purchased parts. Stages continued in the 200 series, but a new type of fully enclosed 25-passenger bus for local use, with a rear baggage compartment and steel paneling over oak framing, made its debut as the second 400 series.

Dillingham and Cregar Lines. More than 150 route miles were added to the Motor Transit system on April 5, 1924, by the lease of two widely separated properties. The Dillingham Transportation Co. lines between Pasadena and Long Beach complemented Motor Transit's own routes out of Los Angeles to the east and southeast. There were three routes, the most direct being by way of Mountain View Heights and Bandini (now Commerce) and the others via Alhambra, El Monte, and Rivera, and via Alhambra, Montebello, and Rivera. Through passengers naturally preferred the direct route, the other two carrying mainly local riders. Dillingham also operated two routes between Whittier and Long Beach, one via Downey and the other via Norwalk.

The lines of E.B. and H.L. Dillingham originated prior to 1917 with operation of service between Pasadena and Long Beach. The Whittier lines were started in 1918 and 1920. The competing Liberty Stage Line route between Pasadena and Long Beach via El Monte was purchased in 1921 as previously mentioned. A line from Long Beach to Santa Monica was operated from August 1921 until Octo-

To provide a focal point for its newly enlarged Orange County operation, Motor Transit purchased the Meyer Hotel at 3rd and Spurgeon streets in Santa Ana for $113,000. The street floor was remodeled as a bus terminal, and the remainder of the hotel was leased out. The depot was soon being used as well by erstwhile competitor Pickwick Stages. *California Historical Society*

ber 1923, when it was sold to Motor Coach Co. (of Lomita). Dillingham's buses were mainly 25-passenger bodies on Menominee truck chassis, which were soon replaced by Motor Transit's usual Whites.

The Cregar Stage Line routes were Riverside–San Jacinto via Eden Hot Springs and Gilman Hot Springs, San Jacinto–Idyllwild via Oak Cliff and Keen Camp, and from Keen Camp and Idyllwild to Banning, Beaumont, and Riverside. No local service was allowed between Banning, Beaumont, and Riverside to protect United Stages. The Riverside–San Jacinto service had been leased by Cregar to West and Clark in 1923, and the line was not taken over by Motor Transit until January 1925.

Richard Bruce Cregar started operating buses between Riverside and Santa Ana in June 1919 but sold this line to J.C. Best in January 1920. His subsequent absence from the motor stage business was not a long one, for he acquired operating rights between San Jacinto and Idyllwild from R.E. Williams in June 1920.

A new line connecting his existing route with Riverside via Gilman Hot Springs and Eden Hot Springs was authorized early in 1921, and an extension over a new road from Oak Cliff to Idyllwild soon followed. Through operation from Riverside, Beaumont, and Banning to Idyllwild and Keen Camp was authorized in July 1922, and by the end of that year Cregar was running three daily round trips to connect with the trains of the Pacific Electric in Riverside.

Motor Transit Co. in 1925. Operating statistics for the year 1924 showed more than six million miles operated using 118 cars and carrying 2,337,000 passengers, the average ride being 2¾ miles. Motor Transit's total revenue for the year was $1.6 million. The first abandonment of a marginal service occurred during 1924 (Chino–Ontario). Riverside–Loma Linda followed in January 1925, and the little-used Los Angeles–Long Beach connection to the San Pedro–Long Beach–Santa Ana–San Diego line was discontinued in April. The Taft–Maricopa connection, purchased less than two years earlier, was leased to Charles Sansome.

With increasing traffic over the Valley Route, Motor Transit identified itself more closely with California Transit in 1925 by adopting a distinctive shield-shaped emblem that was shared with the other company. Using the name of its predecessor on the Northern Division, Motor Transit called itself the "El Dorado System"; California Transit styled itself as the "Pioneer Stage."

Use of the emblem as a radiator ornament led to Motor Transit's home-built buses being called El Dorado coaches, and the name was later used without the emblem. Much the same thing happened on California Transit, which built Pioneer Stages in Oakland.

Consolidation of the leased Dillingham and Cregar lines was accomplished in January 1926. The Dillingham routes were merged with the Eastern and Southern Divisions, except that no through service was allowed from Riverside or Pomona to Long Beach (to protect Crown Stages) or between Los Angeles and Long Beach by any route (to protect PE). New routes made possible by this merger were Pasadena–Whittier–Santa Ana and Pasadena–Whittier–Long Beach, the latter a routing that had been denied to Dillingham by the Railroad Commission in 1920. The Cregar routes were merged into the Eastern Division, per-

An analysis of the commodities moving into and out of Los Angeles by bus during August of 1922 showed newspapers making up almost half of the items shipped; automobile accessories made up half of the remainder. The crew of the Los Angeles freight and express depot (located behind the Union Stage Depot on Maple Ave.) is captured on film in 1927. Closeup shows agent and driver loading express packages into the rear compartment of a 700-series bus.
Both: Motor Bus Society

mitting the establishment of through service from Los Angeles to the San Jacinto Mountains via Riverside.

Crown Stages. Next to Motor Transit itself, the largest interurban operator in Orange County was the Crown Stages system of A.B. Watson. The original route from Santa Ana to Anaheim was supplemented before 1917 by service to Long Beach via Greenville, Talbert, Westminster, and Seal Beach, and early in 1918 an alternate route via Garden Grove was authorized. Crown's operating territory was extended south in September 1918, when rights to Laguna Beach via Irvine were authorized.

Entry into Los Angeles was gained in 1920 by the previously described purchase of Valley Stage Line, and a new route between Pomona and Long Beach via Anaheim and Los Alamitos (which did not pass through Santa Ana) was

The bin of laundry, new bedsprings, crates of eggs and boxes of produce, all point toward a successful season for the Big Bear Lake resorts, if this view inside the Big Bear Lake Motor Transit station is any indication. MT's freight service provisioned the mountain camps and resorts. The indoor loading bay was required by the winter weather when access was possible only by the desert routes through Victorville and Hesperia. The exterior photo shows bus 207 about to leave for the lowlands with a full load and a sister 200-series stage converted to a six-passenger combo loading in the bay.

Both: Motor Bus Society

started soon thereafter. By the end of 1920, Crown Stages was also operating from Santa Ana to Balboa via Newport Beach. A line from Santa Ana to Huntington Beach was acquired from the estate of Charles J. Crosby in February 1924, which was also the date of the Railroad Commission decision authorizing lease of the ex-Valley Los Angeles–Santa Ana "Short Line" to Pickwick Stages.

In April 1924, Crown Stages acquired the Santa Ana–Riverside route that had been started by R.B. Cregar in 1919 and then purchased by J.C. Best, who became manager of what Crown called its Riverside Branch. An attempt to extend the Santa Ana–Huntington Beach route to Seal Beach and Long Beach was denied in deference to the protests of the Pacific Electric, which ran a connecting service to Laguna and San Juan Capistrano over this route in conjunction with the Pacific Coast Motor Coach Co. A second effort two years later was successful, PE having found the bus service to be unremunerative, but Crown was not permitted to carry local passengers between Huntington Beach and Seal Beach.

The Tri-Stage Merger. It was evident by 1926 that competition over Southern California's motor stage routes was neither economical nor efficient, in spite of an ever-increasing amount of interlining and joint operation. Toward the goal of consolidating territories for economy of operation, the so-called "tri-stage merger" was proposed and approved by the Railroad Commission. An exchange of rights among Motor Transit, California Transit, and Pickwick Stages was authorized, and specific areas of service for each company were defined.

Motor Transit retired from the long-distance field by giving up its Northern Division to California Transit and its San Diego line to Pickwick. In return, local lines owned or controlled by Pickwick in the territory south of Los Angeles were transferred to Motor Transit. California Transit purchased from Pickwick its local rights in the Fresno area. The lease of Packard Stages by Pickwick was canceled, and Packard's operating rights via Mojave were transferred to Motor Transit, so that when California Transit purchased Motor Transit's Bakersfield line it included the circuitous Packard operation.

By entering into this agreement, Pickwick gave up its foothold in the inland territory and California Transit succeeded in consolidating the Valley Route. Pickwick in turn gained sole operation of the Coast Route south to San Diego, and Motor Transit consolidated its hold on Orange County.

On April 24, 1926, Pickwick Stages gained control of Crown Stages by signing a conditional bill of sale for the remainder of the system (other than the leased Los Angeles–Santa Ana "Short Line"). By putting the extensive Crown network into the merger agreement, and by offering to abandon its local operations between Los Angeles and Santa Ana on the Coast Route and between Los Angeles and Riverside on the Inland Route to San Diego, Pickwick made the deal impossible for Motor Transit to resist.

Accordingly the exchanges were made on May 13, Motor Transit's 200-mile Northern Division and 16 stages passing to California Transit and the 135-mile San Diego line to Pickwick. Motor Transit assumed operation of the 106-mile Crown Stages system as well as the 37-mile "Short Line," and acquired Crown's 23 buses and three trucks. The purchase price was approximately $167,000; presumably Motor Transit received an equivalent amount for the rights and buses it contributed to the three-way deal.

In the words of the Railroad Commission, completion of the merger left Motor Transit as "a specialized local operator of motor transportation in the territory in and around Los Angeles, Santa Ana, and the San Gabriel Valley, from the ocean to and including the San Bernardino and San Jacinto Mountains."

Express and Freight. In 1924, when divisional operation was imposed on Motor Transit, all existing tariffs were revised as part of a new single certificate to limit the weight of express packages to 40 pounds. Permission to carry any overflow in trucks was denied. Tariffs previously in effect had included a wide range of size and weight limitations, as well as a diversity of rates. In fact, there were instances of rates and limits that had no basis in actual certificates, even though they were in most cases inherited from predecessor companies.

The 40-pound limit might have been objectively considered a kindness extended by the Railroad Commission, since it was authorized systemwide, even on routes where no previous express service had existed. The decision had no effect on the Mountain Division, where specific freight rates had been in existence since Mountain Auto Line's independent days.

In keeping with the philosophy that there is nothing new under the sun, it seems worth a few lines to quote part of the 1924 recertification decision insisting that Motor Transit "shall name one rate for the transportation of baggage, packages, and express, which rate shall be applicable and not subject to increase by reason of the holding out on the part of applicant of a guarantee to forward a particular baggage express, or package shipment on the first car scheduled following the receipt of the baggage, express, or packages." Almost 50 years later, Greyhound instituted "Next Bus Out" double-or-nothing guarantees on certain package express shipments, with great fanfare.

Soon after the 1924 decision, Motor Transit requested a higher weight limit on package and baggage shipments, and new authority was awarded in 1927. Inconsistencies still existed, notably the absence of any express rights at all on the former Dillingham routes, but basically the 1927 rights provided that baggage up to 150 pounds per piece could be carried free on any one-way fare of $3 or more. Express up to 100 pounds per package was authorized to be carried on passenger vehicles.

Motor Transit had gotten into the business of hauling freight with purchase of the Mountain Auto Line in 1920. A second freight operation, from Riverside to the San Jacinto Mountains, came with the former Cregar lines, and a third (minor) freight route was inherited with Crown Stages (Santa Ana–Laguna Beach). While the extent of these rights was small, just over 100 miles in a 1,200-mile system, the mountain territory was the most difficult served, as exemplified by the 5,200-foot climb from San Bernardino to Lake Arrowhead in 15 miles.

The first significant tonnage handled from the valley to the San Bernardino Mountains was cement from the plant at Slover Mountain (Colton) to Lake Arrowhead. The trucks replaced six 12-horse mule teams. One two-ton White truck could make three trips to Lake Arrowhead in one day against one round trip by mule train every two days.

The matter of rates was always a problem on these lines. Due to the great variation in demand with the changing seasons, as well as varying road conditions, both freight and passenger rates on the Mountain lines were higher in the winter. When the desert routes had to be used, double rates were charged; when the normal routes were passable, but weather conditions precluded maintenance of normal schedules, an hourly flat rate was imposed. Prior to the establishment of this rate structure, the use of standard tariffs and commodity classifications had produced continuous disputes over rates and an expensive and complicated billing system.

Freight Equipment. Motor Transit's continuous equipment rebuilding program was nowhere as evident as in the freight hauling area. The first freight equipment consisted of convertible White trucks which came with the purchase of the Mountain Auto Line. These were reworked with 12-speed transmissions and were mechanically similar to the so-called "compound" stages which worked the mountain lines in early years. The arduous physical requirements of that service soon took their toll and the rebuilding efforts resulted in combos converted from both stages and from streetcar-type buses as well as purpose-built trucks.

The first rebuilds used chassis which were under early 21-passenger buses. As these were put into service, they replaced worn-out vehicles which were returned to the Market Street Shops. There, the body and all components were stripped from the chassis which was reconditioned, received a new engine and transmission and was completed as an express truck or a service vehicle.

In 1925, the same year that it turned out its first complete bus, Motor Transit built its first truck. Like the bus, it was powered by a White GR engine. Trucks continued to be produced until 1929 ranging in size from two to five tons; at least one of the five-tonners was a tandem-wheel design.

The assortment of freight equipment on the roster in 1929 comprised two combos with a capacity of six passengers and 2,500 pounds of freight, three carrying nine passengers and two tons, and 12 trucks ranging in capacity from three to five tons. The trucks were used primarily in the summer months, when 90 percent of the Mountain Division's freight was handled. In the winter, the combos were sufficient to handle the schedule.

The year 1927 saw White 75 rebuilt as a 9-passenger combo. The spacious rear compartment could accommodate the largest express package as well as most freight shipments.
Both: Motor Bus Society

The New Look. The 1926 operating statistics reflected the changed character of the operation, as 400,000 more passengers were carried than in 1925 while 400,000 fewer vehicle-miles were operated. The Dillingham lines, formerly leased, were purchased in December 1925 for $20,000 and the Cregar lines followed in September 1926 for $5,000. Three additional small local lines were added to the Eastern Division during that year: Pomona–La Verne–San Dimas from City Transit Co. in March, San Bernardino–Victorville–Oro Grande from Victorville Stage in July, and Redlands–Yucaipa from Yucaipa Stage Line in November.

The Victorville line had been started by Carl D. Hodge and Joseph H. Santen in February of 1924; Hodge bought out Santen in December of 1925. The Redlands–Yucaipa line was started by D.I. Stewart in July of 1918. It passed through several changes of ownership until it was acquired by G.A. Schoen, a Redlands merchant, in July of 1922.

Meanwhile another line was taken over by lease; that of the Verdugo Hills Transportation Co., running 20 miles north from Los Angeles to Sunland via Glendale, Montrose, La Crescenta, and Tujunga. This company had succeeded A.J. Richardson as operator of the route in May 1922; Richardson had started with Studebakers in 1920. In effect, the Sunland line was a local service over the inner portion of the Northern Division, the rest of which had already been given up by the time of the lease. It became one of Motor Transit's busier lines and was purchased in 1928 for $20,000.

On the grounds that consolidation of the Cregar routes had left the San Bernardino Mountains resorts at a disadvantage, one through trip a day (with overload accommodation permitted as required) from Los Angeles over each of three access routes was allowed in the summer season starting in 1926.

For the 1927 season, Pasadena and South Pasadena were added as points of origin for resort-bound riders, and Foothill Blvd. was accordingly made an alternate route for these summer-only through runs. Once-daily Chino–Corona service was abandoned on September 21, 1926. Pomona–San Dimas and Pomona–Chino local routes were leased to J.O. Maupin on November 4, 1927.

An abortive effort to enter the sightseeing and tour market began on May 15, 1927, when a daily "Golden Orange Scenic Tour" was initiated. The $3.50 ride started in Los Angeles and proceeded via Downey, Seal Beach, Huntington Beach, and Newport to Laguna Beach, where lunch was served. In the afternoon, the return route was by way of Santa Ana, Anaheim, and Whittier. After a hope-

Ticket trailer T-100 was yet another product of the Motor Transit Shops. It was used at the Pomona Fair, the Orange Show and other events that merited special service. *SCRTD Collection*

See America First'

MOTOR TRANSIT COMPANY

SHORT ONE-DAY

SIGHTSEEING TOURS FROM LOS ANGELES

The following short sightseeing tours offer the visitor the most economical, convenient and delightful way of seeing California.

Golden Orange Scenic Tour

"The Most Interesting Trip in Southern California" takes you through bearing orange groves, along picturesque beaches, producing oil fields, cities of Whittier, Fullerton, Anaheim, Santa Ana, Laguna Beach, Newport-Balboa Beach, Long Beach. Personally conducted—$3.50, including lunch. Leave Los Angeles 9:00 a.m. daily.

Pasadena—Redlands—Riverside—Pomona

This is the most comprehensive tour of the great Orange Kingdom going via the scenic Foothill Boulevard to Redlands and returning through Riverside, Pomona and Valley Boulevard.—$2.80.

Pomona—Riverside—Santa Ana

Takes you thru El Monte, Pomona, Riverside, returning via beautiful Santa Ana River Canyon, Santa Ana and oil fields.—$3.00.

Sunland and the Green Verdugo Hills

This tour through Glendale, La Canada, La Crescenta, Verdugo to Sunland is through the romantic and historic Green Verdugo Hills.—$1.00.

Two Day "Rim of the World Tour"

An exploration of a mountain land of crystal clear lakes, pine scented peaks and tumbling streams—a tour thru the vacation resorts of the San Bernardino Mts. Overnight accommodations range from tents and housekeeping cabins to luxurious lodges. Ninety day stopovers permitted. Round trip fare from Los Angeles, $13.95. From San Bernardino $11.50. Tour operates daily June 15 to Sept. 15.

Motor Transit heavily promoted its sightseeing tours, as witness this ad appearing on March 15, 1928. *Author's Collection*

ful beginning the daily tour soon became an on-demand service and was finally discontinued in 1929.

In addition to promoting special-rate triangle sightseeing trips on its own lines, Motor Transit also sold a circle tour over the routes of two other companies using its own route from Pasadena via San Gabriel and Whittier to Long Beach as the first leg. At Long Beach a transfer was made to the Motor Coach Company's line to Ocean Park via Wilmington and Redondo Beach. The third leg began at Ocean Park where a change was made to the coaches of the Pasadena–Ocean Park Stage Line which returned to Pasadena via Hollywood and Glendale. The circle trip could be started and completed from any point on the route.

Operations. From its earliest days Fuller's company was operated in a methodical and workmanlike manner. Starting with creation of a uniform fare structure as the system grew larger and carrying through to the design and erection of buses specially conceived for each intended service, the company's endeavors bore the stamp of sound management. Even in the early 1920s, scheduling was done by time and position charting, still an excellent graphic method.

Motor Transit maintained 30-minute service within a 40-mile radius of Los Angeles with hourly service provided beyond that distance. Far-flung branches and less-used alternate routes received two-hour service. The bulk of Motor Transit business, however, was handled within a radius of 15 to 20 miles of Los Angeles. Service on these routes was provided at 7- to 15-minute intervals during peak periods. More than 40 trips departed from the Union Stage Depot between 4 and 6 p.m. each evening. Counts showed an average of eight passengers per minute leaving the terminal during this time.

By Motor Transit's estimate some 75 percent of these passengers were required to change buses before reaching their final destination, a primary reason for the continued

Even after the Tri-Stage merger, Motor Transit retained some of its compound-geared 200-series stages for mountain service. This view of the 247 shows the newly striped belt rail where the cities served in the days of long-distance operation had been listed.
Motor Bus Society

applications to consolidate the system allowing through-routing of lines. Roadside business was always protected by picking up and discharging passengers and express at any point along the lines. Extra equipment was maintained at 14 locations on the system to relieve overloads or replace breakdowns.

The El Dorado Works. By the mid-Twenties, commercially built streetcar-type buses had made inroads into the California market. White was in first place with Fageol a close second among the higher-priced vehicles, while Reo was the front runner among the less expensive makes. No commercially built stage-type equipment was considered satisfactory and operators requiring such equipment built their own, including Motor Transit. Even in the area of streetcar-type buses, Motor Transit chose to build its own using the 45,000 square feet of floor space available in the Market Street Shops.

By 1925, it was evident that the disproportionately large number of modifications required to make stock buses satisfactory for service was making the purchase of such equipment uneconomical. Needing a more rugged chassis, and more powerful drive train than White could supply, Motor Transit was forced to turn to other sources. Starting in that year, six-cylinder Buda engines and Brown-Lipe transmissions were first assembled on Motor Transit-fabricated frames. The first vehicle produced using these components was a new, more substantial, side-door stage design.

The epitome of the passenger stage as far as Motor Transit was concerned was the 500 series of 1925. Fully enclosed and boasting luxuriously upholstered seats and a leather-lined smoking compartment at the rear, these fine stages were fully up to the demands of long-distance service to San Diego or along the Valley Route. California Transit and Pickwick Stages were busy turning out their own buses too, while smaller California operators mostly bought Fageols after the Safety Coach was introduced in 1921.

Only five 500s were built, because with the tri-stage merger of 1926, Motor Transit ceased to be a long-distance carrier. The 16 buses that California Transit acquired in the deal were 200s, as the newer 500s were retained for limited-stop service to the mountains, and for other special uses. They were soon joined by the seven equally plush central-aisle buses of the 550 and 575 series.

Changes under the hood were soon reflected on the radiator shell where the White logo was replaced—first on 500s by an arrowhead enclosing the initials ORF (undoubtedly standing for O.R. Fuller) and later by the Motor Transit Company shield with its prominent EL DORADO ROUTE legend. White radiators continued to be used for several years (along with a few Fageols) but were replaced with a smoother-shaped shell bearing the legend EL DORADO COACH.

By mid-1926, Buda engines also appeared in the new suburban 400 series then being assembled; they became standard from that time on. Even in its streetcar-type buses, Motor Transit was reluctant to give up the center-aisle to open space. Portable stools and later fold-down jump seats provided accommodations for hardy passengers who decided not to wait for the second section or the next schedule. Although the 400s were described as 29-passenger buses, only 25 seats were permanent.

Motor Transit's 600 series included eight Fageols acquired with Crown Stages and the Reos which came in the same deal were numbered in the 100s along with other diverse used equipment. More than 40 buses of the suburban 400, 450, and 475 series were produced and were joined in 1927 by the first buses of the improved 700 class.

Further Rights Acquired. The fall of 1927 brought expansion of operating rights within Motor Transit's established territory. What started out as a contest with United Stages for competitive rights along Foothill Blvd. between Pasadena and San Bernardino and between Riverside and Redlands via Loma Linda ended in an amicable settlement. Pickwick Stages had acquired United Stages in November 1926, and in the spirit of the tri-stage merger

The police band, complete with tubas, proved no obstacle to Motor Transit on this charter movement. The bus is 575, an interurban central-aisle 1925 product of the Market Street Shops; note the Fageol radiator shell.
California Historical Society

ROSTER OF BUSES

Motor Transit Co.
(1925–1930 only)

Numbers	Make	Engine	Seats	Built	Notes
180	Reo	Reo	25	1919	(1926) Crown Stages
181	Reo	Reo	25	1922	(1926) Crown Stages
182-183	Reo	Reo	25	1923	(1926) Crown Stages
400-407	El Dorado	White	25/4	1925	
408-412	El Dorado	Buda	25/4	1926	
450-456	El Dorado	Buda	25	1926	
475-488	El Dorado	Buda	25	1926	
489-495	El Dorado	Buda	25	1927	
500-502	El Dorado	Buda	20	1925	Side-door bodies
503-504	El Dorado	Buda	20	1926	Side-door bodies
550-551	El Dorado	Buda	21	1925	
575-578	El Dorado	Buda	25	1925	
579	El Dorado	Buda	21	1926	
600, 602	Fageol	Hall-Scott	29	1923	(1926) Crown Stages
601, 603	Fageol	Hall-Scott	29	1922	(1926) Crown Stages
604-605	Fageol	Hall-Scott	29	1923	(1926) Crown Stages
625-626	Fageol	Hall-Scott	22	1922	(1926) Crown Stages; side-door bodies
700-706	El Dorado	Buda	33/5	1927	
707-708	El Dorado	Buda	33/5	1928	
800-805	El Dorado	Buda	33/5	1928	
806-811	El Dorado	Buda	33/7	1929	
850-853	El Dorado	Buda	25/5	1929	Compound transmissions
875	El Dorado	Sterling	33/7	1929	
876-881	El Dorado	Sterling	33/7	1930	

This lineup features four different types of Motor Transit Equipment. In the foreground are four brand-new 475-series suburban coaches, beyond are one 575- and one 550-series interurban and four older suburban coaches. The inspector and drivers are nattily attired right down to the inspector's "El Dorado System" shield. *California Historical Society*

requested transfer only of the through rights from Riverside via Loma Linda and Redlands to Imperial Valley points, not the local service.

Motor Transit thus received both sets of local rights applied for, over the strenuous objections of the Pacific Electric, which had twice before frustrated the company's efforts to gain Riverside–Loma Linda–Redlands authority. The Foothill Blvd. route was restricted against local passengers west of Upland to protect the PE rail line and the Pasadena–Pomona Stage Line.

In a second action, Motor Transit acquired from Pickwick Stages its local rights from Riverside to Beaumont via Box Springs Grade, Moreno, and the Jack Rabbit Trail,

The 700 series of 1927 was a substantial forward step: a 33-passenger suburban bus with ample baggage and express capacity. The first of the line was photographed when new at the Union Stage Depot.
Motor Bus Society

thus extending local service to a former Cregar line. A third application requested rerouting of certain segments of the former Dillingham lines through more populated areas and the removal of local service restrictions along these routes. Restoration of the abandoned Downey–Norwalk segment as an alternate through route and establishment of a new service on Euclid Avenue between Anaheim and Bolsa via Garden Grove, also as an alternate through route, were also requested, and all the appeals were granted without amendment.

Events of 1928. Connecting service between Gilman Hot Springs and Soboba Hot Springs in the San Jacinto Mountains was authorized in May 1928, though very likely the number of passengers wishing to avail themselves of this connection was quite small. A Fullerton–Placentia route started by Cory G. Hoff in 1924 was purchased in July 1928, and its extension to Yorba Linda was approved.

On July 10, 1928, service was added on Whittier Blvd. (part of the original route of White Bus Line) to replace the city of Montebello's bus line between that municipality and the terminus of the Los Angeles Railway's R streetcar line. The municipal bus service, in operation since 1922, was discontinued when a referendum failed to provide continued funds. The Maupin lease was terminated on November 20, 1928, returning the minor Pomona–Chino and Pomona–San Dimas lines to the fold.

December 3, 1928, was the date of a significant event, as Motor Transit was awarded new rights between Pasadena and Long Beach via Atlantic Avenue and PE's competing application was dismissed. This line was not far from the former Dillingham routes and had almost the same terminal points, but it was more direct and competed directly with an important Pacific Electric bus line between Hunt-

SYSTEM TIME TABLES and PASSENGER FARES

Effective March 15, 1928

MOTOR TRANSIT STAGES

and Connecting Stage Lines

UNION STAGE DEPOT

5th & Los Angeles Sts.

MEtro — 3850

LOS ANGELES

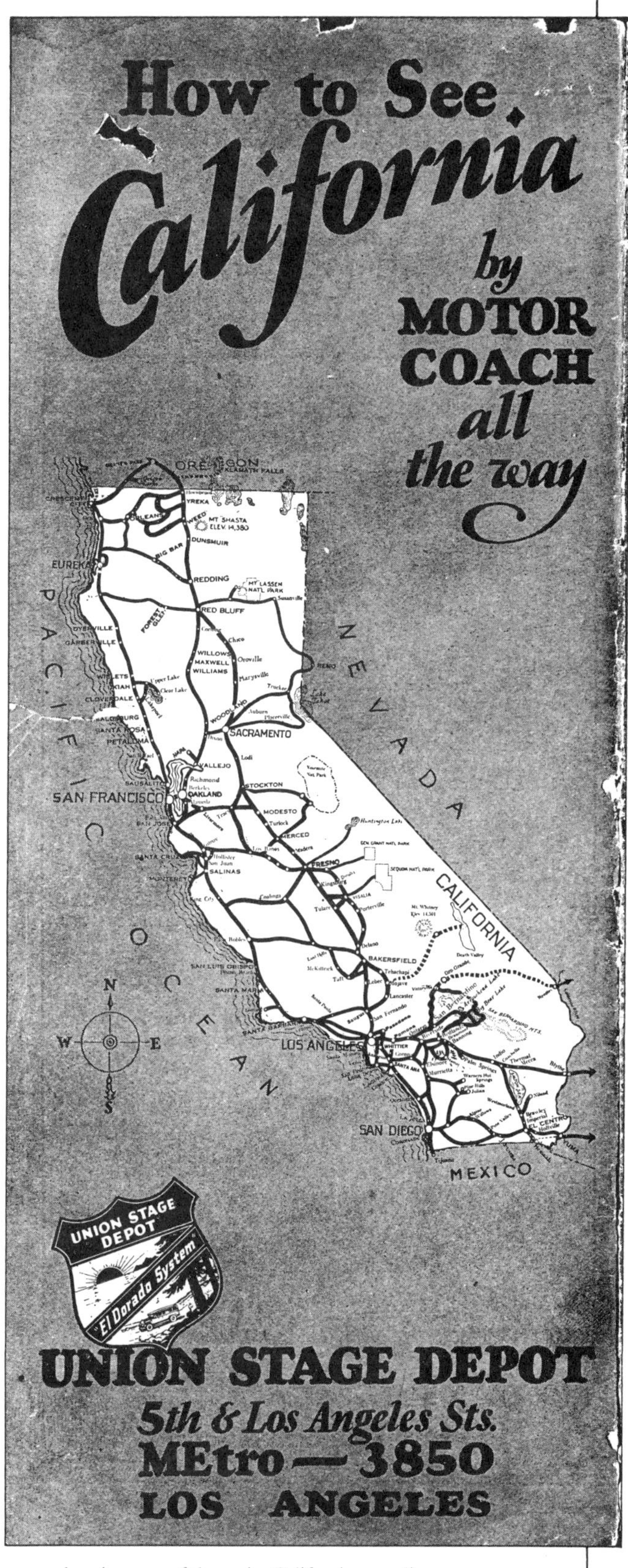

This 1928 Motor Transit timetable listed connecting lines and included a comprehensive map of the major California stage lines.

Author's Collection

Pomona was an important junction point for MT's Eastern Division routes and, as such, required facilities to perform light repairs and to store spare equipment. This combination terminal and garage at 3rd and Main streets served satisfactorily for many years. Customarily, Motor Transit leased out the newsstand and lunch counter concessions in the larger terminals which it owned. Commission agents were used in smaller towns which did not rate dedicated terminals; these were most commonly in cafes, drugstores or other sundry storefront locations. The interior photo is of the Pomona terminal, circa 1924.
Both: Motor Bus Society

ington Park and Long Beach. Another new line authorized at that time ran from the Biltmore Hotel at 5th and Olive Streets in Los Angeles to the Biltmore Hotel in Flintridge; it lasted just six months.

Pasadena Pomona Stage Line. Motor Transit Co. purchased the 30-mile Pasadena–Pomona Stage Line from J. Hatch Lord for $10,000 early in 1929 and soon merged the Pomona–San Dimas line into it. This purchase, coming soon after the award of the Atlantic Avenue route, must have disturbed PE, for Lord's route was listed in the PE timetable as a connection between the Northern District Foothill route, which ended at Glendora, and the main line to San Bernardino. The rights between Pasadena and Pomona via Foothill Blvd. had been granted to D.E. Hamilton and Charles R. Lusby in 1920. Hamilton, later a principal in the Pasadena–Ocean Park Stage Line, sold his interest to Lord in January 1921, and Lusby followed suit in August.

Improved Motor Transit service in the growing industrial area east of Los Angeles was undertaken in March 1929, when alternate routes between Los Angeles and Downey via Maywood, Bell, and Cudahy, and between Los Angeles and Whittier via 9th Street, Mines Avenue, and Washington Blvd. were secured. The most strenuous objection to the new Downey route was presented by PE, which oper-

The short-wheelbase, 25-passenger, 850-series of coach was specially geared for mountain service. The first of the class meets an earlier form of mountain transportation at Lake Arrowhead.
California Historical Society

ated 33 schedules daily from Walker Avenue (on the Maywood–Bell boundary) to Los Angeles on its Whittier line. The Commission felt that the railway's lower fare would protect its traffic.

Minor reroutings took place on various lines during 1929, and the winter of that year brought Motor Transit's last expansion. Whitcomb Stages, operating through East Los Angeles from El Monte to 1st and Indiana (connecting there with LARy's P car line), ceased on October 5 due to bankruptcy. William F. Whitcomb had started in 1915 between Wilmar and Belvedere, extending east to San Gabriel and west to 1st and Indiana in 1920 and on to El Monte in October 1928.

Belvedere Gardens Bus Line, a local operator since 1921, applied to take over the feeder line as such; Motor Transit offered to provide through service from El Monte to Los Angeles, restricted within the city limits, and was awarded the rights, so gaining an alternate route into Los Angeles via Garvey Road and Brooklyn Avenue.

End of the El Dorado. Construction of the 33-passenger 800-series interurban buses began in 1928. A slightly larger bus on a longer (253-inch) wheelbase, the 800s featured mahogany interior trim and an above-roof extension of the exhaust pipe to reduce the possibility of drawing fumes into the buses. Seven aisle jump seats increased the passenger capacity to 40. Six of these behemoths were built in 1928; six more built in 1929 introduced full-length interior parcel racks in addition to a rear baggage compartment.

The 850 class, also built in 1929, were smaller buses (25-passenger) than the standard then being produced and were specially fitted with 5.66:1 rear axles for mountain service. Their shorter wheelbase (20 inches) and overall length (15 inches) compared to the 475-series buses of the same capacity made them prime equipment for the mountain routes. Five aisle jump seats made their capacity 30.

The last El Dorados built were the seven 1875-series interurbans built in 1929 (one) and in 1930 (six). These, too, were 33-passenger buses with seven jump seats and full-length interior racks. They differed from the 800 series, however, in having Sterling Petrel engines (like the Pickwick buses being constructed at that time) and more metal replacing wood in structure and sheathing.

A Last Try. Motor Transit never ceased its efforts to reach a position from which it could effectively compete with PE. In a final attempt to achieve parity, the company applied in 1929 for removal of the requirement for divisional operation, so as to permit through service between any two points, and to lift all local service restrictions.

Pasadena–Pomona Stage Line 24 was a Reo Speed Wagon with possibly a FitzJohn body. It is shown here in May 1926. Motor Transit did not acquire any buses with the purchase of this line in 1929.
Pasadena Historical Society

Some logical routes that might have been started in competition to PE were Los Angeles–Long Beach, Los Angeles–Pasadena, and Los Angeles–Santa Ana–Laguna Beach. Through service between Eastern and Southern Division points, such as San Bernardino–Riverside–Santa Ana–Laguna Beach, was also contemplated.

Naturally PE objected, claiming that bus competition with its principal Northern and Southern suburban lines would divert $75,000 to $100,000 of revenue per month and jeopardize what it said was a two percent annual return on an $85 million investment in facilities. Motor Transit's $3.5 million investment in facilities and equipment was meager by comparison. The question was whether the Railroad Commission would permit Motor Transit to take any further steps along the road to competitive parity.

The answer came in several parts, and it is not unlikely that the Commission was sending a message to PE within its ruling. Removal of restrictions was authorized in several specific areas: through service to Victorville and Oro Grande from Eastern Division points and to Yucaipa via Redlands was permitted; full local service and freight rights were awarded between San Bernardino or Redlands and the San Bernardino Mountains and between Riverside, Hemet, and the San Jacinto Mountains. All-year service over the "winter routes" to the San Bernardino Mountains was approved. Additional local restrictions were removed from the summer service between Los Angeles, Pasadena, and the San Bernardino Mountains.

Local service was authorized between Glendale and Sunland, between Olive and Corona, and between Huntington Beach and Seal Beach. Merger of the former Crown Stages lines into the Southern Division was approved, with revision of the inherited Crown rate structure. Restrictions against local service on the former Dillingham lines were lifted between Whittier and Long Beach, Norwalk and Santa Fe Springs, and Alhambra and Pico. Full local rights were awarded on existing through lines between Pomona and Long Beach and between Riverside and Long Beach. Through and local service was authorized between Los Angeles and Laguna Beach via Santa Ana.

A change in attitude on the part of the Commission was evident, and parity of operation appeared to be assured. The bars of full competition were being removed one by one, and Pacific Electric did not fail to recognize the signs. Furthermore, by the end of the decade of the 1920s in Southern California, the enemy of both common carriers was the private auto.

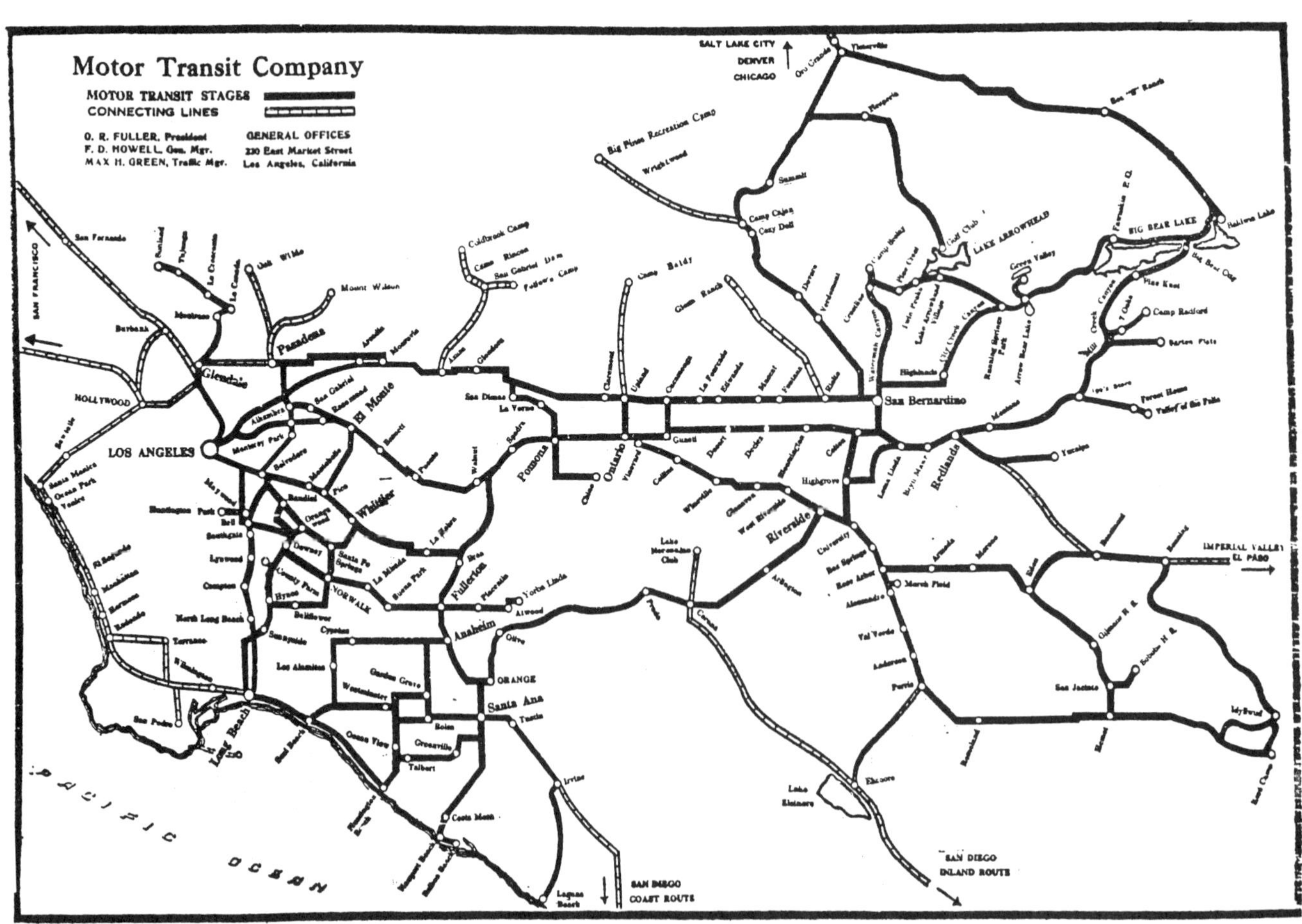

This map shows the Motor Transit System in 1929, at its height as a suburban carrier, just prior to its sale to Pacific Electric. PE's subsequent abandonment of less profitable branches and rerouting of lines paralleling its electric interurbans soon reduced MT to the status of a secondary and feeder operation for its former competitor. *Author's Collection*

CHAPTER THREE

LOS ANGELES MOTOR COACH 1923-1949

Motor bus to motor coach; double-deck doings

By 1930, the new University of California of Los Angeles campus at Westwood was a major destination of motor coach service. Its importance was such that Pacific Electric made it the subject of a cover photo in its November 1930 magazine. *Interurban Press Collection*

THE RAIL ARTERIES that enabled the early growth of the Los Angeles metropolitan area were of three kinds. Oldest, and by the first decade of the twentieth century least important, were steam railroads. Their suburban passenger service was greatly overshadowed by that of the Pacific Electric Railway, which reached its greatest extent with a merger of three large predecessor companies in 1911.

Most of the PE lines were interurban trunk routes, while territory closer to the central city was effectively served by the purely local streetcar lines of the Los Angeles Railway. There was little overlap between the two systems, and furthermore there were no inter-company transfer privileges.

A move toward a trunkline bus service similar to those already in existence or contemplated for a few other major cities resulted in the formation of Pacific Motor Coach Co. in Los Angeles in April 1914, apparently by interests allied with New York Motor Bus Co., which was then vying with Fifth Avenue Coach Co. (unsuccessfully, as it turned out) for long-term bus franchise in New York.

The new company proposed to place 100 double-deckers on trunk routes from Los Angeles to Venice, Long Beach, Pasadena, San Pedro, "and other points," and the St. Louis Car Co. was given an initial order for 34 bodies.

One of PE's most popular rail routes was the Venice Short Line, particularly on the Fourth of July when thousands flocked to the beaches. A parallel bus line along

Washington Blvd. from Pershing Square in downtown Los Angeles to Santa Monica (17 miles) was inaugurated by Pacific Motor Coach Co. during July 1914—presumably in time for the holiday rush. The double-deckers might well have been enough of a novelty to draw a share of the traffic, but the proprietors evidently hoped to enhance their attraction by undercutting PE's fare and so charged 40 cents for a round trip as compared to 50 cents on the train.

Neither state nor local public utility regulations had anything to say about buses, a fact whose significance was not lost on a solitary automobile owner whose name seems to be lost to history. According to a later reconstruction of events by Los Angeles Railway management, the first "jitney" driver piloted his Ford auto over a four-mile route competing directly with LARy streetcars on July 1, 1914. The streetcar was an established, conventional means of travel; the jitney was something new, and the phenomenon spread nationwide within months.

Although most of the entrepreneurs who tried their hand at providing jitney service in the Los Angeles area and elsewhere failed to endure, and the average duration of their attempts was said to be 60 days, the appeal of the jitney to potential operators and customers was immense. Riders gladly put up with overcrowding and unsafe conditions for which trolley companies were roundly criticized.

Some 1,400 rent permits for autos were issued in Los Angeles from April 1914 (when Pacific Motor Coach received its few) to February 1915, when the first attempt at a regulatory ordinance was passed by city council.

Among the transit services adversely affected by the jitney phenomenon was the Pacific Motor Coach Co.'s bus line to Santa Monica. The round-trip fare was cut to a quarter in an effort to compete, but to no avail. In December 1914 the buses were repossessed and the enterprise went into receivership, which was terminated by voluntary bankruptcy in February 1915. Meanwhile a follow-up order for 48 additional double-deck buses was canceled.

Pacific Motor Coach No. 17 is ready to leave for Los Angeles on a flatcar. The solid rubber tires and chain drive are up-to-date features of its Kelly-Springfield chassis along with its St. Louis Car Co. body. The bus would soon be in service on Washington Blvd. *Motor Bus Society*

The original fleet made its way north to San Francisco and operated in a jitney-style service to and from the Ferry Building during the Panama-Pacific Exposition of 1915.

A Second Competitive Effort. The Pacific Electric Railway entered the bus business in 1917 and by 1923 was operating extensive feeder service to its rail lines in San Bernardino, Redlands, Glendale, Alhambra, Santa Ana, Pasadena and Beverly Hills. LARy had started its first bus line, San Pedro Street, in December 1922. Rapid growth of the region in those postwar years—Los Angeles itself expanded from 576,000 people in 1920 to 987,000 by 1923—also attracted the attention of Richard W. Meade, formerly with Fifth Avenue Coach Co. and directly responsible for starting new and popular bus services in Detroit and St. Louis.

Needing local partners, Meade formed an association with William Gibbs McAdoo, Woodrow Wilson's son-in-law and first Treasury Secretary (and administrator of the railroads during World War I), who was then head of the United Artists motion picture studio, and with local banker Marco W. Hellman, whose father had been financially involved with the Pacific Electric in its early days. This group proposed a citywide system of trunklines using 125 double-decker buses competing directly with both PE and LARy car lines.

Their Peoples Motor Bus Co. put its application in the form of a referendum petition, requiring an election to settle the question, so that the electric railways had to offer an opposing plan if they were to keep the rivals out. As a result, PE and LARy agreed to cooperate against the common opponent.

Believing that responding to public demands would involve them in loss-making routes into thinly settled neighborhoods, the railway companies agreed with the Board of Public Utilities and Transportation that bus lines started at the request of the Board and failing to earn operating expenses could be discontinued after a suitable trial period.

Public and press agitation centered about the lack of direct service and of transfer privileges between the rapidly developing west side of Los Angeles (LARy territory) and Hollywood, a short distance away to the north but served exclusively by PE. The two railway companies formed a bus operating subsidiary called Los Angeles Motor Bus Co. and laid plans for routes that would connect their respective territories.

Once this step had been taken, the local press came out in support of PE and LARy, playing to civic pride by pointing out (as had been argued in 1915) that fares paid to the railways represented money that would stay in Los Angeles. The "eastern capitalists," like the jitneymen earlier, would spend their income elsewhere.

The contest for votes was waged with newspaper advertisements, pamphlets and public appearances, and despite an admitted expenditure of $125,000 by the rival group, the voters favored PE and LARy by 12,000 votes out of 86,000 cast.

Railway-Owned Buses. The referendum was held on May 2, 1923, and on August 1, Los Angeles Motor Bus Co.

Unable to compete with Los Angeles jitneys, No. 7 and other Pacific Motor Coach double-deckers moved to San Francisco in 1915 to help handle service to the Panama-Pacific Exposition. Driver and conductor confer at the Ferry Terminal amid a crowd of streetcars and taxis. *Motor Bus Society*

became a functioning organization with a general manager, Frank Van Vranken. Well known to both parent companies, Van Vranken had risen from Southern Pacific brakeman to Pacific Electric Los Angeles Division superintendent and had then served as general superintendent of Los Angeles Railway.

His first task was to arrange construction of a bus garage at Virgil Avenue and Santa Monica Blvd., for which bids were asked in September. Bus operation began on August 18 with ceremonies and a parade, the first route being the Western Avenue line between Hollywood and Slauson Avenue (9½ miles) and the first buses 10 single-deck Morelands purchased for the new company and several Whites obtained from LARy and PE. Plans were announced for the purchase of single-deck and double-deck Morelands, built in nearby Burbank.

PE had two 6-cent fare zones between downtown Los Angeles and Hollywood, and LARy's fare was 5 cents. The Western Avenue bus line offered 6-cent local rides within Hollywood and 10-cent through rides, for which fare a free transfer was given to any intersecting PE or LARy east-west rail line (of which no less than 12 were crossed). Within two weeks the new route was carrying 10,000 passengers a day.

Its buses were housed in a corner of LARy's Division 5 carhouse at 5th and Arlington Streets pending completion of the Virgil Avenue garage. The custom was to persist, however, for many years after Virgil became an active facility. Meanwhile LARy had started its second bus line on Lincoln Park Avenue and was preparing to inaugurate others.

By the end of November, the first of 32 new Moreland single-deckers had arrived and been sent to LARy's South Park Shops for outfitting. Mechanically similar to the first 10, they had more modern bodies similar in design to PE's Whites. On December 20 they were operating over 16 additional route miles on the Sunset Blvd. and Vermont Avenue lines between 7th and Grand Streets and Hollywood. The first experimental Moreland double-decker was on the property before the end of 1923 and was placed in service on the Sunset Blvd. line on January 11, 1924.

Meanwhile Fageol had designed and constructed a double-decker bus which arrived in March. After several test trips, it went into service on the Sunset line along with a second Moreland double-deck. An early decision was made to try both makes and in April, authorization was given to order 20 double-deck buses for LAMB.

In the meantime too, on October 10, 1923, Los Angeles Railway had started a major trunk bus line of its own running from 5th and Olive Streets out Wilshire Blvd. to La Brea Avenue at a 10-cent fare. Here again both Moreland and Fageol double-deckers were ordered, as Van Vranken was simultaneously general manager of the railway's own bus division, based at 16th and San Pedro Streets. LARy, rather than LAMB, operated the Wilshire route because it complemented streetcar service without touching a PE car line.

Troubles in operation of the double-deckers during 1924

Los Angeles Motor Bus had 42 single-deck Morelands, all built in 1923 on modified 5-ton truck chassis with Continental L-4 engines. Bodies for 201-210 (with off-center destination signs) were of typical Moreland design. The bodies of 211-242 were also built by Moreland but the design followed that of the ex-LARy and PE White 50s such as the one seen fifth from the left, which was built in the Torrance car shops.
Both: Burbank Historical Society

indicated the need for some improvements and the fleets of both operating companies were reworked between January and March of 1925; the Fageols received new axles and the Morelands, an improved braking system. The results of the modifications were satisfactory and early in May, 10 more double-deck buses were ordered—six more from Fageol and four more from Moreland.

With bus service between Los Angeles and Hollywood established to supplement rail lines, the densely populated urban region was better served than it had been, and the threat of outside competition arising as a result of the tacit understanding between PE and LARy not to compete with each other had been beaten off. Further expansion of the Los Angeles Motor Bus system was to come about through the acquisition of existing bus lines and the initiation of relatively minor feeder services, rather than by starting additional main routes.

In January 1924, a 6.6-mile line operating from Vermont and Sunset to and through Griffith Park was taken over from the city parks department, with two buses, and was later operated as a branch of the Vermont Avenue line. With continued growth of the west side, a second crosstown route was inaugurated on Vine Street and Rossmore Avenue between Hollywood Blvd. and Wilshire Blvd. on December 1, 1924. The Vermont Avenue line was made into a feeder by being cut back from downtown on October 1, 1925; it connected with PE's Hollywood Blvd. car line as well as with the Sunset Blvd. bus line, which had turned out to be the much more heavily traveled of the two bus lines.

The first double-decker on the property was this Moreland, delivered in December 1923 for trials and numbered 501. It had a six-cylinder Continental 14H motor and Westinghouse air brakes front and rear. *Los Angeles Times*

Below: The first two Fageol double-deck buses were also experimental when they first arrived, and many alterations were made in subsequent groups. Equipped with Hall-Scott model 75 six-cylinder engines, the Fageols also had air brakes, but only on the rear wheels. *Security Pacific National Bank*

As the motor coach became recognized as a dependable means of transport, it began to be favored for private, as well as public, use. Los Angeles Motor Bus double-deckers were particularly in demand for charters due to their large capacity and the novelty of the open upper deck. A 1920s group is snapped here in the mandatory pose of the day. LARy-owned Fageols were numbered upward from 601 and PEs from 651; each partner contributed 17 of these buses for Sunset Blvd. service between 1924 and 1926. These two photos capture one each of the PE and LARy units.
658: California Historical Society; 610: SCRTD Collection

From Vermont and Melrose the feeder route continued east and then north to Hillhurst and Avocado. Both the Hillhurst Avenue and Vine Street lines were started at the request of the Board of Public Utilities and Transportation and thus were subject to quick abandonment if they turned out to be unable to pay their own way.

Another feeder line was inaugurated on Riverside Drive in the Silver Lake district on February 1, 1926, connecting the PE's Glendale and Edendale rail lines with LARy's Eagle Rock (E) and Garvanza (W) car lines. In May, six more Fageol double-deckers were ordered for Sunset Blvd. At this time, it was decided to add buzzers to the double-deck fleet so that passengers (particularly on the upper deck) would not have to depend on the conductor's memory for their stops.

At the end of 1926 there were 40 double-deckers (six Morelands and 34 Fageols) and 46 single-deckers (four Whites and 42 Morelands) being operated by Los Angeles Motor Bus. Peak-hour requirements were 30 double-deckers on Sunset Blvd. and 34 single-deckers on Western Avenue, plus five on Vermont Avenue, three on Vine Street, and one on Riverside Drive.

In January of 1927, Fageol 608 was repainted at LARy's South Park Shops with a wide cream band under the windows brightening up the original all-green color scheme. The experiment was considered a success and the rest of

The graceful lines of Moreland's final double-deck design are demonstrated by 553. The addition of a windshield to the upper deck was the most prominent improvement for passengers. The tandem rear axles did not work out well from the point of view of tire wear and the Morelands were the first double-deckers retired from service.
Dave Garcia Collection

the fleet followed. In November, the company was renamed Los Angeles Motor Coach Company, which was considered more dignified.

Double-Deck Service Consolidated. Bus service in the western part of the Motor Coach territory was rearranged and simplified on May 4, 1928, when four routes were replaced by two. Development of Wilshire Blvd. as a shopping and commercial street required better transportation access from the high-quality residential district to the west, and at the same time the territory to the north of the boulevard had been developed with elegant homes on large tracts, still one of the finest neighborhoods in Los Angeles.

The LARy Wilshire Blvd. trunk bus line was extended from its previous terminus at Fairfax Avenue west to Beverly Hills, replacing a small part of the PE Wilshire–Sunset (or Hollywood–Beverly Hills) bus line, and was formally transferred from LARy to LAMC because it was now operating partly in PE's territory since it reached Santa Monica Blvd. With it came LARy's fleet of 25 Fageol, eight Moreland and 13 Yellow double-deckers; however, the line continued to be based at the 16th and San Pedro Streets garage.

At the same time, the La Brea Avenue crosstown bus line of Los Angeles Railway, which had replaced a branch of the Wilshire line in 1927, was turned over to Motor Coach. It was subsequently combined with the Vine Street line to create a long U-shaped north-south service which

Special service was offered on the Wilshire line for events at the Carthay Circle Theater. Fageol 708 was snapped at Wilshire and Berendo bound for McCarthy Vista and the Carthay Center. Note the unique street lamps along this stretch of the boulevard.
G. L. Squier

Double-Deck Details
. . . or . . .
Learning to Live With a Two-Story Bus

BULLETIN No. 233 March 24th, 1925

The ornamental light electroliers on Olive Street, between 5th and 8th St., are so placed that there is danger of striking passengers on the upper deck.

Operators will therefore be very cautious when pulling in close to the curb for any reason.

F. VAN VRANKEN, Manager

BULLETIN NO. 242 April 16, 1925

The spring fastener and the housing in the rear end of the Double Decks will not clear the traffic buttons at intersections; therefore great care must be exercised by drivers not to split these buttons with the rear wheels. To do so results in expensive damage to the equipment.

BULLETIN NO. 353 NOV. 20th, 1925

The new type of Acme Traffic Signal being installed at various intersections along the route of the Wilshire Boulevard Bus Line are low enough to come in contact with Double Deck Buses and operators must be especially careful when stopping at these points so that damage will not be done to these signals.

BULLETIN NO. 369 1/4/26

Your attention is called to Bulletin No. 150 issued in October, 1924, which permits a passenger to stand on the lower deck if he presents a reasonable excuse that he does not care to sit on the upper deck but that in no event will the seating capacity of the bus be exceeded.

There has been several complaints recently from passengers who would rather stand on the lower deck than to sit in the cold and your attention is called to this so that there will be no further complaints.

BUS 3/27
NO. 16

Conductors of Double Deck Buses must not permit more passengers to board the bus than the seating capacity provides except in cases where the bus ahead is broken down and then an additional 15 may be carried.

Conductors are required to use their very best efforts to discourage any passengers from standing up on the lower deck when there are seats on the upper deck unoccupied. This does not refer to times when it is raining.

Conductors' attention is again directed that they must keep a strict account at all times of whether there are any vacant seats on the upper deck, which condition will change from time to time as passengers leave the bus and board it. This in order that waiting passengers may not be refused passage by reason of a capacity load being aboard the bus when such is not the case.

Employes will be held strictly responsible for carrying out these instructions.

Los Angeles Railway transferred its 46 double-deckers along with the Wilshire and La Brea lines to LAMC in 1928. LARy's 700-series Fageols were identical to LAMC's own 600s and the Morelands of LARy's 800 series were identical to LAMC's four three-axle Morelands. All, however, kept their original equipment numbers after the transfer. The 722 is seen at Pershing Square in the mid-30s; 801 is shown as delivered to LARy in this 1924 scene and 1010 is also laying over at Pershing Square. LARy's 1000s were one window shorter and four seats smaller than other Yellow double-deckers built after 1924. Unit 1010 was one of the last, built in 1928. *722, 1010: Security Pacific Bank; 801: Joe Corbin*

Left: Excerpts from Company Bulletins to Drivers

was later further extended and designated Crenshaw–Vine–La Brea.

Also in 1928 the dual-motor Twin Coach made its debut in Los Angeles, LAMC starting with 10 of them to replace Morelands in base service on Western Avenue. The receipt of LARy's own Model 40s in May had allowed the release of the Figueroa line double-deckers to Los Angeles Motor Coach. At this time a separate fleet number series was started for Motor Coach to keep its equipment apart from that of parent companies, though existing buses were not renumbered.

The practice began of having PE-owned buses carry odd numbers and LARy-owned buses even numbers in the same number group. Finally the paint scheme was changed to the "negative" of that previously used, becoming LARy yellow with a green stripe below the windows. This lasted less than two years before the green was replaced by PE red, giving a combination that was to last (in various schemes) until the end of the subsidiary's separate existence.

In March 1929, the Wilshire line was extended to the new Los Angeles campus of the University of California in Westwood. Soon PE's Sunset Blvd. buses began serving the campus from Hollywood, and then PE extended this route to Santa Monica, paralleling its rail service on Santa Monica Blvd.

In July 1932, the two bus lines exchanged western terminal points: the PE line was cut back to Wilshire and Westwood in favor of through LAMC Wilshire Blvd. service from downtown Los Angeles to Santa Monica. Alternate buses continued to terminate at UCLA, and no local traffic was permitted beyond Westwood Blvd. to protect Bay Cities Transit Co.

This change came about in response to a request from the Santa Monica City Commissioners. After two years of agitation by the traveling public of Santa Monica for better transportation to downtown Los Angeles, a Transportation Committee report was issued favoring new service by the Santa Monica Municipal Bus Lines. Increasing losses on the Muni Pico line due to the depressed state of the local economy precluded this solution and the request for extension of the Wilshire service resulted.

Moving the Movies. By the late 1920s a partnership had been formed between Southern California's motor coach industry and its growing motion picture industry. When the movie business took root in the area there was no reliable way to transport the actors and technicians to remote locations for filming. Horse-drawn vehicles, electric and steam railroads and, to some degree, automobiles, had all been tried and found wanting. Most trips required two or more modes of travel with the consequent awkward transfers.

The establishment of the motor coach as a dependable

Looking north along the Hill Street side of Pershing Square in 1929. The LAMC buses are 663 and 665 on the Sunset Blvd. line and 1008 on Wilshire; both interim color schemes are represented. In the foreground, one of LARY's model 40 Twins basks in the sun at the terminal of the Figueroa line—once operated by double-deck Fageols. *Motor Bus Society*

ROSTER OF BUSES

Los Angeles Motor Bus Co.
(1923–1927)

Owner	Numbers	Make	Model	Seats	Built	Notes
LARy	(?)	White	50	25	1923	(1923) LARy
PE	106-107 (at least)	White	50	25	1923	(1923) PE
PE	201-205	Moreland	AC	25	1923	
LARy	206-210	Moreland	AC	25	1923	
LARy	211-226	Moreland	AC	25	1923	PE body design
PE	227-242	Moreland	AC	25	1923	PE body design
?	(2)	Fageol	—	?	?	(1924) City of Los Angeles
PE	501	Moreland	DD	56	1923	Two axles
PE	502-503	Moreland	DD	58	1925	Three axles
LARy	551	Moreland	DD	58	1924	Two axles
LARy	552-553	Moreland	DD	58	1925	Three axles
LARy	601	Fageol	—	58	1924	sample
LARy	602-611	Fageol	—	58	1924	
LARy	612-614	Fageol	—	58	1925	
LARY	615-617	Fageol	—	58	1926	
PE	651	Fageol	—	58	1924	sample
PE	652-661	Fageol	—	58	1924	
PE	662-664	Fageol	—	58	1925	
PE	665-667	Fageol	—	58	1926	

ROSTER OF BUSES

Los Angeles Motor Coach Co.
Double-Deck Buses
Assigned from Los Angeles Ry., May 4, 1928

Owner	Numbers	Make	Model	Seats	Built
LARy	701	Fageol	—	58	1924
PE	702	Fageol	—	58	1924
LARy	703	Fageol	—	58	1924
PE	704-705	Fageol	—	58	1925
LARy	706	Fageol	—	58	1925
PE	707	Fageol	—	58	1925
LARy	708, 710	Fageol	—	58	1925
PE	709, 711	Fageol	—	58	1925
LARy	712-718 even	Fageol	—	58	1926
PE	713-719 odd	Fageol	—	58	1926
PE	720	Fageol	—	58	1927
LARy	721	Fageol	—	58	1927
LARy	722, 724	Fageol	—	58	1928
PE	723, 725	Fageol	—	58	1928
LARy	801-803	Moreland	DD	59	1924
PE	804	Moreland	DD	59	1924
LARy	805	Moreland	DD	59	1924
LARy	806	Moreland	DD	59	1925
PE	807-808	Moreland	DD	59	1925
LARy	1001	Yellow	Z-AD-256	63	1924
LARy	1002	Yellow	Z-AD-256	63	1926
PE	1003-1004	Yellow	Z-AD-256	63	1926
LARy	1005	Yellow	Z-AD-256	63	1926
LARy	1006, 1008	Yellow	Z-AAJ-305	63	1927
PE	1007, 1009	Yellow	Z-AAJ-305	63	1927
LARy	1010, 1012	Yellow	Z-AAAM-354	63	1928
PE	1011, 1013	Yellow	Z-AAAM-354	63	1928

Later Changes

Owner	Numbers	Make	Model	Seats	Built	Notes
LARy	1801	Moreland	DD	59	1924	(1928) Ex-802 (Hall-Scott engine)
LARy	726-730 even	Fageol	—	58	1926	(1933) Ex-615-617
PE	727-731 odd	Fageol	—	58	1926	(1933) Ex-665-667
LARy	732	Fageol	—	58	1926	(1935) Ex-613?
PE	668-669	Fageol	—	58	1925	(1935) Ex-704-705

means of transportation caused the movie studios to take notice and begin to use this new method to reach their remote locations. Twelve local bus companies soon formed an association to meet the varying equipment demands of the studios. The association established standard rates and the companies provided a pool of 250 buses to enable 24-hour response to the requirements of the studios. When the demands of a single movement exceeded the equipment available from one company, other members of the association were contacted until the requirements were filled.

Five of the firms were primarily common carriers; the others had come into being solely to serve the studios. The largest of the common carrier members was the Motor Transit Co. whose specially geared buses were most often used for trips to the San Jacinto and San Bernardino Mountains. A typical specialized carrier was D.G. Henderson's Standard Transfer Company which operated primarily in support of the movie industry; Standard Auto Tours, an associated company, ferried prospective buyers to newly opened areas for local land developers.

Buses were usually employed for movements between 10

One of the original group of Motor Coach model 40 Twins photographed at Virgil Ave. garage in 1935. The colors are LARy yellow and PE red with a chocolate-brown roof. Behind the Twin is one of the original single-deck Morelands in green and cream.
SCRTD Collection

and 300 miles. Even Death Valley, some 375 miles away, saw several incursions by busloads of movie folk. Perhaps the largest movement took place on one busy day in 1928 when the Famous–Paramount–Laskey Studio decided to film two mob scenes at separate locations. It took 217 buses belonging to all 12 cooperating companies to move the 1,987 people involved. Single-deck buses were normally used, but on occasion, Los Angeles Motor Coach double-deckers were pressed into service. The large buses were available at standard (but higher than single-deck) rates and were used for "short" locations within the city limits which could be reached by paved roads.

The Other Side of the Camera. Like so many other prominent features of the Los Angeles scene, the double-deckers did not escape the cameras of the early movie-makers. Like good character actors, they quietly accepted background roles—often masquerading as Fifth Avenue Motor Coach or London General Omnibus vehicles, but when called upon, they became foils for the comedians of the day. A few, in fact, became featured players.

One of the more frequent users of the double-deckers was Harold Lloyd, a frenetic comedian of the Twenties. In *For Heaven's Sake,* filmed in 1926, the bespectacled Lloyd starred in a get-me-to-the-church-on-time chase scene staged on the upper deck of a commandeered Fageol. When the film was released at the Million Dollar Theater, the double-decker was driven across the stage before each performance—perhaps the shortest movie charter of all time. When the battery failed before one performance, stage hands were forced to push the behemoth—surely earning their pay for that day. (Lloyd also used streetcars—the Pacific Electric playing a supporting role in several Lloyd comedies.)

Charlie Chase, another comedian of the time, pioneered a new method of passenger loading in one of his films; he

Standard Transfer Co. was formed by Daniel G. Henderson to transport movie personnel to remote locations. This side-door Sierra stage was typical of the equipment used in this type of service.
Motor Bus Society

Fageol double-decker 613 was just a year old when snapped on the Sunset Blvd. line in 1925. The longitudinal seats on the upper deck were distinctly different from the cross seats of the Morelands. *Dave Garcia Collection*

stepped out of a second-story window onto the top deck of a bus. Another facet of the business involved the sale of buses to the studios for use in wreck scenes. It was estimated that several dozen tired pieces of equipment met untimely ends each year while being immortalized on celluloid. The buses were sold at a nominal fee and were usually wrecked beyond repair—mostly in comedies.

The all-time epic scene, however, was filmed on Wilshire Blvd. where one enterprising moviemaker staged a head-on crash between two double-deckers by driving one through a huge mirror set in the middle of the street. A mockup was built on the movie lot showing the coach completely demolished and the two comedians, Charlie Murray and George Sidney, were photographed emerging from the wreck.

Another double-decker was featured in *Pennies From Heaven* along with Bing Crosby. In the *Garden Murder Case,* filmed in 1935, Edmund Lowe and Virginia Bruce starred along with two double-deckers. The mystery centered around the driver of the first bus who committed a murder by jerking his vehicle to throw a rider off the top deck. The passenger was then run over by the bus behind —ah, those close headways on Wilshire!

Purchase of West Side Transit. The summer of 1930 brought a different kind of competitive threat to the established electric railways, which was again answered through Los Angeles Motor Coach Co. Harbor Stage Line, a new company, proposed a parlor bus service from Los Angeles to the steamship docks at San Pedro, in direct competition to PE's Catalina Dock trains.

The service was never started, but LAMC was led to propose a route of its own from the Hollywood bus terminal (1627 Cahuenga Blvd.) to the Union Bus Depot in Long Beach with a branch to the San Pedro docks. West Side Transit Co., operating since 1924 between Western and Manchester (near the southwest corner of LARy's territory, and southern terminus of LAMC's Western Avenue line) and Long Beach, saw this application as a peril to its continued existence and promptly petitioned to extend its line to Hollywood.

Two such routes would have been one too many, but by June 1931, West Side had agreed to sell out to Los Angeles Motor Coach for $15,000. The sale, as well as the extension to Hollywood and the branch to San Pedro, was authorized on October 11, and Motor Coach operation started on November 1. No transfers were offered to local lines and the new line was operated as an independent interurban route between Hollywood, Torrance, San Pedro, Wilmington Docks, Catalina Terminal and Long Beach.

Included in the purchase were two buses, a 1926 Studebaker which was never used by LAMC and a 1930 Federal

LAMC acquired two small ACF parlor cars in 1931 and 1932 to operate the Hollywood–Long Beach–San Pedro line. It is believed that they originated with PE's sister subsidiary Southern Pacific Motor Transport Co. which had just been merged into Pacific Greyhound Lines. *SCRTD Collection*

Morelands were replaced on the lighter lines by a variety of different buses including 14 3100-series Yellow Coach U's. They entered service in September of 1931 on the Crenshaw–Vine–La Brea line. *SCRTD Collection*

When the Pickwick bus lines were merged into the growing Greyhound system in 1929, its chief engineer, Dwight Austin, bought the bus manufacturing facility in Inglewood. The first product of Austin's Utility Coach Co. was this unique compact vehicle—the prototype of the modern rear-engined transit coach. The engine was mounted transversely under the bustle (which can be seen protruding from the rear) driving through Austin's patented angle-drive. His efforts caught the eye of the management of Yellow Coach and before long Austin and his patent became the key ingredients of new Yellow rear-engined transit and over-the-road coach designs. *SCRTD Collection*

which was. Later two small ACF parlor cars were purchased second-hand for this route, which never had more than a few trips a day.

Several motor coach lines were rerouted in March of 1931 as the terminal of the Vermont–Griffith Park–Hillhurst service was changed to connect with the LARy V car line at Monroe and Vermont instead of the H line at Melrose and Heliotrope. At the same time, the Vine–La Brea line was extended southward from Wilshire and Rossmore to 54th and Crenshaw and renamed Crenshaw–Vine–La Brea. In August, 14 Model U Yellow coaches were ordered to replace aging Morelands on the newly extended line. The other end of the line was extended from Pico and La Brea to the Vineyard and Washington terminal of LARy's W car line in April of 1933.

During 1931, Glendale real estate promoters endeavored to establish a through bus line to Los Angeles through the Silver Lake district, served by PE feeder buses. To obtain support from the Silver Lake community, the promoters promised a 5-cent fare between Silver Lake and Los Angeles. Motor Coach started a new service to combat this attempt on July 1, 1932. Pacific Electric handed over its Glendale Blvd.–Hyperion Avenue feeder line, and the Glendale Blvd. segment was made part of the Vermont Avenue line.

A new connection along Silver Lake Blvd. linked the Hyperion Avenue portion of this route with the rest of the LAMC system at Beverly Blvd. and Vermont. If not through service, the new route was the next best thing: direct feeder service by an established and reliable operator.

Neither of these feeders was heavily traveled, and both operated through hilly territory; Yellow type U's purchased in 1931 were usually assigned, and Austin Utility Coaches later succeeded them. In 1933 the Riverside Drive line was also combined into the Vermont Avenue service.

Trial Routes. At the request of the Board of Public Utilities and Transportation, Motor Coach started two trial routes during the early Thirties. The first, Crescent Heights Blvd., was a short loop in the Fairfax section started in February of 1932 for a 60-day trial period. In fact, it ran almost a year (until January of 1933) before expiring due to lack of patronage. A second trial line, the Beverly Hills local, was started on September 1, 1933, between Wilshire and La Cienega and 3rd and Robertson; it did not last beyond the 60-day trial period.

Los Angeles hosted the summer games of the Xth Olympiad during 1932 and, as usual, when a need could not be handled by one of the parent companies, PE and LARy did so jointly, through Los Angeles Motor Coach. Opening day found 69 coaches from the three companies ferrying participants and contestants to the ceremonies from a half-dozen residence and assembly locations.

Subsequently, more than 34,000 passenger movements were handled during the next two months including some to Oxnard and Pasadena for cycling and Long Beach for rowing. The high standard of maintenance during this period was demonstrated by the fact that on July 30 every coach owned by LARy was operating. The fact that this service was provided without one personal injury, or delay to any competition, must be considered a credit to all concerned.

When the Los Angeles Railway numbered its bus routes in 1934, LAMC routes were also numbered and became lines 81 to 87. At least some of the early routes had had numbers in the 1920s, but this system had been discontinued.

LAMC ROUTE NUMBERS (1934)

81	Hollywood–Long Beach–San Pedro
82	Wilshire Blvd.
83	Sunset Blvd.
84	Western Avenue
85	Crenshaw–Vine–La Brea
86	Vermont Avenue
87	Silver Lake–Hyperion–Talmadge

Los Angeles Railway started a feeder bus line beyond the end of its L car line on Olympic Blvd. in 1931 and transferred it to Los Angeles Motor Coach on April 8, 1934, as Rt. 88. As a Motor Coach route it was extended to connect with the Wilshire Blvd. line at both ends. Finding a shortage of equipment, LARy and PE each provided a vintage 29-passenger Fageol (3501 and 3502) to temporarily reinforce the Motor Coach fleet so it could operate the new line; the borrowed buses were soon returned to their owners.

A further expansion of the connecting bus service in this region took place in 1936, when the Olympic Blvd. line was extended north at its western end and then turned east along Beverly Blvd. and West 3rd Street to meet LARy's R car line at La Brea Avenue, and the crosstown Fairfax Avenue line (89) was started, providing new service to a previously untapped residential district.

Motor Coach then had four north-south lines, operated as three routes, connecting Hollywood with the west side of Los Angeles. A later effort to operate a fifth such line (90), on La Cienega Blvd., was unsuccessful. After a brave start in January 1941, it was sparsely patronized and was abandoned in December.

Motor Coach was once again called upon to provide extra service for a local event when the National Air Races were held at the Municipal Airport on September 4-7, 1936. The peak crowd was handled on Labor Day when 72 buses were used to provide direct service to the race grandstand. Those who chose to drive themselves were forced to trudge a dusty half mile from the parking lot.

Double-Deckers Phased Out. When Yellow Coach introduced its "Type 41" or Model 718 with a transverse rear engine in the fall of 1934, Los Angeles Railway and Pacific Electric were quick to place trial orders for the new model. The 718 is generally identified with New York City Omnibus Corp., which used 366 of the 426 built to convert Manhattan car lines, but the second largest fleet operated in Los Angeles (taking the three operating companies together). The Motor Coach 718s were used to initiate express service on the Wilshire line, carrying no local passengers between downtown and Fairfax Avenue, in October 1934.

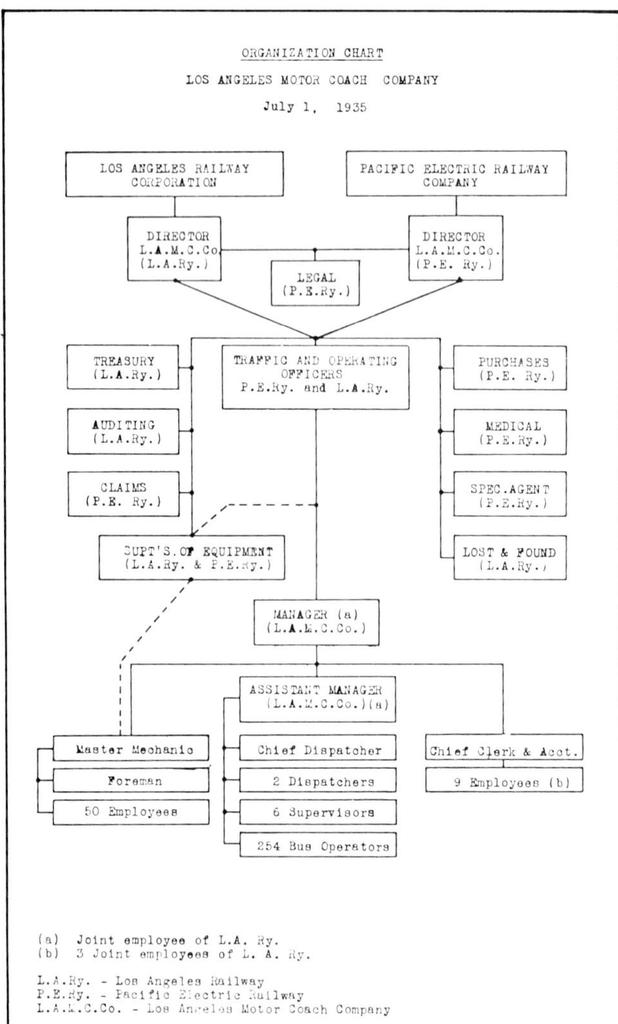

LAMC was an operating agency of PE and LARy and line operating rights were awarded jointly to the partners rather than to LAMC. The administrative functions were handled by one partner or the other as shown by this 1935 organization chart. *Author's Collection*

LOS ANGELES MOTOR COACH CO.

JUNE 1, 1939

LOS ANGELES MOTOR COACH ROUTES

Full-time service

Part-time service

OTHER ROUTES

Los Angeles Railway car lines

Los Angeles Railway bus lines

Pacific Electric car lines

Pacific Electric bus lines

One Mile

AEM 2-76

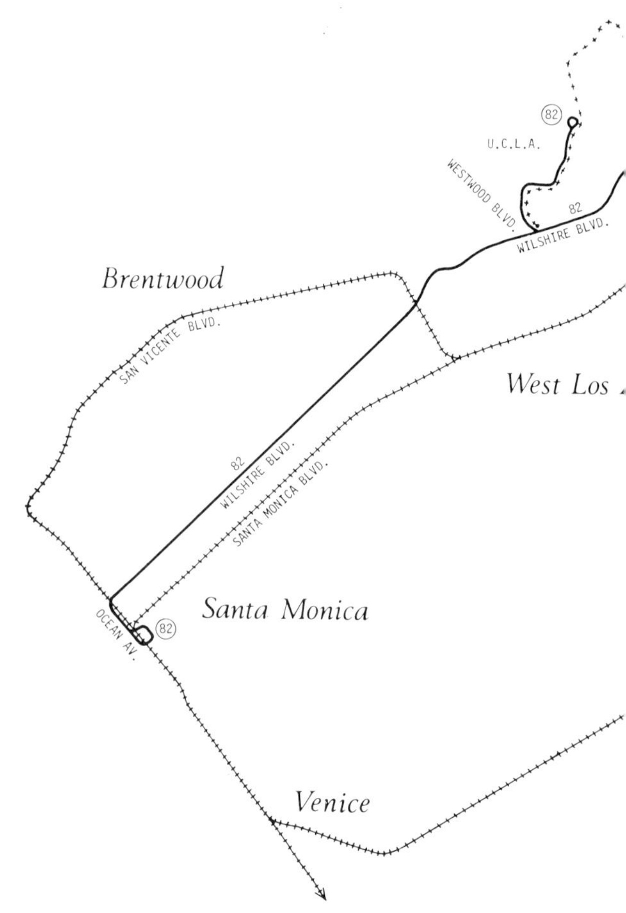

The routes of LAMC dovetailed with LARy and PE rail and bus lines mostly as crosstown or feeders; only the Wilshire and Sunset lines came downtown. *A. E. Meier*

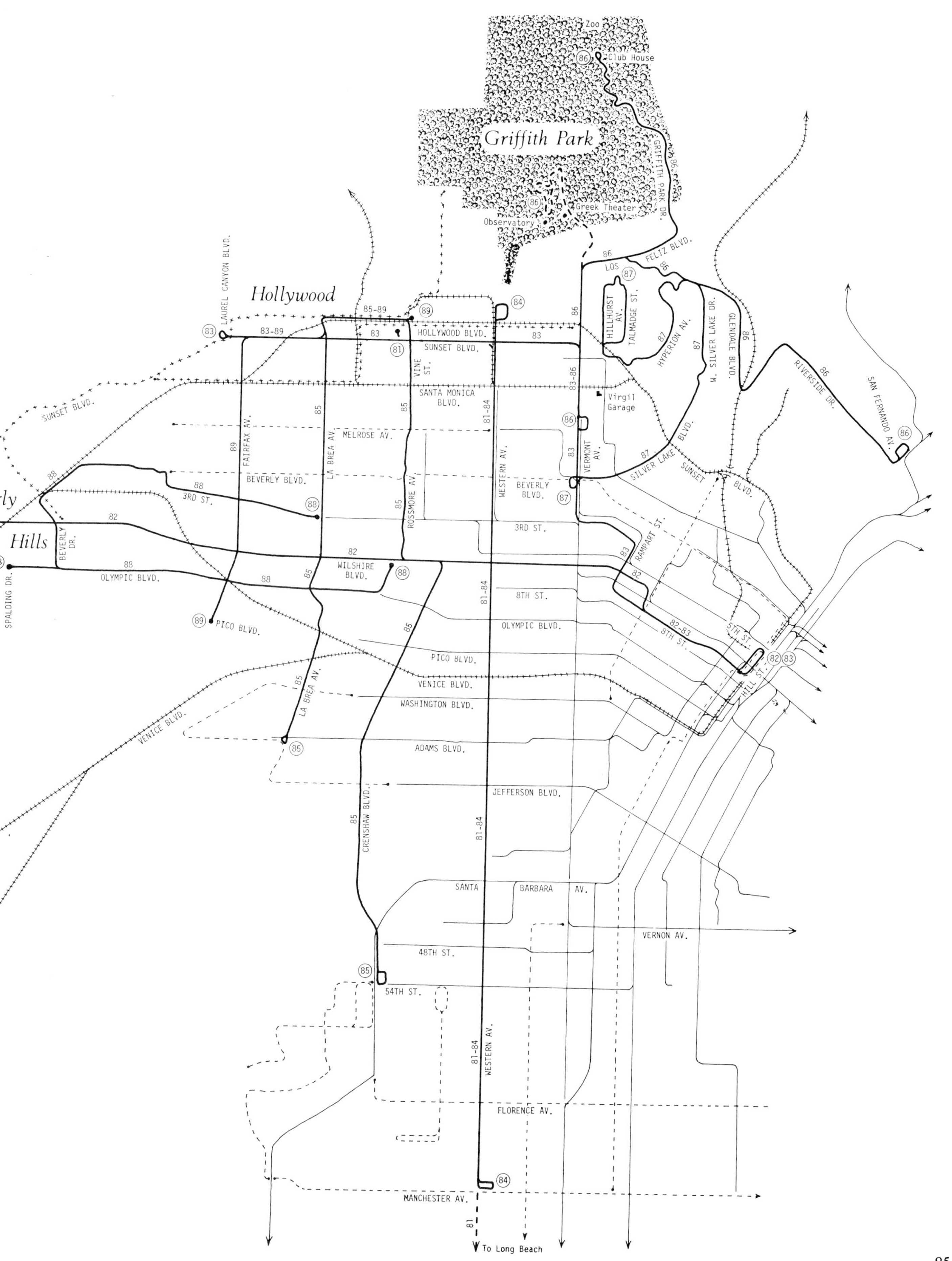
Griffith Park
Zoo
Club House
Greek Theater
Observatory
GRIFFITH PARK DR.
Hollywood
LAUREL CANYON BLVD.
LOS FELIZ BLVD.
HOLLYWOOD BLVD.
SUNSET BLVD.
SANTA MONICA BLVD.
Virgil Garage
MELROSE AV.
BEVERLY BLVD.
3RD ST.
WILSHIRE BLVD.
OLYMPIC BLVD.
8TH ST.
PICO BLVD.
VENICE BLVD.
WASHINGTON BLVD.
ADAMS BLVD.
JEFFERSON BLVD.
SANTA BARBARA AV.
VERNON AV.
48TH ST.
54TH ST.
FLORENCE AV.
MANCHESTER AV.
To Long Beach
Hills
SPALDING DR.
BEVERLY DR.
FAIRFAX AV.
LA BREA AV.
VINE ST.
ROSSMORE AV.
WESTERN AV.
VERMONT AV.
CRENSHAW BLVD.
HILLHURST AV.
TALMADGE ST.
HYPERION AV.
W. SILVER LAKE DR.
GLENDALE BLVD.
SILVER LAKE BLVD.
RIVERSIDE DR.
SAN FERNANDO AV.
RAMPART ST.
5TH ST.
HILL ST.

Eight Yellow 718s were purchased in 1934 and six more in 1936. At first used to start the Wilshire express service, they were later assigned to Sunset Blvd. All had double front and no center doors and were the only known 718s so fashioned. This photo was taken in July 1936.
SCRTD Collection

A 1935 view of 3804, one of eight Yellow 728s. The livery during the mid-1930s was mostly yellow with a red belt stripe, black pin stripes and a gray or silver roof. *SCRTD Collection*

WILSHIRE BOULEVARD COACH LINE

Route No. 82

TIME TABLE

BETWEEN LOS ANGELES
(5th and Hill Streets)

CARTHAY CENTER

BEVERLY HILLS
(Cor. Wilshire and Santa Monica Blvds.)

UNIVERSITY OF CALIFORNIA
(At Westwood)

SANTA MONICA
(Ocean and Broadway)

In addition to schedules shown herein, frequent local service is operated between 5th and Hill Sts. and Fairfax Ave. (Wilshire Blvd.).

Sunday Schedules will be operated on New Year's Day, Memorial Day, Fourth of July, Labor Day, Thanksgiving Day and Christmas Day.

EFFECTIVE NOVEMBER 11, 1934
Subject to Change Without Notice

LOS ANGELES MOTOR COACH CO.

1023 North Virgil Ave.
Los Angeles, Calif.
Telephone OLympia 2144

10M—9-26-34

Differing from other 718s, the Motor Coach buses were hastily modified by Yellow Coach with double-width front doors and no rear exits; they also incorporated air-shift. A second order arrived in 1936 with more carefully modified bodywork and mechanical transmissions. Fourteen smaller buses (eight Yellow 728s and six twin 30-Rs) were also received during this time for the Crenshaw–Vine–La Brea line where they replaced Model U's which were used to start the new Fairfax Avenue route.

Further purchases of large single-deck buses followed late in 1937: 18 Twin 40-RC buses permitted withdrawal of double-deckers from base service on Sunset Blvd. and 20 Yellow 740s with semi-automatic Banker transmissions completed replacement of double-deckers on Wilshire. The 15 Model 718s used by Pacific Electric to provide replacement base service on its Glendale–Burbank car line after 1936 were transferred to LAMC in 1942, when full-time streetcar service (partly operated with PCCs) had been restored on that route by order of the Railroad Commission. Although the double-deckers were all out of service by 1940, several survived in storage, and some were operated again during World War II.

From Wilshire Boulevard to the Sonora Desert.

The Ferrocarril de Nacozari was opened on May 15, 1904, by the Phelps Dodge copper interests to haul copper ore from Nacozari over the high desert of northern Mexico to smelters in Bisbee, Douglas and El Paso. It was at first

Daily Except Sunday Schedule

Westbound — Los Angeles to Beverly Hills, University of California at Westwood and Santa Monica — Westbound

STATIONS	Miles	AM	AM	AM	AM	AM	AM	AM	Ex AM	Ex AM	Ex AM	‡-Ex AM	Ex AM	Ex AM	Ex AM
Lv. Los Angeles (5th & Hill Sts.)	.00	5.30	5.45	5.55	6.00	6.10	6.20	6.30	6.40	6.50	7.00	7.05	7.15	7.20	7.30
" Wilshire and Western	4.11	5.45	6.00	6.10	6.15	6.25	6.35	6.45	6.55	7.05	7.16	7.21	7.31	7.36	7.46
Ar. Beverly Hills (Sta. Monica Blvd.)	9.92	6.03	6.18	6.28	6.33	6.43	6.53	7.03	7.14	7.24	7.36	7.41	7.51	7.56	8.06
Ar. University at Westwood	13.02	.....	.....	.....	.....	6.52	.....	7.12	.....	7.33	.....	7.50	.....	.....	8.15
Ar. Santa Monica (Ocean & B'dway)	17.00	6.23	.....	.....	6.53	.....	7.13	.....	7.34	.....	7.56	.....	.....	8.16	.....

STATIONS	‡-Ex AM	Ex AM	Ex AM	Ex AM	Ex AM	Ex AM	Ex AM	Ex AM	Ex AM	Ex AM	Ex AM	Ex AM	Ex AM	Ex AM	Ex AM
Lv. Los Angeles (5th & Hill Sts.)	7.38	7.40	7.50	8.00	8.10	8.20	8.31	8.40	8.51	9.00	9.11	9.20	9.31	9.40	9.51
" Wilshire and Western	7.54	7.56	8.06	8.16	8.26	8.36	8.47	8.56	9.07	9.16	9.27	9.36	9.47	9.56	10.07
Ar. Beverly Hills (Sta. Monica Blvd.)	8.14	8.16	8.26	8.36	8.46	8.56	9.07	9.16	9.27	9.36	9.47	9.56	10.07	10.16	10.27
Ar. University at Westwood	.....	.....	8.35	.....	8.55	.....	9.16	.....	9.36	.....	9.56	.....	10.16	.....	10.36
Ar. Santa Monica (Ocean & B'dway)	.....	8.36	.....	8.56	.....	9.16	.....	9.36	.....	9.56	.....	10.16	.....	10.36	.....

STATIONS	Ex AM	Ex AM	Ex AM	Ex AM	Ex AM	Ex AM	Ex AM	Ex AM	Ex AM	Ex AM	Ex AM	Ex AM	Ex PM	Ex PM	Ex PM
Lv. Los Angeles (5th & Hill Sts.)	10.00	10.11	10.20	10.31	10.40	10.51	11.00	11.11	11.20	11.31	11.40	11.51	12.00	12.11	12.20
" Wilshire and Western	10.16	10.27	10.36	10.47	10.56	11.07	11.16	11.27	11.36	11.47	11.56	12.07	12.16	12.27	12.36
Ar. Beverly Hills (Sta. Monica Blvd.)	10.36	10.47	10.56	11.07	11.16	11.27	11.36	11.47	11.56	12.07	12.16	12.27	12.36	12.47	12.56
Ar. University at Westwood	.....	10.56	.....	11.16	.....	11.36	.....	11.56	.....	12.16	.....	12.36	.....	12.56	.....
Ar. Santa Monica (Ocean & B'dway)	10.56	.....	11.16	.....	11.36	.....	11.56	.....	12.16	.....	12.36	.....	12.56	.....	1.16

STATIONS	Ex PM	Ex PM	Ex PM	Ex PM	Ex PM	Ex PM	Ex PM	Ex PM	Ex PM	Ex PM	Ex PM	Ex PM	Ex PM	Ex PM	Ex PM
Lv. Los Angeles (5th & Hill Sts.)	12.31	12.40	12.51	1.00	1.11	1.20	1.31	1.40	1.51	2.00	2.12	2.20	2.32	2.40	2.52
" Wilshire and Western	12.47	12.56	1.07	1.16	1.27	1.37	1.48	1.57	2.08	2.17	2.29	2.37	2.49	2.57	3.09
Ar. Beverly Hills (Sta. Monica Blvd.)	1.07	1.16	1.27	1.36	1.47	1.57	2.08	2.17	2.28	2.37	2.49	2.57	3.09	3.17	3.29
Ar. University at Westwood	1.16	.....	1.36	.....	1.56	.....	2.17	.....	2.38	.....	2.58	.....	3.18	.....	3.38
Ar. Santa Monica (Ocean & B'dway)	.....	1.36	.....	1.56	.....	2.18	.....	2.38	.....	2.58	.....	3.18	.....	3.38	.....

STATIONS	Ex PM	Ex PM	Ex PM	Ex PM	Ex PM	Ex PM	Ex PM	Ex PM	Ex PM	S-Ex PM	‡-Ex PM	Ex PM	‡-Ex PM	S-Ex PM	‡-Ex PM
Lv. Los Angeles (5th & Hill Sts.)	3.00	3.12	3.20	3.32	3.40	3.52	4.00	4.12	4.20	4.32	4.33	4.39	4.48	4.52	4.57
" Wilshire and Western	3.17	3.29	3.37	3.49	3.57	4.09	4.17	4.29	4.37	4.49	4.50	4.56	5.06	5.09	5.14
Ar. Beverly Hills (Sta. Monica Blvd.)	3.37	3.49	3.57	4.09	4.17	4.29	4.37	4.49	4.57	5.09	5.12	5.17	5.27	5.29	5.36
Ar. University at Westwood	.....	3.58	.....	4.18	.....	4.38	.....	4.58	.....	5.18	5.21	.....	5.36	5.38	.....
Ar. Santa Monica (Ocean & B'dway)	3.58	.....	4.18	.....	4.38	.....	4.58	.....	5.18	.....	.....	5.38	.....	.....	.....

STATIONS	Ex PM	‡-Ex PM	S-Ex PM	‡-Ex PM	Ex PM	‡-Ex PM	S-Ex PM	‡-Ex PM	Ex PM	Ex PM	Ex PM	PM	PM	PM	PM
Lv. Los Angeles (5th & Hill Sts.)	5.00	5.06	5.12	5.15	5.18	5.24	5.31	5.34	5.39	5.50	6.00	6.11	6.20	6.30	6.40
" Wilshire and Western	5.17	5.23	5.29	5.32	5.35	5.41	5.48	5.51	5.54	6.07	6.17	6.28	6.37	6.47	6.57
Ar. Beverly Hills (Sta. Monica Blvd.)	5.37	5.45	5.49	5.54	5.57	6.03	6.08	6.13	6.17	6.27	6.39	6.49	6.58	7.08	7.18
Ar. University at Westwood	.....	5.54	5.58	.....	.....	6.12	6.17	.....	.....	6.36	.....	6.58	.....	7.17	.....
Ar. Santa Monica (Ocean & B'dway)	5.58	.....	.....	.....	6.17	.....	.....	.....	6.38	.....	6.59	.....	7.18	.....	7.38

STATIONS	PM	PM	PM	PM	PM	PM	PM	PM	PM	PM	PM	PM	PM	PM	PM
Lv. Los Angeles (5th & Hill Sts.)	6.50	7.00	7.15	7.30	7.45	8.00	8.15	8.30	8.45	9.00	9.15	9.30	9.45	10.00	10.22
" Wilshire and Western	7.07	7.17	7.32	7.47	8.07	8.17	8.32	8.47	9.02	9.17	9.32	9.45	10.00	10.15	10.37
Ar. Beverly Hills (Sta. Monica Blvd.)	7.28	7.38	7.53	8.08	8.23	8.38	8.53	9.08	9.23	9.38	9.53	10.05	10.20	10.35	10.57
Ar. University at Westwood	7.37	.....	8.02	.....	8.32	.....	9.02	.....	a9.30	.....	a10.00	.....	a10.27	.....	.....
Ar. Santa Monica (Ocean & B'dway)	.....	7.58	.....	8.28	.....	8.58	.....	9.28	.....	9.58	.....	10.25	.....	10.55	.....

STATIONS	PM	PM	PM	PM	PM	PM	AM	AM							
Lv. Los Angeles (5th & Hill Sts.)	10.30	10.45	11.00	11.15	11.30	11.47	12.07	12.30	.....	.....	.....	.....	.....	.....	.....
" Wilshire and Western	10.45	11.00	11.15	11.30	11.45	12.02	12.22	12.45	.....	.....	.....	.....	.....	.....	.....
Ar. Beverly Hills (Sta. Monica Blvd.)	11.05	11.20	11.35	11.50	12.05	12.22	12.42	1.03	.....	.....	.....	.....	.....	.....	.....
Ar. University at Westwood	.....	a11.27	.....	.....	.....	a12.29	.....	.....	.....	.....	.....	.....	.....	.....	.....
Ar. Santa Monica (Ocean & B'dway)	11.25	.....	11.55	.....	12.25	.....	1.02	.....	.....	.....	.....	.....	.....	.....	.....

Eastbou

STA

Lv. Santa Moni
" University a
" Beverly Hill
Ar. Wilshire an
Ar. Los Angeles

‡—Daily except Saturday and Sunday.
S—Saturday only.
a—Operates to or from Westwood Blvd. and Le Conte Drive only.
c—Operates to Eighth and Olive only.

Ex.—Express Service between Los Angeles (5th & Hill Sts.) and points west of Fairfax Ave.—Stops will be made as follows: Westbound to pick up passengers destined to points west of Fairfax Ave. and eastbound to discharge passengers originating at points west of Fairfax Ave.

R
west
2nd S
R
rever
N
West

In addition to schedules shown above, frequent local service is operated between 5th & Hill Sts. and Fairfax Ave. & Wilshire Blvd.

Wilshire Blvd. was undoubtedly the busiest transit corridor in Los Angeles never to have had rail service. Motor coach service on that artery grew rapidly in the 1920s and 1930s and it enjoyed both local and express service. Here is part of a 1934 timetable showing a basic 10-minute headway plus "frequent local service." *Author's Collection*

owned by the El Paso & Southwestern Railroad, and after 1924 by the Southern Pacific. It continued in existence until August 1965, when it was sold to the Mexican government, so that it was one of the very last foreign-owned railroads in Mexico.

The Mexican railway enterprises of the Southern Pacific were never particularly lucrative. With the demand for copper reduced during the depression and because of depletion of the better copper deposits at Nacozari, ways were sought to reduce the cost of passenger train operation but still provide reasonable levels of service. Operation of buses was a possible answer, but no direct highways existed, and the roads in the region were unimproved and primitive.

In 1933 the Southern Pacific, already using five similar buses on the SP de Mexico, directed that subsidiary Pacific Electric sell to subsidiary F.C. de Nacozari a White Model 50 and rebuild its running gear to operate on standard railroad track. The work was carried out at PE's Torrance Shops, and the resulting creation was placed in service on

Above, left and right: LAMC turned to medium-sized buses for the Crenshaw–Vine–La Brea and Vermont lines in the mid-'30s to replace small Yellow Coach Model U's. Eight YC 728s and six Twin Coach 30-Rs were bought in 1935 and 1936; four more Twins, 31-Rs this time, were added in 1937. Units 3206 and 4102 appear in original paint and lettering about to go into service.
Both: SCRTD Collection

Left: An elaborate paint scheme with more red was featured on the large new single-deckers bought for Sunset and Wilshire in 1937-1938. The 3900s, owned by PE, were Yellow 740s with semi-automatic transmissions and the same peculiar door arrangement as the 3700s. *SCRTD Collection*

the 77-mile run in place of a steam passenger train. The White worked out well on an undemanding schedule, and two more were pulled out of storage in 1935 and 1936, rebuilt by PE and assigned to the Nacozari. By 1940, because of the age and uninspired maintenance, a replacement for the Whites became necessary.

Again the SP turned to Pacific Electric, but this time the result was quite different. PE-owned Los Angeles Motor Coach double-deck Fageol 723, made surplus by the arrival of new Yellow TD-4502s, was rebuilt with a front truck (a modified Birney streetcar truck with 19-inch wheels) and cast steel 43-inch rear wheels on redesigned hubs. Numbered A504 and painted bright maroon, the railbus was shipped from Torrance on October 2, 1941.

On much the same schedule as the predecessor Whites, the Fageol operated north from Nacozari on Monday, Wednesday and Saturday at 8:30 A.M. and south from Agua Prieta (across the border from Douglas) at 1:00 p.m. on Tuesday, Thursday and Sunday. It was joined by a second Fageol numbered A505 in the summer of 1945. This service continued until at least 1950 and possibly later, until removal of the connecting trains at Douglas, declining patronage and the age of the Fageols caused discontinuance of the "motor bus" service.

It is not known whether the upper deck proved as popular in Sonora as it did on Wilshire Blvd., but the fierce desert climate must have been a moderating influence on the enthusiasm of any travelers desiring to ride there during the warmer months. The railway company soon added a corrugated metal roof over the front part of the upper deck of A504 and a tiny window at the front for ventilation.

Seats at the rear of the lower deck were removed, the windows were covered over, and the area was used for baggage and express. In this form, the bus lasted until the end of service. Its exact disposition is unknown, but a visitor to Nacozari in 1956 found A504 retired and rusting on a spur.

One of the more unusual jobs attempted by Pacific Electric's Torrance Shops involved the conversion of five double-deck buses (three Whites from PE and two Fageols from LAMC) into railbuses for the Ferrocarril de Nacozari, Mexico. The A-505 was one of the LAMC Fageols and is shown at the shops in July 1945, awaiting shipment to Mexico. *Pacific Electric Magazine*

Use of converted buses as railcars was not common in North America, but the Southern Pacific, besides using Whites on the SP de Mexico, also sent six MTCo Pickwick Duplexes there for use as railcars, and the affiliated St. Louis–Southwestern Railway operated at least two White 54-As, acquired from its subsidiary, Southwestern Transportation Co., as railcars in Texas.

Rail Replacements. On May 26, 1940, Los Angeles Motor Coach buses (as route 90) replaced Los Angeles Railway streetcars on the West 10th Street–Olympic Blvd. line between downtown Los Angeles and Mullen Avenue (Los Angeles High School). On July 1, LAMC buses replaced PE interurbans on San Vicente Blvd. between West Los Angeles (Federal Avenue) and Santa Monica, operating as a branch ("Santa Monica via Brentwood") of the Wilshire Blvd. line.

These changes constituted a major increase in the size of the bus operation, for no fewer than 88 Yellow TD-4502s were placed in service on these routes and replaced the last double-deckers on Wilshire Blvd. The resulting need for additional storage space required construction of a maintenance building and 164 bus storage yard on four acres of PE's Vineyard property near Venice Blvd. and La Brea Avenue, opened on July 13, 1941. LAMC buses previously housed at 16th and San Pedro and at 54th St. (LARy Division 5) were transferred to Vineyard as well.

In spite of this considerable expansion, there was a sign that the days of Los Angeles Motor Coach might be numbered in that PE put its own buses in service in place of the Santa Monica via Sawtelle interurban in 1940. This line ran through the heart of the Motor Coach territory, and its routing into downtown Los Angeles was via Olympic Blvd.

In 1941 the Brentwood branch of the Wilshire line was returned to PE, which made it into an alternate routing of the recently motorized Santa Monica via Sawtelle line. The

Eighteen 40-passenger Twins arrived in 1937 and were immediately put into service on the Sunset Blvd. line in place of double-deckers. *SCRTD Collection*

The 4340 was one of 88 Yellow TD-4502s delivered in the spring of 1940. This fleet was one of the very first to be built with Yellow's stressed-skin design, which lasted until the introduction of the "New Look" in 1959. The view was taken on Wilshire Blvd. eastbound at Park View Street; the bus is about to cross what is now MacArthur Park. In the background is the Otis (now Los Angeles County) Art Institute, still in the same location but now in a modern building. The LAMC color scheme was again simplified during World War II to yellow and silver-gray with a red stripe; coach 4241 models this along with the new oval emblem adopted around 1939. *Both: SCRTD Collection*

Olympic–West 3rd feeder line was abandoned in 1941, when through route 90 was extended to cover part of it, and the sparsely utilized Hollywood–Long Beach service last ran in June 1942.

About a year later, in July 1943, the Talmadge–Hyperion portion of the Silver Lake route was reestablished as a separate line (Route 80). When 5th and 6th Streets downtown were made one-way, the Sunset and Olympic lines were through-routed, effective October 5, 1947, as a matter of operating convenience.

Los Angeles Motor Coach started four defense plant routes during the spring of 1942 under contract to Lockheed Aircraft. Three of the lines connected with the terminals of Los Angeles Railway car lines and by the end of April, a fourth line had been added from Ocean and Broadway in Santa Monica. Equipment for the lines was supplied by LARy in the form of new diesels.

Although patronage was slow at first (582 passengers on 13 trips), more than 2,000 passengers were being carried on 40 trips by the end of May. By 1945, the lines were operating from Olympic and Doheny (92), Olympic and Fairfax (93), Pico and Rimpau (94), and the Virgil Garage (95) to the Lockheed and Vega plants in Burbank. They ran for one more year, serving each shift change, until they were discontinued.

Dissolution. By 1948 the original purpose of Los Angeles Motor Coach Co. remained valid, but the circumstances within which the jointly owned subsidiary had to function were greatly changed from those of 1923. Los Angeles Railway had become Los Angeles Transit Lines, under National City Lines control, in 1945; it had several major bus lines of its own and would soon have more.

Conversion to buses of principal PE routes was continuing in earnest, and it became clear that operating economies could be realized by dissolving Motor Coach. In anticipation of this division, the Sunset–Olympic through-routing was discontinued on December 12, 1948.

ROSTER OF BUSES

Los Angeles Motor Coach Co. (1928–1949)

Owner	Numbers	Make	Model	Seats	Built	Notes
PE	3001-3009 odd	Twin	40	40	1928	
LARy	3002-3010 even	Twin	40	40	1928	
PE	3011-3025 odd	Twin	40	40	1929	
LARy	3012-3026 even	Twin	40	40	1929	
PE	3027	Twin	40	40	1930	
LARy	3028	Twin	40	40	1930	
PE	3029	Twin	40	40	1929	(1934) PE
LARy	3030	Twin	40	40	1929	(1934) LARy 2014
PE	3101-3113 odd	Yellow	U-M-662	25	1931	
LARy	3102-3114 even	Yellow	U-M-662	25	1931	
½ & ½	3201	Federal	A-6	25	1930	(1931) West Side Transit Co.
½ & ½	3301	ACF	602-1	16	1928	(1931) (To PE ownership 1939)
½ & ½	3302	ACF	602-1	21	1928	(1932) (To LARy ownership 1939)
PE	3401, 3403	Austin	Utility Coach	22	1933	
LARy	3402, 3404	Austin	Utility Coach	22	1933	
PE	3501	Fageol	—	29	1924	(1934) PE 201
LARy	3502	Fageol	—	29	1924	(1934) LARy
PE	3601	Yellow	U-N-665	23	1934	
LARy	3602	Yellow	U-N-665	23	1934	
PE	3701-3707 odd	Yellow	718	41	1934	
LARy	3702-3708 even	Yellow	718	41	1934	
PE	3709-3713 odd	Yellow	718	42	1936	
LARy	3710-3714 even	Yellow	718	42	1936	
PE	3715-3729	Yellow	718	40	1936	(1942) PE 415-429
PE	3801, 3803	Yellow	728	32	1935	
LARy	3802, 3804	Yellow	728	32	1935	
PE	3805, 3807	Yellow	728	32	1936	
LARy	3806, 3808	Yellow	728	32	1936	
PE	3201-3205 odd	Twin	30-R	31	1936	
LARy	3202-3206 even	Twin	30-R	31	1936	
PE	3901-3920	Yellow	740	41	1938	
LARy	4001-4018	Twin	40-RC	40	1937	
LARy	4101-4104	Twin	31-R	31	1937	
LARy	4201-4248	Yellow	TD-4502	45	1940	
LARy	4249-4259	Yellow	TD-4505	45	1941	
LARy	4260-4274	Yellow	TD-4505	45	1942	(To LATL 6186-6199, 6100)
LATL	4260	Yellow	TD-4505	45	1942	(1948) LATL 6100
PE	4301-4340	Yellow	TD-4502	45	1940	
PE	4341-4362	GM	TD-4506	45	1945	
PE	3311-3325	White	798	44	1944	ODT allocated
LATL	3351-3365	White	798	44	1945	
LATL	3366-3380	White	798	44	1945	(1947) LATL 2422 down to 2408
LATL	3381-3387	White	798	44	1945	(1949) LATL 2407 down to 2401
LATL	3401-3402	White	784	31	1939	(1947) LATL 2904-2905
LATL	4401-4423	GM	TD-4506	45	1945	(1945) LATL 6206, 6208, 6211, 6229-6238, 6241-6247, 6249, 6250, 6254
LATL	4424	GM	TD-4506	45	1945	(1948) LATL 6269
LATL	4425-4433	GM	TD-4506	45	1946	(1948) LATL 6400-6408
LATL	4434-4443	GM	TD-4506	45	1945	(1949) LATL 6268 down to 6259
PE	4500-4519	GM	TD-4507	45	1946	
PE	4520-4538	GM	TDH-4507	45	1947	

ROSTER OF BUSES

Los Angeles Motor Coach Co.
Disposition of Buses
May 1, 1949

To Pacific Electric Ry.
(128 buses)

3311-3325	798	to	2395-2409
(3351-3387)	798	to	2410-2422*
4301-4314,			
4316-4340	TD-4502	to	2639-2677
4341-4362	TD-4506	to	2678-2699
4500-4519	TD-4507	to	2638 down to 2619
4520-4538	TDH-4507	to	2618-2605, 2600-2604

To Los Angeles Transit Lines
(127 buses)

(3351-3387)	798	to	5101-5124*
4201-4248	TD-4502	to	6025-6072
4249-4260	TD-4505	to	6073-6083, 6100
4401-4424	TD-4506	to	6200, 6259-6281
4425-4433	TD-4506	to	6292-6300
4434-4443	TD-4506	to	6282-6291

3351*	LATL 5109	3370	LATL 5120
3352	LATL 5110	3371	LATL 5118
3353	LATL 5105	3372	PE 2413
3354	LATL 5104	3373	LATL 5124
3355	LATL 5101	3374	LATL 5123
3356	PE 2420	3375	LATL 5119
3357	PE 2421	3376	PE 2414
3358	LATL 5106	3377	PE 2415
3359	LATL 5103	3378	LATL 5117
3360	LATL 5102	3379	PE 2416
3361	PE 2410	3380	PE 2417
3362	LATL 5112	3381	LATL 5115
3363	LATL 5107	3382	LATL 5113
3364	LATL 5108	3383	PE 2418
3365	LATL 5111	3384	LATL 5116
3366	PE 2411	3385	LATL 5114
3367	LATL 5122	3386	PE 2419
3368	LATL 5121	3387	PE 2422
3369	PE 2412		

PE favored big Whites in the 1940s, and both owners bought 798s for LAMC. PE's 15 were numbered 3311-3325 and came in 1944 with ODT numbers. *Motor Coach Age*

CHAPTER FOUR

PACIFIC ELECTRIC/ MOTOR TRANSIT • 1930-1940

Consolidation; if you can't beat 'em, buy 'em

PE extended bus service to the Rose Hills station (at Huntington Drive and Monterey Road) during 1931. In 1935, when the South Pasadena car line was given up, the replacement bus service was through-routed with this segment providing an alternate route to South Pasadena. Here is the transfer point in later days, complete with timetable posted for the convenience of passengers. *SCRTD Collection*

This unit illustrates two phases in the gradual rebuilding of the Avery-bodied Whites. As No. 60, with added air springs, balloon tires, steel wheels, and window sashes (about 1925) and as 1060 with steel disc wheels, a smaller rear freight compartment and new paint (1933). Here, the 1060 appears in the new Motor Transit colors of Greyhound blue and PE red—a far cry from the beach sand and forest green of former days.
60: SCRTD Collection
1060: Motor Bus Society

AT THE TIME of Motor Transit's organization in 1916 as White Bus Line, 50,000 shares of $1 par value common stock were issued. The amount of stock authorized to be issued was increased to $500,000 in 1920 and to $1.5 million in 1923, the additional shares being used to buy other companies and manufacture buses. Though certain purchases were made for stock, by December 1929, O.R. Fuller owned all but three of the 1,306,926 outstanding shares, the other three being in the hands of other company officers.

On December 12, 1929, Motor Transit Terminal Corp., the legal owner of the stock and itself wholly owned by Fuller, granted an option to purchase all of the outstanding shares to Robert C. Gillis as agent for Pacific Transportation Securities. Gillis assigned the option to the Securities Company on January 30, 1930, and it was exercised on the following day for an estimated price of $3 million, the exact amount to be determined by appraisal.

Pacific Transportation Securities, soon to be renamed Pacific Greyhound Corp., was owned one-third by Greyhound, one-third by Pickwick, and one-third by the Southern Pacific, PE's parent, which had already contributed its own bus operations to the new combine. Announcement of the sale of Motor Transit prompted the trade press to assume a coordination of its service with Greyhound's, but this was not to be and had never been intended. What was not generally known was that upon receipt of authorization from the Railroad Commission, the Pacific Electric Railway had agreed to buy two-thirds of the Motor Transit stock.

The Commission reluctantly authorized the purchase on April 3, 1930, and thus provided PE with control of its former competitor. No property was transferred, and no curtailment of service by either PE or Motor Transit was at issue, though the Commission did recognize in its decision that certain economies might be realized by consolidation

El Dorado 1881 (ex-881) arrives at Lake Arrowhead with a load of vacationers. Direct service from downtown Los Angeles allowed San Bernardino Mountain resort travelers a one-seat ride starting in the summer of 1926. This prospect did not delight the PE, whose passengers still had to transfer from cars to buses at San Bernardino.
California Historical Society

of specific properties and services. Any subsequent application along these lines, however, was left to be dealt with on its own merits.

Immediate results of the sale were the move of Motor Transit offices to the Pacific Electric Building at 6th and Main, the abandonment of the 220 E. Market Street headquarters, and the appointment of T.B. Wilson, president of Pacific Transportation Securities, as president of Motor Transit. F.D. Howell stayed on as vice-president and general manager, and PE President D.W. Pontius became chairman of the board. Directors included Charles F. Wren of Pickwick, Frank Karr of PE, and of course O.R. Fuller. The final sale price was $3,337,500.

Motor Transit purchased six Pickwick Duplex 53-passenger buses from Pacific Greyhound lines in 1933 and assigned them to its heaviest suburban routes. The Sterling engine supplied with the Duplex was also used in Motor Transit's last home-built buses, the 875-881 series, completed in 1930. Soon after the purchase by PE, all Motor Transit buses were renumbered in the 1000 series (so that 60 became 1060, 475 became 1475, and so on), to avoid conflicts with Greyhound and PE buses.

Another change was modification of Motor Transit's shield-shaped emblem. "Motor Transit Stages" became "Motor Transit Lines," and "El Dorado System" lamentably disappeared, replaced by "Comfortable Courteous Service" to complement PE's own "Comfort–Speed–Safety."

Consolidation. Full-time PE rail passenger service to the Orange County points of La Habra, Yorba Linda, Stern, and Fullerton ceased soon after the acquisition, because the Motor Transit route between Fullerton and Los Angeles was more direct, and patronage did not warrant continuation of both services. The Railroad Commission first had to authorize extension of the bus line out to Yorba Linda.

The largest buses ever operated by Motor Transit were Pickwick Duplexes like 1901, waiting here under the elevated deck behind PE's Main Street station. They were all gone by 1938 with at least six being converted to railcars for sister subsidiary SP de Mexico.
Security Pacific National Bank

Local streetcar service between Santa Ana and Orange ended on September 15, 1930, replaced by increased Motor Transit bus service.

During the next three years, Motor Transit contracted into fewer but stronger routes that complemented rather than competed with the PE rail network. Under common management, Motor Transit's 1,400-mile system of alternate routes (some with little service from the start) was pared down until only 600 miles of the strongest lines remained, and sparsely patronized feeder bus lines beyond PE's service area were abandoned, routes to Banning and Yucaipa on the eastern fringe of the system being the earliest casualties. The route from Santa Ana to Laguna Beach via Irvine traversed relatively unpopulated territory and was given up before the end of 1930 in favor of an extension of the Newport Beach line along the Coast Highway.

Withdrawal from the San Jacinto Mountains was undertaken in 1931, and in that year passenger miles dropped 28 percent under the total for 1930, but total passengers carried decreased only 16 percent. However, 1931 was to be the best year for Motor Transit under PE ownership. In January 1932, service was suspended on alternate routes between Ontario, Upland, and San Bernardino, and the San Bernardino–Victorville–Oro Grande line was sold to Pickwick–Greyhound Lines. The route from Pasadena to Pomona via Monrovia was suspended on May 1, at which time also the final routing of the Riverside–Long Beach line via Bolsa and Westminster was put into effect and the Pasadena–Long Beach route via Atlantic Avenue was given up.

The County Farm branch of the Santa Ana line was abandoned on April 24, 1933, and in that summer the Fullerton–Yorba Linda extension, added in 1930 and cut back to Placentia in 1932, was abandoned. Motor Transit was authorized to share depots with Pacific Electric in Pasadena, Orange, Fullerton, Whittier, and San Bernardino. The operating results for 1933 showed 40 fewer buses being operated than 10 years previously (78 as against 118), while only 10 percent fewer passengers were carried.

Santa Ana–Newport Beach–Laguna Beach service was sold on January 29, 1934, to Robert P. Kellogg, who operated it as the Laguna Beach–Santa Ana Stage Line and soon afterward, the Pomona–Chino line was abandoned because of a lack of business.

The most important aspect of the takeover was that experienced operators of trunkline bus service became part of Pacific Electric management for the first time. More effective coordination of rail and bus lines was demonstrated in 1934, when a new Motor Transit line between Glendale, Montrose and Verdugo City replaced an extension of the Rossmoyne local line and provided feeder service to the Glendale rail line from the central portion of the Motor Transit Los Angeles–Sunland route.

Glendale and Pasadena Developments. Wherever Pacific Electric operated local bus service, a classic dilemma had to be faced: how to accommodate a growing and shifting population as well as political pressure while minimizing the operating losses incurred by overexpansion. As early as 1927, PE had discovered that by achieving a monopoly in Pasadena, it had committed itself to a level and an extent of service greater than required. It was only the faster growth of neighboring Glendale that kept the lines there solvent for a longer time. The 1930 census found the population of Glendale to be 62,000, five times the 1920 figure.

On September 9, 1928, service in Glendale was extended into the rapidly growing Rossmoyne district and into the Lake St. district passing the new Grand Central Airport. Service was also diverted to pass the newly opened Hoover High School in the Northwest section. On June 1, 1930, routes and schedules were extensively revised with the

PE made a series of "record shots" before changing Motor Transit's red, blue and gray to its own red in 1936; the photos are from the collection of Bob Burrowes.

Generally similar to the 700s, Motor Transit's 800-series coaches were more deluxe with curtains, rooftop baggage racks, and wider seat spacing. When the 800s were introduced in 1928 they were the first Motor Transit buses with hot air instead of exhaust pipe heat, and they had the longest wheelbase (253 inches) of any buses being built in the U.S. at that time. The 1877 (ex-875 series) is shown here in side and front views.
Both: Bob Burrowes Collection

major change being an extension into the Atwater district providing direct service between the East Side and downtown.

Glendale buses were stored and maintained at East Broadway and Chevy Chase Drive, where there was also a railcar storage yard. Thirteen buses were needed to provide base service on the system of 16.4 route miles, with four more buses added to take care of morning and afternoon school loads. As of 1931, almost 60,000 miles were operated and 134,000 passengers were carried in Glendale each month.

It was apparent by 1930 that the Whites used in Glendale and Pasadena since 1923 were due for replacement. The consensus was that they were hard-riding, drafty and smelly, and their four-cylinder engines left much to be desired in the way of performance in the hilly parts of both cities. The first relief came on October 12, 1930, when 12 new Model 20 Twin Coaches went into service in Glendale.

The seriousness of the financial situation on the Pasadena lines was demonstrated in January 1931, when an application was submitted to adjust fare zones and reduce service in response to a $93,000 operating loss run up during the previous fiscal year, when 9.5 million passengers had been carried on these routes. The company agreed to buy new buses and thus secured local approval for the proposed fare adjustments. Instituted in April, the new fare structure replaced two 7-cent zones with three 5-cent zones and incorporated a maximum fare of 10 cents (eight tickets for 50 cents) for two or more zones. The hope was that patronage would increase as a result of the lower zone fare, but this was not to be.

The promised new equipment was ordered in April and started arriving in June. Included were 23 Fageols (all for Pasadena) and 12 Twin 30s (10 for Pasadena and two for Glendale), relegating the Whites to standby duties and providing both cities with improved service standards. Route changes included elimination of the El Molino and Del Mar lines and revision of through-routing arrangements so that only five purely local routes were operated instead of nine.

From 1923 into the 1930s, local bus services of Pacific Electric were dominated by White model 50 chassis with bodies built at the Torrance Shops. This view shows such a bus at the Glendale yard in 1928.

Magna Collection

Several further changes were made in April of 1932 including the replacement of single-track interurban operation on N. Lake Ave. by the Mendocino shuttle bus. At the same time, the El Molino line was reestablished and the Allen Ave. line again established as a separate route. Operating losses still totaled over $70,000 in 1933, and further service adjustments were made, in February and June of 1934 and in January 1935, all to no avail.

On March 1, 1936, the eastern portion of the Colorado Blvd. car line between Sierra Madre Blvd. and Daisy Avenue was replaced by a shuttle bus line, which ran through to Rosemead Blvd., in order to end operation of streetcars against the flow of motor traffic on a single-track segment. New Twin Coach 23-Rs were added to the Pasadena fleet in 1936 and served as the first-line equipment, backed up by the Fageol "box cars." Local service in Pasadena and Glendale was to bear the PE name for another five years before disposition.

Modernization of the Glendale service was carried out in October 1930 with 12 Twin model 20s having angled perimeter seating and painted red and gray with ivory window trim and brown roof. Traffic picked up, and two larger model 30s were added to the Glendale fleet in 1931.

Twin Coach

Other Changes of the Early 1930s. Feeder service was resumed in North Hollywood on October 1, 1930, after an independent operator had applied to serve Hollywood by a direct route from the center of North Hollywood, some distance from the PE station. PE's new route was in the form of a loop, and rail service was increased; a year later the bus line was extended to Hollywood and rail service was again reduced to its former level. The Ventura Blvd. line, also in the Western District, was diverted to Northridge via Reseda Blvd. in 1932.

The minor Pomona–Claremont car line was replaced by buses on January 1, 1933, but the most significant substitution of buses for cars so far made by PE occurred on January 2, 1935. The South Pasadena interurban line was discontinued except for a short spur south of Mission Road, serving the General (now Los Angeles County) Hospital. The decision was based solely on economics, as patronage on the once-busy line had fallen significantly and the costs for necessary repairs to a bridge over the Arroyo Seco represented an impressive expenditure.

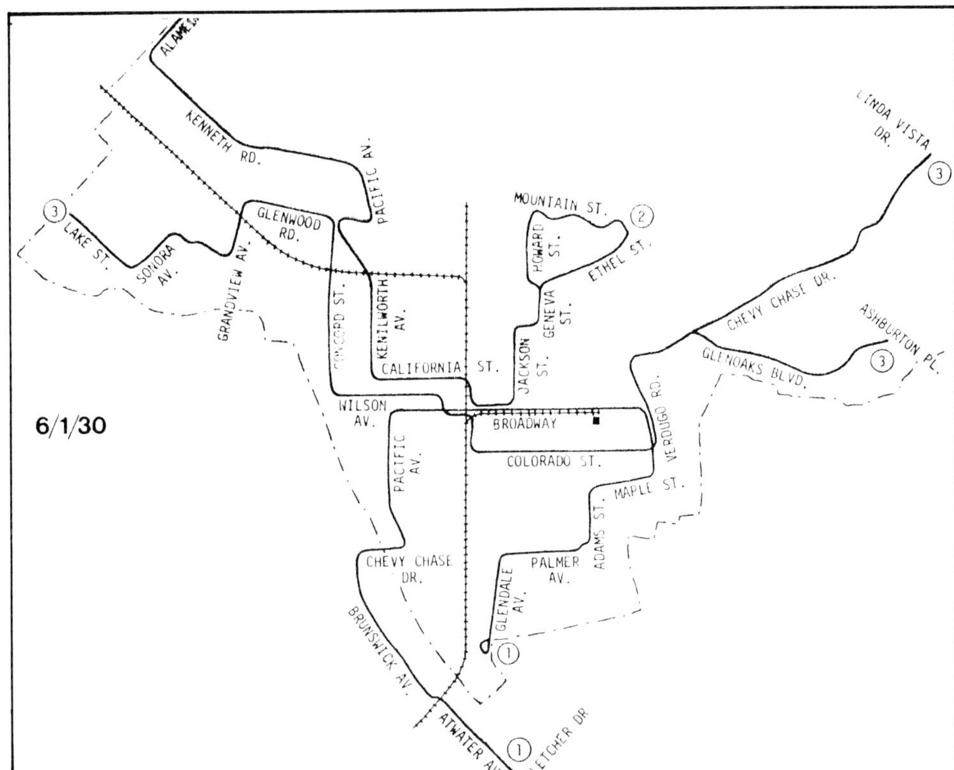

The Glendale lines as revised in June of 1930 with new Route 3 taking over Lake St. and Chevy Chase services along with new service on Glenoaks Blvd.
A. E. Meier

Sweeping changes in Pasadena during 1931 included adjustments to routes and fares as well as new buses in place of aging Whites. PE 262-273 were the first Twin 30s, and 10 of them with 23 similar Fageols took over the Pasadena service in that year. *Twin Coach*

Opened in 1895, the South Pasadena line was the first interurban railway in Southern California, but its route was roundabout compared to later lines built between Los Angeles and Pasadena. The inner portion of the line, from the General Hospital to Avenue 64, was replaced by a Los Angeles Railway bus line. The remainder was covered by a new PE bus route from South Pasadena to Highland Park. From there, it ran to Rose Hills station in place of the Avenue 64 line, extended there in 1931.

Joint Fares. Prior to 1934, there was no method by which a passenger could transfer between lines of the Pacific Electric and the Los Angeles Railway unless Los Angeles Motor Coach was used as an intermediate carrier. As the result of a committee studying local transportation problems, a 10-cent joint fare went into effect on February 1; this allowed direct transfers in the Los Angeles Railway inner zone and any two PE zones within zone 3. Along the Hollywood Blvd. line, zone 1 was bounded by Alvarado St., zone 2 by Vermont Ave. and zone 3 by Fairfax Ave. The PE lines on which the joint fare was effective included Hollywood, Edendale, Echo Park, Vineyard, Venice Blvd., Watts, Sierra Vista and South Pasadena.

Buses to Glendale. As the national and local economy emerged from the Depression, Pacific Electric was faced

Pressured by competition, Fageol finally introduced a forward-control bus in 1931, officially model 500 but referred to as the "Metropolitan" type. Featured was an electrically operated mechanism for sliding the engine out of the front of the bus for maintenance. Here are right, left and inside views.

Joe Corbin Collection

Pacific Electric also had Austin Utility Coaches No. 101 and two sisters, which spent most of their time on Pasadena-based feeder lines. Smallest of all PE buses in the 1930s were four tiny Yellow 714s seating just 17 passengers. Based at the Pasadena garage, they served the Flintridge, Lamanda Park and South Pasadena-Highland Park routes. Unit 151 is illustrated. In 1936, PE bought two new buses for its North Hollywood lines. Beneath the elongated bodies of 130 and 131 were Ford V-8 chassis reworked by school bus builder Patchetts & Charastensen. By 1937 they had migrated to Pasadena along with most other non-standard equipment.

Two: Floyd Hayhurst Collection; 151: Magna Collection

PE's allegiance to Twin Coach continued in 1934 with purchase of nine streamlined 30-S buses, which operated in both eastern and western districts. The color scheme was red and ivory with a brown roof.

Twin Coach

PE's Yellow Coach 718s were delivered in two groups, with 437 being the last in 1937.
Joe Corbin

with the need to improve standards of service on several principal suburban and interurban rail lines. Routes that had not received new cars in the 1920s still had wooden cars, some dating to 1902. Continuing development of outlying areas had led to numerous grade crossings on routes that had once been unobstructed. Major engineering improvements were out of the question except for the most important lines, and the Motor Transit system was providing daily evidence of the ability of buses to handle substantial volumes of traffic. Few electric railways had as yet made extensive substitutions of buses for cars on heavily traveled routes when, on July 12, 1936, PE placed 15 new Yellow Coach 718s on the Los Angeles–Glendale–Burbank route to provide base service.

In order to provide a downtown terminal, PE converted an elevated deck south of the Subway Terminal into an off-street bus depot. The deck had been built as an auto parking lot in 1931 and also served to shelter the Hill Street Station surface tracks. The Olive Street Bus Deck, as it became known, was later used by other lines as well.

Despite the fact that most off-peak rail runs were replaced by buses, hourly midday rail service continued between Los Angeles and Burbank, and the portion of the line south of the Los Angeles River, primarily on private right-of-way, continued to be frequently served by cars of the Edendale local line.

Handicapped by the lack of private right-of-way and the inability to use the subway, the replacement buses were slow and unpopular. By 1939, public clamor had risen to the point where the Railroad Commission ordered PE to reinstate full-time rail service and buy modern cars. Trackage was upgraded at substantial cost, and PCC cars entered service on November 24, 1940. The 718s were used elsewhere on the system until 1942, when most of them were transferred to the Los Angeles Motor Coach Co.

A little-known proposal to supplement another inter-

Yellow Coach 718s lay over at the East Broadway and Chevy Chase terminal between trips on the Glendale line. The ill-fated trial bus service partially replaced interurban cars from 1936 until 1940. At that time complaints forced a return to full-time rail service, with brand-new, multiple-unit PCC cars. *Interurban Press*

Fifteen new Twins, 23-Rs 240-249 and 31-Rs 310-314, were assigned to the West Hollywood "terminal" for the Ventura Blvd., Hollywood-North Hollywood, Beverly Blvd. and Hollywood-Beverly Hills-University routes in the fall of 1937.
244: Western Transit Society
310: Interurban Press

urban rail line with bus service was made by PE in the summer of 1937. As construction proceeded on the new Arroyo Seco Parkway, later to be known as the Pasadena Freeway, Pacific Electric proposed an express bus line from the Olive Street loading area (across the street from the Subway Terminal) to Broadway and Colorado Street. It was expected that the grade-separated highway would allow express buses to save 10 minutes over the Short Line rail schedule. But the adamant stand of the city of South Pasadena not to allow commercial traffic on its segment of the parkway put a halt to plans for the new line.

San Fernando Valley. During 1936, Pacific Electric was forced to reevaluate its San Fernando Valley operations. The stimulus, as usual, was external: an application by the Original Stage Line to operate a meandering interurban bus route from downtown Los Angeles via Riverside Drive, North Hollywood and Van Nuys to San Fernando.

In the face of mounting losses and deteriorating cars and track, PE offered a counter proposal: to replace its San Fernando Valley rail line with two new through bus lines and two feeder routes. One feeder would run between North Hollywood and Sunland, tapping Original Stage

Painted in PE red as if to symbolize the subsidiary nature of the formerly independent company, Motor Transit 1600-1614 were Mack BCs with Crown bodies introduced on the Redlands line in 1936. Each had 29 forward-facing seats on platforms.
Bob Burrowes Collection

Line territory, and the second between North Hollywood and Burbank, paralleling an existing OSL route. The through lines would both have started from the Olive Street Bus Deck and left the downtown area via Glendale Blvd. One would have closely paralleled the route of the rail line via Hollywood and the Cahuenga Pass, splitting at Van Nuys to serve San Fernando and Canoga Park (formerly Owensmouth). The second line was proposed to run along Riverside Drive through North Hollywood and Van Nuys to Ventura and Van Nuys Blvds., mainly duplicating the proposed OSL line.

The Pacific Electric application was immediately answered by the Original Stage Line, which offered its own proposal for an alternate route between Burbank and North Hollywood as well as routes along Ventura Blvd. from Hollywood via Reseda to San Fernando and via Girard to Canoga Park. Various communities took sides, the most vocal being San Fernando for the PE plan and North Hollywood against it. The California Railroad Commission and the Los Angeles Board of Public Utilities and Transportation both disapproved of PE's scheme to abandon the rail line, and that part of the application was denied.

The outcome of the skirmish definitely favored Original Stage Line. PE came away only with permission to extend its North Hollywood line to Van Nuys along the route of the proposed Riverside Drive line—a routing PE chose not to implement since it would only have diverted passengers from the interurbans. OSL, meanwhile, gained an alternate route from Burbank to North Hollywood complementing its existing line through Magnolia Park.

Rehearings resulted in a compromise plan which strengthened the PE rail line by converting its lightly patronized branches to buses and rerouting existing bus lines to feed it at the Universal City station. On June 1, 1938, the rail line was cut back to Van Nuys and two new bus lines replaced the discontinued branches. The Canoga Park and San Fernando feeder lines followed the former rail routes with little change. At the same time the Ventura Blvd. bus line was cut back at both ends to operate from Universal City to Tarzana, and the North Hollywood route was similarly shortened to terminate at Universal City.

PE Becomes Sole Owner. In the spring of 1936, it was decided by PE and PGL that the railway should become the sole owner of Motor Transit and complete the consolidation without passing every decision through a joint executive committee. An agreement to transfer the 5th and Los Angeles Streets terminal to Greyhound for its one-third stock interest was approved by the Railroad Commission on May 25, and the exchange took place in July. PE paid Motor Transit $330,000 to complete the three-cornered deal and keep its subsidiary's books in balance.

In June, PE acknowledged the increased scope of its bus activities by appointing Roy R. Wilson, previously Superintendent of Motor Transit, to the newly created post of Superintendent of Motor Coach Operations. Wilson had started out with Motor Transit in 1917, had gone into trucking in 1920 and joined the new Greyhound system in 1929 when it was getting established in California. He served as a Division Superintendent for Greyhound in Oakland, Phoenix and El Paso before returning to Motor Transit.

An experimental route between El Monte and the government tract near Cogswell Road, three miles northeast, lasted just 90 days in the summer of 1936. July 20 of that year brought transfer of PE's San Bernardino–Highland–Patton bus line to Motor Transit along with a requirement for increased service between San Bernardino and Redlands to replace streetcar service given up on that day. The Brockton Avenue car line in Riverside was abandoned by PE in May of 1936 and was replaced by Motor Transit bus service.

New Equipment. Once Pacific Electric had acquired Greyhound's minority interest in Motor Transit, the first new buses since 1930 were purchased. Motor Transit's tra-

Suburban Twins and Macks of 1937 brought Motor Transit into the modern era of rear-engined buses. The Twins (left) were completed at the Kent, Ohio, plant but many special parts for the Macks (above) were manufactured by Crown Coach and the modifications were carried out in Crown's Los Angeles plant. *1661: Interurban Press. 1684: Mack.*

ditional disdain for standardized equipment was evident in the initial order for 15 Mack BC front-engine chassis with CT engines and with custom bodies designed and built by Crown Coach, Los Angeles. To the modern eye the result looks uncomfortably like a school bus, but in fact there were 29 high-backed seats upholstered in brown leather and all on platforms facing forward (entirely over the wheels), as well as inside, underfloor, and rear baggage space.

Two orders were placed in 1937 and brought Motor Transit into the modern era of rear-engine buses. Fifteen Twins were far from stock 40-Rs, having forward-facing, leather-covered seats mounted on platforms as well as underfloor loaders for baggage. Ten Mack CTs were set up on the same general plan, with Crown fabricating many special parts. Out of about 105 Motor Transit-built buses on hand in 1930, some 50 had been disposed of without replacement during the period of retrenchment, and another 27 of the oldest were now withdrawn. The Duplexes were sold to the SP's Mexican affiliate after conversion to railbuses at PE's Torrance Shops, two going south in 1937 and four in 1938. The Mack-Crowns were originally assigned to the San Bernardino-Redlands line, later being used throughout the system, while the Twins provided all base service on the Sunland and El Monte lines and the CTs were used primarily on the Los Angeles-Whittier-Santa Ana route.

Final Contraction. Sale of marginal lines in 1937 included return of the Mountain Division to Max Green for $7,500. Despite attempts to increase operating efficiency the division had never shown a profit. Green felt that his familiarity with the territory and long acquaintance with the resort owners would enable him to reduce the overhead and increase traffic. With the rights went station facilities and six vehicles, none built later than 1929. The special relationship of the Mountain Auto Line to Motor Transit and PE was not ended, however; Mountain Auto Line timetables continued to appear in the joint PE-MTCo folders (the only foreign ones so honored), and interline ticketing persisted for years between the successors to both operators.

The Brockton Avenue line in Riverside was abandoned on December 20, 1937, and on January 17, 1938, PE transferred its three Pomona area local bus lines and three Twin 30-Ss to Motor Transit. Effective February 1, Motor Transit contracted to provide connecting bus service for the Southern Pacific between San Bernardino and Riverside via the Colton SP station, in addition to its regular route through the same territory. Five round trips a day were operated over the whole line and four more between Colton and Riverside; one 30-S was rebuilt as a 12-passenger combo.

ROSTER OF BUSES

Motor Transit Lines (1930–1939 only)

Numbers	Make	Model	Seats	Built	Notes
1900-1905	Pickwick	Duplex	53	1930	(1933) Pacific Greyhound Lines
1501-1503	Twin	30-S	26	1934	(1938) PE 280-282; 1501 to 12-passenger combo
1600-1614	Mack	6-BC-3S	29	1936	CT engines, Crown bodies
1650-1664	Twin	40-R	41	1937	All forward-facing seats
1675-1684	Mack	6-CT-3S	39	1937	Crown modified bodies

Buses turned over to Pacific Electric Railway 9/1/39: 1478, 1485, 1492, 1495, 1501-1503, 1600-1614, 1650-1664, 1675-1684, 1700-1708, 1800-1811, 1850-1852, 1875-1877, 1879-1881 (77 buses).

Service over the alternate through route to San Bernardino via Bloomington and Colton was suspended for six months and then discontinued formally on December 5, 1937. The Ontario–Upland route (ex-PE) was sold to R.P. Kellogg on February 5, 1939, and the San Bernardino–Highland–Patton line to Frank Snell on March 1. The last Motor Transit line to be disposed of was Riverside–Hemet, leased to P.C. Cross in August 1939 and subsequently sold. Cross continued to operate the Hemet Bus Line until 1973, when it was sold to Roesch Lines.

Through the years of PE control, Motor Transit operations did not change in method or philosophy from the independent days. Fuller's distaste for deadhead mileage still showed in 1939, when buses were based at 11 different locations although there were then only 79 vehicles in the fleet. Cleaning, servicing, and overhauls were done under contract at the Decatur Street Garage of Pacific Greyhound.

One of three Twin 30-Ss turned over to Motor Transit with PE's Pomona local lines; this one was rebuilt as a 12-passenger combo for SP train connection duties. *Bob Burrowes Collection*

Motor Transit service crews were stationed at the Los Angeles and Riverside depots to handle minor repair work. As had been the case 20 years before, peak-hour loads were handled by scheduled extra sections, 16 of which were operated each weekday. Several ran on the Whittier line between Los Angeles and Montebello High School.

Dissolution. Although PE and Motor Transit were separate corporations, the general officers and supervisory personnel were shared after 1936. In effect, Motor Transit existed in name only, and on September 1, 1939, it was dissolved and its 77 buses and other assets transferred to PE. A "Motor Transit District" joined the several geographical regions that made up the railway's Passenger Traffic Department. These bus lines maintained an identity because of different tariffs and restrictions. Intrastate tickets reading "via Southern Pacific Lines" or "via Pacific Greyhound Lines" were honored on these routes interchangeably with Motor Transit's own. They were also the only PE bus lines on which baggage could be checked and stopovers made. Sharing of depots and agencies with Greyhound on routes where both had rights was another custom, which survives in some cases to the present day.

The Railroad Commission Survey. Beset by increasing labor costs, rising taxes and declining patronage, Pacific Electric applied for a fare increase in December 1937. Equivalent increases were sought for Motor Transit and Los Angeles Motor Coach lines in order to maintain the existing relationship between the fare structures. An interim increase was granted in April 1938, but only after a series of public hearings had revealed widespread dissatisfaction with the company's operations.

Recognizing that a fare increase by itself could not provide a real solution to PE's financial plight, the commission instituted a comprehensive survey of all phases of PE's operation. The primary objective was to determine what economies might be effected in order to put operations on a better paying basis while maintaining reasonable fares and service levels. The study was carried out under the

WEEKDAY OPERATING DATA
March 2, 1939

	NO. TRIPS DAILY		RUNNING TIME		SCHEDULE SPEED Miles Per Hour		
Line	Outbound	Inbound	Minimum	Maximum	Minimum	Maximum	Route Miles
Los Angeles-Sunland	26	26	60 m	1 hr-11 m	19.2	20.0	20.0
Glendale-Verdugo City	10	10	20 m	20 m	17.7	17.7	5.9
Los Angeles-El Monte							
Via Brooklyn & Garvey	19	18	39 m	49 m	18.0	22.6	14.7
Via Valley	27	25	37 m	50 m	16.6	22.4	13.8
Via Ramona	13	15	31 m	38 m	22.1	27.1	14.0
LA-San Bernardino-Redlands	14	15	2 hr-59 m	3 hr-14 m	24.7	26.7	79.8
Los Angeles-Whittier	20	20	38 m	43 m	19.0	21.5	13.6
Los Angeles-Santa Ana							
Via Whittier	9	9	1 hr-45 m	2 hr-0 m	21.0	24.0	42.0
Via Santa Fe Springs	9	8	1 hr-19 m	1 hr-40 m	23.3	29.5	38.8
Via Downey (Norwalk)	6	7	1 hr-45 m	1 hr-47 m	22.3	22.7	39.8
Long Beach-Pasadena	4	4	2 hr-3 m	2 hr-3 m	21.0	21.0	43.1
Long Beach-Riverside	4	4	2 hr-10 m	2 hr-10 m	29.5	29.5	63.9
Riverside-Hemet	2	2	1 hr-10 m	1 hr-10 m	32.5	32.5	37.9
San Bernardino-Colton-Riverside	5	5	29 m	33 m	19.6	22.3	10.8
Pomona-Claremont	11	11	15 m	18 m	15.3	18.4	4.6
San Dimas	9	9	10 m	10 m	12.6	12.6	2.1

Rails and rubber coexisted for many years in Pasadena. In this mid-'30s scene at Colorado and Raymond, Birney 365 heads west for the Lincoln Ave. route while baby Twin 285 is destined for Orange Grove Ave. *Bert Ward; E. R. Mohr Collection*

The Pacific Electric name was added on a diverse variety of buses when Motor Transit Co. was dissolved in 1939. Here are three examples: 1811 was built by MT in 1929 (as 811) with an all-steel body and a Buda engine. The 1610 was one of 15 Mack BC's with Crown bodies purchased in 1936, and 1684 was a modified CT Mack acquired for the Whittier Blvd. line in 1937.
All: Joe Corbin Collection

supervision of senior transportation engineer Arthur C. Jenkins, and it took 16 months to complete. The result was a 10-volume report of more than 1,100 pages which concluded with 50 specific recommendations dealing with over 90 individual items.

The study recommendations covered Pacific Electric's financing, organization and management as well as its operations and service. They were first published in April of 1939 and modified in June due to passage of the Los Angeles one-man car ordinance. PE's position on the recommendations was presented to the Commission in October by O.A. Smith in the form of an application. It was in general agreement with the recommendations and outlined the beginning of what the commission first called PE's "program of rehabilitation."

Management aspects of the "Jenkins Report" mainly considered what was said to be an unnecessary duplication of organization between PE and SP, stressing the resulting excessive control over policy by the SP. There was also an internal organizational deficiency which resulted in inadequate supervision of day-to-day operations. Criticism was also leveled at the overly complicated financial relationships between PE and its parent, which precluded any accurate accounting of expenses. Financial reorganization was recommended in order to relieve Pacific Electric of large and disproportionate bond interest payments and in the process to remove restrictive clauses in the debt instruments which prohibited abandonment of certain loss-producing rail properties.

Concerning the rail lines, the report recommended abandonment of the least-used passenger and freight operations, substitution of buses for rail service which did not

Representative of the last buses built by Motor Transit in its Market Street Shops, 1880 shows little resemblance to its wooden-bodied ancestors. The steel behemoth weighed in at 18,000 pounds and could seat 40 when all the folding aisle seats were occupied. These buses lasted well into the era of PE control and by the early '40s were used mostly for rush-hour trippers. They were best known for the roar of their Sterling Petrel engines. *SCRTD Collection*

return the cost of maintenance and taxes, and modernization of electrical facilities. The pressing need for replacement of the wooden interurban cars and Birneys as well as modernization of the 600-class cars were the most important points made about the equipment. A third group of recommendations dealt with the obviously unsatisfactory condition of track and roadbed because of deferred maintenance, and the need for an improved standard of janitorial service for equipment and stations throughout the system.

Another class of recommendations dealt with PE's relationship with the traveling public. Included were suggestions for a campaign to improve public relations, increase advertising and implement new sales promotions. One last item of interest was the recommendation to discontinue the practice of carrying lighted kerosene lanterns in the passenger compartments of interurban cars.

Local Lines. The thrust of the Railroad Commission's recommendations regarding PE's local lines was that obsolete equipment should be replaced, rail lines abandoned and unprofitable bus lines cut back in terms of service and mileage. The most radical of the specific suggestions was that Birney cars on Pasadena's two remaining rail lines as well as Hill Avenue buses should be replaced with trolley coaches. While Pacific Electric began to implement the commission's simpler suggestions at once, an equally radical but different solution to the problem of its marginal local lines was being explored.

The three minor Alhambra local lines had already been discontinued—City Park in 1933; Granada Park in 1937; and South Marengo in 1938. Only the Garfield Avenue line remained, providing a crosstown connection to each of the Northern District interurban lines.

Responding to requests for reinstatement of the former Motor Transit bus route between Pasadena and Long Beach via Atlantic Blvd., PE proposed an extension of the South Pasadena–Monterey Park local line to Huntington Park via Atlantic Blvd. A through trip could then be made by transferring twice, an arrangement that would surely not have satisfied travelers wanting the return of a one-vehicle ride instead of having to change cars at 6th and Main.

The bus line was duly extended on January 15, 1940, for a trial period, in accord with the Railroad Commission's recommendations. It operated at a loss but survived until August, when it was discontinued. The short-lived extension served PE's purpose by making the interurban cars look good by comparison. P.C. Cross, who had leased and then bought the Riverside–Hemet route from Motor Transit in 1939, applied to operate a replacement service, but his Atlantic Blvd. bus line lasted only four months.

Pacific Electric's largest remaining local streetcar system was in Long Beach, where operations were carried out in competition with the Lang Motor Bus Corp., the descendant of the 1914 jitneys. The outcome of the rivalry had never been in doubt, for Lang and its predecessors consistently offered a lower fare than PE. Spurred by the Railroad Commission, the two companies and the city began negotiations in 1938 leading to withdrawal of the car lines and their replacement by Lang Motor Bus routes. After many delays the changeover was carried out on February 24, 1940.

Pacific City Lines. Local bus lines in Glendale and Pasadena endured longer than any others of the original

The small Twins had comfortable interiors featuring spring-cushion leather seats. Some (like 249, shown here) were delivered with rear doors but rebuilt with the step-wells filled in and a pair of seats added.
Magna Collection

PE system. From the beginning they were subject to frequent revisions, changes in through-routing arrangements, extensions and then cutbacks. New routes appeared in both cities during the 1930s because of the growing and shifting residential population. During this period both systems were served primarily by the Fageols of the 350 series and the small Twins of the 250 series. Patronage and service declined as a result of the economic depression, and despite economies and fare increases, mounting losses foreshadowed the eventual sale of both local operations.

Negotiations were completed in 1940 to sell the two systems to Pacific City Lines, a holding company originally formed by National City Lines to finance the acquisition of the Southern Pacific's local streetcar subsidiaries in Fresno, Stockton and San Jose. In March 1940, T.J. Manning, who operated four small city systems in the western states, bought control of PCL from NCL. Manning's own properties were put into PCL in February 1941, and the combine was soon to include systems in Inglewood and Burbank as well.

PE also intended to have Pacific City Lines replace its last local trolley operation in San Bernardino at the same time. PCL's proposed routes, however, did not cover all of the rail mileage, and public protests forced PE to withdraw that part of its application. The rights went instead to the locally owned San Bernardino Valley Transit Co. a year later.

The Glendale bus lines changed hands on January 12, 1941. The purchase price of the garage, four routes and 29 buses was $45,000. Sale of the Pasadena lines was consummated a week later for the price of $104,000. Property involved included 39 buses, the garage at Broadway (now Arroyo Parkway) and Bellevue, and the remaining local trolley lines as well as the bus lines. The leased Flintridge line was abandoned by its owner, and new operating rights over the portion of the route within the city limits were issued to Pacific City Lines. Pasadena City Lines immediately substituted buses for the streetcars, with Pacific Electric retaining trackage on South Fair Oaks and South Lake in order to continue operation of the Short Line and Oak Knoll interurbans.

Fares and transfer privileges remained unchanged on both the Glendale and Pasadena systems, with local service still provided by PE interurban cars and free transfers exchanged with the local lines within the city fare zone. Continuing trips from the local buses to the interurban cars continued to be available at the old combination fare.

Pacific City Lines was reacquired by National City Lines in 1946. The Glendale system continued operation until a protracted strike caused NCL to give it up in November 1962, after which service was provided by the Los Angeles Metropolitan Transit Authority at the request of the city of Glendale. NCL continued operation of the Pasadena system until May 1963, when it was sold to Ray Wilcox and the same T.J. Manning. The Wilcox–Manning Transportation Co. operated Pasadena City Lines until July 30, 1967, when it was sold to the Southern California Rapid Transit District, once again combining local and interurban routes under a single ownership.

Bus 364 was one of the 23 Fageol "box cars" of 1931 which still provided more than half of the Pasadena system base service in 1937. This one is about to pull out on a scheduled school tripper.
Floyd Hayhurst Collection

Pasadena local lines in 1936. Two through-routed lines were served by tiny Birney safety streetcars; all the rest by buses. *A. E. Meier*

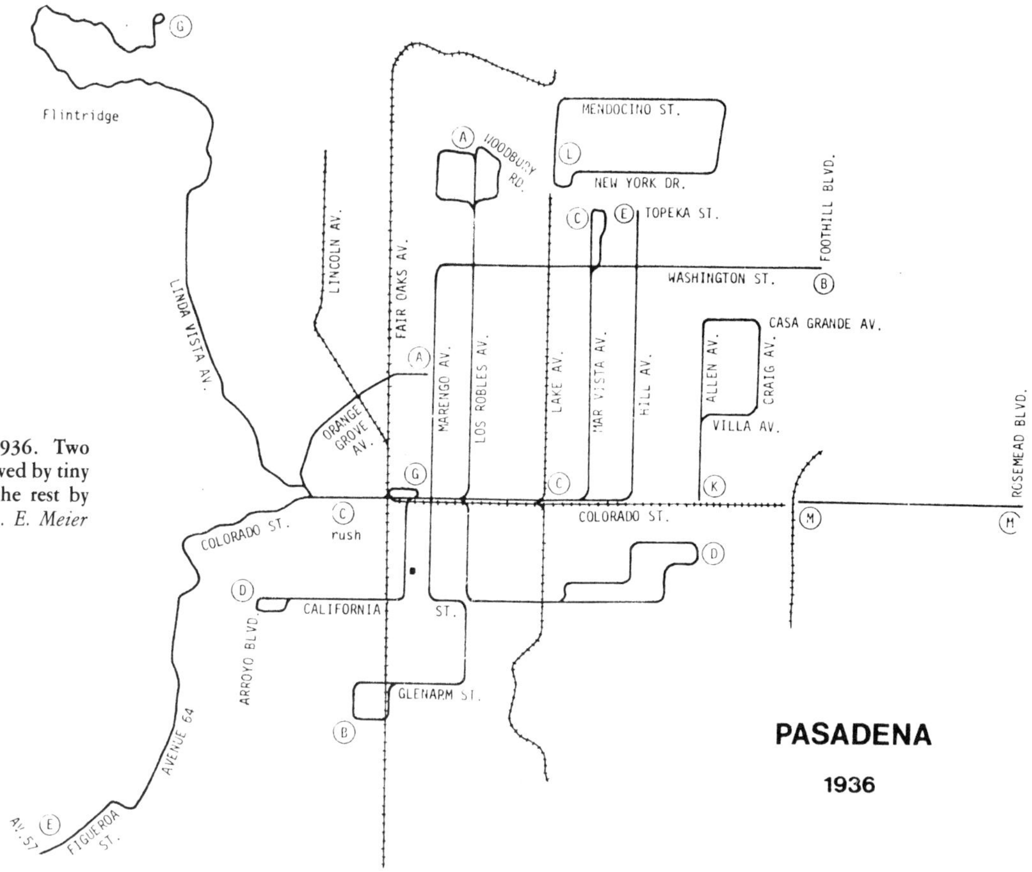

PASADENA

1936

Most of the 16 Twin Coach 23-R buses delivered in two batches during 1936 were also used in Pasadena, releasing some 350-series Fageols to the western district. Routes A, C, E and K regularly used 23-Rs when this view was taken in 1938. *Bob Burrowes Collection*

ROSTER OF BUSES

Pacific Electric Railway (1930–1940 only)

Numbers	Make	Model	Seats	Built	Notes
250-261	Twin	20	24	1930	
89-93	White	50-B	25	1927	(1931) Southern Pacific Motor Transport Co.
262-273	Twin	30	26	1931	
350-372	Fageol	500	28	1931	
100-102	Austin	Utility	22	1934	
274-282	Twin	30-S	26	1934	
150-153	Yellow	714	17	1935	Renumbered 500-503 in 1938
283-288	Twin	23-R	25	1936	
289-298	Twin	23-R	25	1936	
130-131	Ford	BB-18	22	1936	P&C bodies
415-429	Yellow	718	41	1936	
240-249	Twin	23-R	25	1937	
310-314	Twin	31-R	31	1937	
430-437	Yellow	718	41	1937	
500-503	Yellow	714	17	1935	(1938) Ex 150-153
1478, 1485, 1492, 1494	El Dorado	—	25	1926-27	(1939) Motor Transit Co. 1478, 1485, 1492, 1494
1501	Twin	30-S	12	1934	(1939) MTCo 1501; combo
1502-1503	Twin	30-S	26	1934	(1939) MTCo 1502-1503
1600-1614	Mack	6-BC-3S	29	1936	(1939) MTCo 1600-1614
1650-1664	Twin	40-R	41	1937	(1939) MTCo 1650-1664
1675-1684	Mack	6-CT-3S	39	1937	(1939) MTCo 1675-1684
1700-1708	El Dorado	—	33	1927-28	(1939) MTCo 1700-1708
1800-1811	El Dorado	—	33	1928-29	(1939) MTCo 1800-1811
1850-1852	El Dorado	—	25	1929	(1939) MTCo 1850-1852
1875-1877, 1879-1881	El Dorado	—	33	1929-30	(1939) MTCo 1875-1877, 1879-1881

Lamanda Park is the site of this busy scene; the single track in the foreground continues to Sierra Madre and the double tracks turn onto Colorado Blvd. toward downtown Pasadena. One local and one interurban PE rail line connected here, and while the Twin 23-R loads passengers, one of the tiny Yellow Coach 714s waits to make a trip to Rosemead Blvd. on the Lamanda Park shuttle. *Interurban Press*

CHAPTER FIVE

PACIFIC ELECTRIC • 1940-1953

Feeder to interurban; red to black and back

The scene is 9th and Olive in downtown Los Angeles and the semaphore arm of the Acme traffic signal has just moved to GO. Wartime White 2349 moves through the intersection on its way to Redondo Beach, 26 miles away. *Interurban Press*

IN RECENT YEARS so much has been said, even at high levels, about the "destruction" of "rapid transit" rail systems for the sake of the short-term interests of General Motors and the oil and rubber companies, often using PE as a case in point and sometimes as the leading example. It might be useful in the light of these charges to explore the mechanism of the rail-to-bus transition on Pacific Electric in detail.

Prodded by public complaints, the California Railroad Commission examined the condition of the Pacific Electric Railway in an exhaustive survey during 1938–1939, finding an interurban rail system that was suffering from excessive indebtedness (mainly in obligations to parent Southern Pacific), inadequate maintenance of physical plant, and aging rolling stock. These problems were in addition to a profit squeeze brought about by rapidly rising costs without significant patronage improvements. Southern California was no longer developing at the extraordinarily rapid pace of the 1920s, and modern highways were keeping pace with the travel demands of the public—often at the expense of PE's right-of-way, which had to be relocated or interrupted by crossings.

Local car lines had largely been abandoned or converted to buses by the time of the Railroad Commission report,

Three Twin Coach 30-Gs numbered 315-317 were used to convert the Western and Franklin car line to buses in March 1940. *Magna Collection*

which recommended further cuts; in fact, most of the local routes were sold instead, as previously described. Conversion of interurban rail routes began with Glendale–Burbank in 1936, but this shift from rails to rubber was not successful, and PCCs were placed in service by order of the Commission in 1940. The outer branches of the San Fernando Valley rail line were discontinued in 1938 and replaced by feeder buses. The Commission's report suggested that other lightly traveled interurban lines were suitable for conversion to buses and that the weakest ones of all should be abandoned. The Redondo Beach, Newport Beach, Santa Monica via Beverly Hills, and Alhambra–Temple City rail lines would all be discontinued, and service sharply reduced on the San Bernardino route, during 1940-1941, in response.

Rail to Bus. The concluding years of the 1930s closed one era of Pacific Electric bus operations and opened another, the recommendations of the Railroad Commission bringing about PE's transition from an operator of feeder and local bus lines to a suburban and interurban motor carrier. The mistakes of the San Fernando Valley proposals (too much, too soon) and of the Glendale experiment (ill-suited bus equipment, poor schedule coordination) were not repeated. Instead of trying to scale up the equipment and operating practices of the local lines, or substituting buses for cars on a one-for-one basis, PE introduced the expertise of Motor Transit and Los Angeles Motor Coach to the replacement of its own suburban and interurban rail routes. Within two years 158 new buses were added and six former rail lines were turned over to bus operation.

Interurban rail service from Los Angeles to Redondo Beach via Gardena and a feeder line from Hermosillo to Torrance were discontinued on January 15, 1940, due to sparse patronage. PE did not provide replacement bus service, so the cities of Gardena and Torrance instituted municipal bus lines, both eventually running through to Los Angeles; they still operate.

The short Western and Franklin local line in Hollywood was motorized on March 17, 1940, using three new Twin 30-Gs. The conversion relieved traffic congestion on narrow Franklin Avenue as well as at both terminals, where streetcars had changed ends in the middle of busy intersections. Peak-hour rail service to downtown Los Angeles was not replaced.

Except for franchise runs, the last interurban car ran between Los Angeles and Redondo Beach via Playa del Rey on May 12, 1940. The primary reasons for abandoning the 25-mile line were its circuitous route through sparsely populated territory and the high tax bill on its lengthy beachfront right-of-way. Replacement service was provided with 15 Twin Coach 35-RL suburban buses. A more direct alternate route via La Tijera Blvd. through the developing community of Westchester was inaugurated at the same time.

Two more substitutions were made on June 9, 1940, in widely separated parts of the system. The 40-mile Los Angeles–Newport Beach–Balboa interurban rail line was discontinued in favor of a through bus route from Los Angeles despite the Railroad Commission's suggestion that a feeder line to and from Long Beach would suffice. The bus route via Lakewood Blvd. was longer than the rail line, and perhaps as compensation its riders were treated to PE's plushest new buses, 10 Yellow PG-3701 parlor cars. It was said that the favored treatment afforded the Newport line over the years was due to the fact that PE President, O.A. Smith, maintained his summer residence in Newport Beach.

TIME TABLE

WESTERN-FRANKLIN MOTOR COACH LINE

EFFECTIVE MARCH 17, 1940

Subject to Change Without Notice

WESTERN AVE. AND SANTA MONICA BLVD. TO VINE ST. AND HOLLYWOOD BLVD.

Route:—From Western Ave. and Santa Monica Blvd., west on Santa Monica Blvd., north on St. Andrews Place, east on Virginia Ave., north on Western Ave., west on Franklin Ave., south on Argyle Ave., and west on Hollywood Blvd. to Vine St.

DAILY EXCEPT SUNDAY SCHEDULE

6.09am	10.19am	2.19pm	6.19pm
6.24	10.29	2.29	6.29
6.39	10.39	2.39	6.42
6.49	10.49	2.49	6.57
6.59	10.59	2.59	7.12
7.09	11.09	3.09	7.27
7.19	11.19	3.19	7.42
7.29	11.29	3.29	7.57
7.39	11.39	3.39	8.12
7.49	11.49	3.49	8.27
7.59	11.59	3.59	8.42
8.09	12.09pm	4.09	8.57
8.19	12.19	4.19	9.12
8.29	12.29	4.29	9.27
8.39	12.39	4.39	9.42
8.49	12.49	4.49	9.57
8.59	12.59	4.59	10.12
9.09	1.09	5.09	10.27
9.19	1.19	5.19	10.42
9.29	1.29	5.29	10.57
9.39	1.39	5.39	11.12
9.49	1.49	5.49	11.27
9.59	1.59	5.59	11.42
10.09	2.09	6.09	11.57

SUNDAY AND HOLIDAY SCHEDULE

6.22am	10.57am	3.27pm	7.57pm
6.42	11.12	3.42	8.12
6.57	11.27	3.57	8.27
7.12	11.42	4.12	8.42
7.27	11.57	4.27	8.57
7.42	12.12pm	4.42	9.12
7.57	12.27	4.57	9.27
8.12	12.42	5.12	9.42
8.27	12.57	5.27	9.57
8.42	1.12	5.42	10.12
8.57	1.27	5.57	10.27
9.12	1.42	6.12	10.42
9.27	1.57	6.27	10.57
9.42	2.12	6.42	11.12
9.57	2.27	6.57	11.27
10.12	2.42	7.12	11.42
10.27	2.57	7.27	11.57
10.42	3.12	7.42	......

G. L. Squier Collection

Top: The 15 Twin 35-RLs purchased for the Redondo Beach line in 1940 were numbered 1910-1924 because six Pickwick Duplexes operated earlier by Motor Transit had carried low 1900-series numbers. PE's prewar Twins were all retired by 1953. *Magna Collection*

Above: For the 1940 installment of its conversion program, PE purchased 40 Twins, 24 Whites and 10 Yellows, which were 41-passenger PG-3701s. Converted to diesel in 1951, the series survived almost intact into LAMTA ownership. *Magna Collection*

The second change to buses was a partial one involving PE's newest rail line to San Bernardino. Buses ran via Garvey Avenue, Pomona and Foothill Blvd., and Pomona–Claremont feeder bus service, recommended for abandonment by the Railroad Commission, was absorbed into the new line. Pomona rail service was increased, while the Riverside–Rialto car line was abandoned (except for a franchise car) in favor of through service on the parallel ex-Motor Transit bus line. Both San Bernardino bus lines were equipped with 24 new White 788s; there were eight trips a day along the rail substitution route, and interurban rail trips were cut from eight a day to four. These remaining rail schedules were operated with modernized steel cars (the so-called "butterfly Twelves"), which introduced a bright new paint scheme eventually applied to PE buses too.

The new interurban and suburban buses perpetuated Motor Transit patterns and practices as well as continuing the Motor Transit roster sequence, whereas new local buses continued to bear low three-digit numbers. As PE came to concentrate on Whites, however, all were numbered in the 2000 series regardless of type.

In the Western District the Railroad Commission had called for upgraded rail service to the beaches, using PCC cars and rebuilt 600s on the Venice Short Line, the Hollywood–Venice line and that part of the Santa Monica via Beverly Hills line that was east of Beverly Hills, with the outer end to be converted to buses. PE on the other hand wanted to keep rail service running to Beverly Hills and Culver City via Vineyard and to replace the Culver City–Venice portion of the Short Line as well as the entire Hollywood–Venice line with buses. The company proposed to replace the outer end of the Santa Monica via Beverly Hills line by a branch of the Los Angeles Motor Coach Wilshire Blvd. route.

The final plan was for a Santa Monica via Beverly Hills

PE's first modern Whites were 24 model 788-6 buses purchased for the San Bernardino line in 1940. They had typical suburban features: high-backed seats, all facing forward on platforms, single doors and under-floor loaders. *White*

bus line using Olympic Blvd. instead of Venice Blvd., and the 17-mile rail line from Hill Street Station to the beach (and its branch via Brentwood) was replaced by buses in two steps. Effective July 1, 1940, the Brentwood service was discontinued and taken over by a new branch of the Wilshire Blvd. bus line. Then on July 7 the main line was converted to buses using 25 new Twin 41-Gs. At the end, this car line was served every 20 minutes, with alternate trips via Brentwood except nights and Sundays, when Brentwood was served by shuttle cars and the main line had a half-hour headway. The Brentwood branch was returned from LAMC to PE in 1941.

The compromise provided for extension of the Venice Blvd. local car line to cover the inner portion of San Vicente Blvd., and for continued rail operation of the Venice Short Line, to be through-routed with Hollywood–Venice, using PCC cars and remodeled 600s. The changes were implemented in February 1941, PCCs being used only briefly before the punishment inflicted by the Short Line's rough track sent them to their final home on the Glendale line.

Purchased originally for the Santa Monica via Beverly Hills line but displaced by TD-4505s, the Twin Coach 41-Gs stayed in the western district. *Magna Collection*

Pacific Electric's plan to institute a local bus line from Hollywood and Vermont to Venice in place of the Los Angeles–Hollywood–Venice car line was turned down by the Railroad Commission as being wasteful, since the proposed route paralleled others for its entire length. Permission was granted to abandon the car line without a direct replacement, but PE chose not to do so immediately and continued to run the cars for more than a year, duplicating the Santa Monica via Beverly Hills bus line west of Beverly Hills. PE's contention was that it would lose up to half of its beach traffic if direct bus service from Hollywood was not provided. The Commission was not to be moved and in July 1941 denied a second application that would have cut the car line back to Fairfax Avenue while starting a bus line from Hollywood and Vine to the beaches.

The 74 new suburban and interurban buses added to the fleet during 1940 were supplemented by 90 White 798s during the next two years,(70 suburbans and 20 for city service) and this type then became PE's standard. In 1941, however, presumably owing to the presence of new Yellow Coach diesels on Los Angeles Motor Coach routes serving the same territory, PE ordered 35 suburban TD-4505s for the Santa Monica via Beverly Hills route. Once again these buses were cast in the Motor Transit mold, with no center door or standee windows, all forward-facing seats raised on platforms and overhead luggage racks.

A further step toward implementing the Railroad Commission's recommendations regarding the San Bernardino line was taken on November 2, 1941, when rail passenger service was cut back to Baldwin Park (18 miles from Los Angeles), except for rush-hour trips through to Covina. Alternate routes were added to the existing bus line to serve intermediate points along the rail line, and the San Dimas local line was absorbed at the same time. Rail service to the Los Angeles County Fairgrounds near Pomona was still provided for special events at that location.

Concerning another area of its Northern District opera-

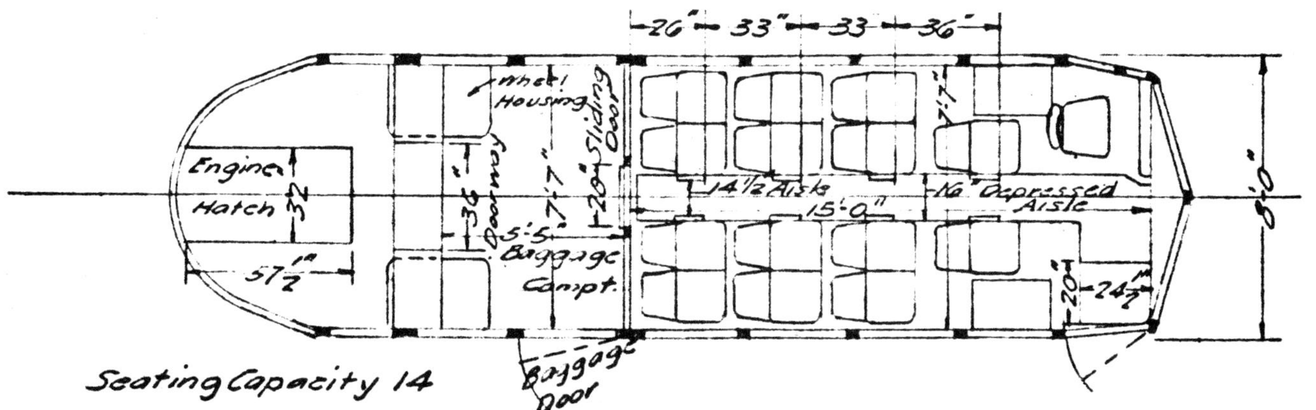

The Pasadena-Shorb (Alhambra) train connection service operated for the Southern Pacific was most commonly served by this Yellow PG-2505 with 14 seats and a rear baggage compartment after 1941. Shown also is a floor plan of this coach.
Both: Magna Collection

tions, Pacific Electric chose to take issue with the Railroad Commission and did not act on a recommendation that the Pasadena via Oak Knoll interurban be replaced by a shuttle bus between Oneonta Park and Colorado and Lake. PE argued that both Pasadena interurban routes and the Alhambra–Temple City car line could wait to be replaced by through bus lines when the Arroyo Seco Parkway was finished. World War II was to interrupt these plans, but the Alhambra–Temple City line was converted to buses on November 30, 1941, mainly due to the poor condition of that line's wooden cars.

The Temple City line was the first PE bus line entering downtown Los Angeles from the east that did not use the Union Bus Depot as a terminal. In attempting to establish a downtown routing for the line, PE ran afoul of Los Angeles' ancient jitney law, which prohibited the use of Spring and Main Streets, the natural routing for Temple City buses. After some controversy over whether the Railroad Commission should attempt to intervene, the company and the city worked out a suitable arrangement for the bus line.

World War II. Pearl Harbor Day found most of the Railroad Commission's recommendations accomplished, although a March 1940 follow-up order requiring retirement of all wooden cars and the oldest buses had not been carried out and could not be. The cutback of San Bernardino service had left electrical facilities intact for freight, and special passenger service over the entire line was to last through the war. It was fortunate that bus substitution had progressed no further, since it would have been much more difficult for Pacific Electric to render adequate service during the war without the rail lines that were still in place. In fact, the rail system was to be rejuvenated by the addition of high-capacity, second-hand cars and forced maintenance of previously neglected trackage.

The Newport Beach line was still physically intact, and it was decided to use its buses elsewhere and restore rail passenger service. A new branch line was constructed to bring shipyard workers to Terminal Island from Long Beach and Los Angeles, and this turned out to be the last expansion of the PE rail system. The Santa Ana line, recently reduced to a single track, was barely able to cope with an increase in traffic to and from the Army airfield in Santa Ana and the nearby Marine barracks.

The Camp at Manzanar. During the summer of 1942, PE buses took part in one of the less memorable episodes of World War II—the evacuation of Japanese-Americans

After participating in a 1940 purchase of Yellow Coach diesel buses for Los Angeles Motor Coach, PE placed its own first diesels in service on the Santa Monica via Beverly Hills line during December 1941. It is noteworthy that no further diesels were bought until 1950. *Motor Bus Society*

Above: Here are examples of the two series of Macks after a 1942 repainting with orange stripes. The "butterfly" stripe design (only partially carried out on the 1604) became the hallmark of Pacific Electric's fleet livery, both rail and bus.
Both: Magna Collection

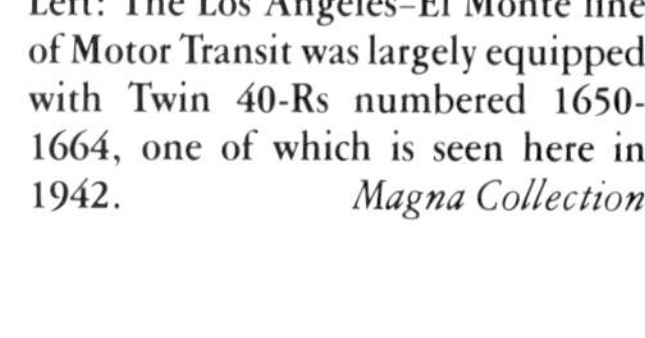

Left: The Los Angeles–El Monte line of Motor Transit was largely equipped with Twin 40-Rs numbered 1650-1664, one of which is seen here in 1942. *Magna Collection*

Units 2025-2049, delivered early in 1942, were to be the last PE Whites with high-backed suburban seats. Later deliveries had ordinary transit seats, all forward-facing in some cases. *White*

City-type White 798s 2200-2219 were delivered in August 1942 and renumbered 2300-2319 in 1947. One is seen on the Long Beach-Huntington Park line.
Magna Collection

Below: This wartime scene was photographed from the roof of the San Bernardino depot in 1943. Even though scheduled passenger service on the LA-San Bernardino rail line was discontinued in November of 1941, troop specials for the San Bernardino Army Air Depot ran until the war ended. Regular service was provided by buses including PG-3701 1693, White 798 2062 and others. *SCRTD Collection*

A military escort was provided for the Japanese-American families during the 243-mile trip to the Owens Valley. The journey through the mountains to the Manzanar settlement was no mean feat for the suburban Whites. It is sad to record PE's role in this unusual movement, though at the time everyone thought it was necessary for the war effort.
Motor Bus Society

from Southern California. The chain of events started on January 29, 1942, when the first of a series of orders issued by U.S. Attorney General James Francis Biddle established security areas along the Pacific coast and required the removal of all enemy aliens from them.

President Roosevelt followed up this action on February 19 by signing an executive order designating areas where the military commanders could exclude certain persons, and authorizing the building of relocation camps to house the people excluded. Prior to this order, the government had encouraged voluntary movement away from the designated strategic areas. On March 27, however, an order was issued halting voluntary emigration and from then on, forced evacuation was carried out in two steps.

Japanese-Americans were first moved to temporary assembly centers such as the Tanforan and Santa Anita race tracks under the control of the Army and the Wartime Civilian Control Agency. They were then moved into permanent camps under the jurisdiction of the War Relocation Authority. On March 24, 1942, 500 Japanese-Americans, both aliens and citizens, had assembled their cars near the Rose Bowl and started the drive to the Owens Valley Center to make it livable for the others to follow. At Manzanar they found a desolate windswept facility with only 38 prefabricated barracks, a temporary field hospital and a small mess hall and administrative office. The camp at Manzanar was one of 10 opened in the summer and fall of 1942 to house the evacuees. In seven weeks the population would grow to over 7,000 people.

PE buses were pressed into service to transport Japanese-American families from Santa Anita to Manzanar during the summer. The suburban White 798s of the 2025 series

This convoy of PE Whites was used to transport Japanese-Americans to Manzonar Camp in 1942. The buses pause for a rest stop at Solemint Junction in Mint Canyon. *Motor Bus Society*

which had been delivered in April now found themselves in the most arduous service that they would see. The 243-mile trip from Los Angeles to Manzanar involved considerable mountain travel. The route to the Owens Valley traversed Mint Canyon and the Tehachapi Pass, both formidable obstacles for the suburban buses. The trip was successfully completed under military escort with several rest stops en route.

The evacuees went on to construct 500 buildings, form their own police force, 50 baseball teams and a dance orchestra, hold regular religious services and found their own newspaper, *The Manzanar Free Press.* By the end of September, the camp population had risen to a peak of more than 10,000. The last resident left and Manzanar was closed, along with the rest of the centers, in November of 1945.

Main Street Station. Until 1942, former Motor Transit interurban routes terminating in Los Angeles continued to use the old Union Bus Depot at 5th and Los Angeles Streets. Starting in February 1941, PE began modifying its 6th and Main station to permit its use by buses. The most important change was made in the main concourse, which was revised to permit bus loading. A parking deck was built adjacent to the elevated structure behind the station, which was reached by a new ramp from Maple Avenue. Buses were thus able to enter the concourse from the new deck and leave via Main Street, and rail operations were confined to the stub terminal on the elevated structure, so that cars entered and left via San Pedro Street. The one exception was New Year's Day, when special Rose Parade service returned interurban cars to the concourse. The cost of the rebuilt station was $175,000. It opened on September 27, 1942, and the Union Bus Depot was closed on the same day after 23 years.

All Pacific Electric routes were officially identified by number in 1943, with interurban rail lines receiving numbers from 1 up, local rail lines 25 up, interurban bus lines 50 up and local bus lines 75 up. When the Riverside–Arlington car line was replaced by buses on January 10, the new line was numbered 62. Later in 1943, service was rearranged in the corridor between Los Angeles and San Bernardino. The old Motor Transit route via Valley Blvd. (57) and the PE rail replacement service (53) were combined into a new Rt. 63, with numerous short turns at and west of El Monte as in Motor Transit days.

The Los Angeles–Newport Beach–Balboa bus line was replaced on May 2, 1943, by rail shuttle service between North Long Beach and Newport, with connecting service to Balboa provided briefly by Circle Taxi Co. Bus service beyond Newport Beach was restored on May 15, along with through rail service from Los Angeles. At the request of the Navy, bus service was again put back between sunset and sunrise effective July 6, since the noise of the passing interurban cars interfered with operation of a submarine listening post at Seal Beach. Full-time bus service returned on September 20, but supplementary rush-hour rail service continued to operate through from Los Angeles during the

PE Route Numbers As Originally Assigned (1943)

1	Los Angeles–Pasadena via Oak Knoll
2	Los Angeles–Pasadena via Short Line
3	Los Angeles–El Monte–Baldwin Park–Covina
4	Los Angeles–Monrovia–Glendora
5	Los Angeles–Sierra Madre
6	Los Angeles–Long Beach
7	Los Angeles–San Pedro
8	Los Angeles–Wilmington–San Pedro Steamship Service
9	Long Beach–San Pedro
10	Long Beach–Wilmington–San Pedro Steamship Service
11	Los Angeles–Santa Ana
12	Los Angeles–Santa Monica via Air Line
13	Newport Beach special service
14	Los Angeles–San Bernardino special service
25	Watts–Sierra Vista
26	Hollywood Blvd./Venice Short Line
27	Subway–Hollywood
28	Subway–Santa Monica Blvd.–San Fernando Valley
29	Los Angeles–Glendale–Burbank
50	Pasadena–Alhambra SP Station
51	Garfield Avenue–Highland Park
52	Los Angeles–Alhambra–Temple City
53	Los Angeles–Pomona–San Bernardino via Garvey Avenue
54	Long Beach–Huntington Park
55	Los Angeles–Newport Beach–Balboa
56	Los Angeles–Sunland (ex-Motor Transit)
57	Los Angeles–El Monte–Redlands via Valley Blvd. (ex-Motor Transit)
58	Los Angeles–Santa Ana (ex-Motor Transit)
59	Long Beach–Riverside (ex-Motor Transit)
60	Riverside–Colton–San Bernardino (ex-Motor Transit)
61	Long Beach–Pasadena (ex-Motor Transit)
75	Los Angeles–Santa Monica via Beverly Hills
76	Beverly–Sunset Blvds.
77	Hollywood–Beverly Hills–University
78	Western and Franklin
79	Los Angeles–Redondo Beach
80	Emery Park
81	Ventura Blvd.
82	North Hollywood
83	Van Nuys–Canoga Park
84	Van Nuys–San Fernando

summer of 1944 and 1945 because of a shortage of buses. The rail service was operated at all times from June 1946 to June 1950.

World War II also taxed PE's regular services to an unprecedented extent. Soldiers and sailors on leave from the numerous bases in the region naturally gravitated to the Hollywood entertainment district, and those newly assigned to area installations used PE rail and bus lines in constantly increasing numbers. This traffic was carried in addition to the workers in defense plants, who depended on PE for their daily commute.

Abandonment of interurban and suburban electric operations by Southern Pacific subsidiaries in the San Francisco Bay area provided PE with its newest and last interurban cars. For electrification of its suburban lines in the Oakland, Alameda and Berkeley area in 1911, SP had specified big 72-foot steel cars, and these were requisitioned by the Maritime Commission in 1942 for service to

Main Street Station was rebuilt for use by buses in 1941-42 and suburban Whites crowd the new parking deck behind the station in the October 1943 scene. Box motors still load at the less-than-carload freight terminal below. *Magna Collection*

Pacific Electric's Main Street Station was a busy spot during World War II. The terminal was filled with uniforms, and servicemen traveling to and from their bases (or seeking the bright lights of the city) swelled crowds which had already grown to 100,000 a day, thanks to the shortages of gasoline and tires. *All: SCRTD Collection*

A model 798 suburban White makes the station stop at Upland inbound on a limited run to Los Angeles. Buses partially replaced San Bernardino interurban cars starting in June 1940. *Interurban Press*

Left: Wartime Whites ran in various non-standard paint schemes until their first postwar overhaul. Nos. 2325 to 2349 were all red with a white roof and large PE emblem; 2344 poses at the North Hollywood station.
Western Transit Society

Left, below: The orange "butterfly" stripes of the 1940 color scheme were imitated on 2350-2379 by a single belt stripe. This group of Whites was also unique in having side destination signs.
Motor Bus Society

Below: Five White 798s delivered in January 1943 were painted solid red because of wartime restrictions. Due to their standard 44-passenger seating arrangement they were renumbered 2320-2324 before being placed in service, to distinguish them from the 45-passenger 2200-2219 series. *White*

Beverly Hills Station in 1944. Bus 2513 will run to Santa Monica via Brentwood, 2521 takes the place of the outer part of the Hollywood Blvd. car line, car 740 is ready to return to Los Angeles, and 2509 is the through bus from town via Vineyard. "Hollywood" car 740 has a hood on its front headlight, mandated by wartime brownout restrictions. *SCRTD Collection*

the California shipyards on Terminal Island. On PE these cars joined a smaller number of similar cars already transferred from the Northwestern Pacific, a third-rail suburban line in Marin County. The NWP cars had been constructed in 1929–1930 to the same general specifications as the earlier equipment, but of aluminum. Their added speed was well suited to the Long Beach, San Pedro and Bellflower (cut back from Santa Ana) routes, where they were mainly used after World War II.

In the Riverside area most of the extra service needed was provided by buses, as special movements to and from March Field and Camp Anza required a larger than normal complement of equipment. An alternate routing of the Santa Ana bus line (ex-Motor Transit) served a Vultee Aircraft plant near Downey, and a new branch of the North Hollywood line served a Bendix plant there. The Army's Birmingham Hospital and Van Nuys Airport were served by a new route (85) early in 1944.

It was necessary for Pacific Electric to make some selective reductions in bus service in order to free up equipment for more essential use elsewhere. The Beverly–Sunset route was cut back to a peak-hour operation east of Beverly Hills in May 1942, and the North Hollywood line was cut back from Universal City to the North Hollywood station in January 1944. By order of the Office of Defense Transportation, operation of the Rose Hill Park spur of the Garfield Avenue–Highland Park line was given up, school tripper and alternate route service on the Hollywood–Beverly Hills–University line was suspended, and the Emery Park loop was cut back.

By 1944, the venerable Main St. Station had been saturated. The 5,000 passengers per day handled in 1905 had been swelled to 100,000 by wartime crowds and PE undertook a major upgrading program. Interior remodeling started with the lobby and proceeded through the waiting room and concession stands to the bus and train gates. Exterior changes included a new marquee and marble facing and concluded in 1947 with enlargement of the bus deck.

Service Expands. Early postwar expansion of bus service in 1946 included extension of the Los Angeles–Alhambra–Temple City line to Arcadia, revival of the 29-mile Pasadena–Pomona line that had been operated by Motor Transit prior to 1935, and reactivation of another dormant Motor Transit route, the alternate Atlantic Avenue line between Pasadena and Long Beach—a route that PE had struggled to avoid operating in earlier years, preferring to require travel via Los Angeles. These improvements reflected the population growth of the San Gabriel Valley.

On January 1, 1947, the SP-subsidized train connection bus between Riverside, Colton and San Bernardino was discontinued. Subsequently the Riverside–Arlington bus line was extended to Redlands via San Bernardino, replacing the outer portion of the through Los Angeles–Riverside–San Bernardino–Redlands route. Finding it little used, PE cut back rail passenger service on the former San Bernardino line from Covina to Baldwin Park in March 1947. The former rail riders were accommodated by the addition of two peak-hour bus trips and the introduction of limited-stop service west of Garvey and Tyler, both effective in February. Additional express runs were instituted on June 6 between Los Angeles and both San Bernardino and Riverside; a week later, rush-hour, limited-stop service via Valley Blvd. was added on the Temple City line.

After several hearings had produced assurances from PE

Twin Coach 1664 is pulling out of Main Street Station, hub of much of the Pacific Electric system, in this 1943 view. *SCRTD Collection*

Another wartime view of PE buses waiting their turn to load on the parking deck behind Main Street Station. The "Motor Transit Lines" legend on the Whites reminds travelers of the heritage of the suburban lines; a Yellow PG-3701 and a Motor Transit Twin also wait their turns.
Motor Bus Society

Left: The postwar remodeling of Main Street Station was not restricted to the interior. This August 1947 view shows the bus deck being enlarged. *SCRTD Collection*

A postwar view of weekend storage at Van Nuys. Wartime Whites share the lot with prewar Twin 41-Gs originally operated on the Santa Monica via Beverly Hills line. *Motor Bus Society*

Right: Ceremonies accompanied the extension of the Temple City interurban line to Arcadia on March 10, 1946. Local dignitaries as well as company officials celebrate PE's first postwar service improvement. *SCRTD Collection*

that abandonment of the San Fernando Valley rail line was not contemplated, expansion of bus service in the area was authorized. In May 1947, the Ventura Blvd. route was once again extended to run from Hollywood to Woodland Hills and Northridge, and a branch on Saticoy Street was added to the North Hollywood line. A new route was started on August 4, 1947, between Los Angeles and Van Nuys via Riverside Drive and North Hollywood, 23 miles; instituted at the urging of the Board of Public Utilities and Transportation and over the objections of Asbury Rapid Transit, the new Rt. 86 was similar to a line proposed in PE's San Fernando Valley plans of 1936. The 86 became a heavy commuter line as the valley filled with immigrants to Southern California's favorable climate and strong job market. Another new San Fernando Valley line (87) was started in 1948 between North Hollywood, Studio City and Sherman Oaks, again similar to a route proposed by PE in 1936.

Buses replaced interurban cars on the Sierra Madre line beyond San Marino except in rush hours effective June 11, 1948. The shuttle (line 65) ran until October 1950, when the entire route was motorized. Buses of Rt. 66 replaced Long Beach–San Pedro cars on January 2, 1949, and on February 21, the Riverside Drive line was extended along Van Nuys Blvd. to Panorama City.

PE's last new Whites, numbered 3000–3024, were purchased in 1948 to provide equipment for new bus routes, and these as well as 2220–2289 of 1947 had hydraulic transmissions like PE's diesels. The changing nature of the Pacific Electric bus sytem may be shown by the fact that only nine small Twin Coaches remained of the prewar feeder bus fleet at the end of 1947. PE bought 284 White 788s and 798s in all between 1940 and 1948, and they were used for most of the system's base service in the late 1940s.

Five dual-motor Twin Coach 44-Ds were purchased in 1946. This view shows 2126 at Beverly Hills Station. *Gerald L. Squier*

Fare Increases. Although World War II had temporarily restored the economic viability of Pacific Electric passenger service, prosperity vanished abruptly thereafter, with a net loss of more than $200,000 recorded in 1946. PE applied for and received permission to institute a 15 percent system-wide fare increase, which took effect on August 20, 1946, and was the first change in fares since 1940. At that time the Railroad Commission once again undertook an investigation of the rates, services, operations and facilities of Pacific Electric (as well as Los Angeles Transit Lines and their joint subsidiary, Los Angeles Motor Coach Co.).

Because of a continuing downward trend in net earnings, the company filed another application to increase fares in June 1947; the operating deficit in that year was $1,760,000. Hearings were held jointly on the fare increase petition and the Commission's investigation, and the increase became effective on February 1, 1948. The previous flat increase had resulted in a confused pattern of odd-penny fares, which were now revised to 5-cent zone increments. Naturally the 1948 tariff was intended to increase revenue, but the opposite was accomplished in certain instances. For example, a 17-cent fare from Los Angeles to such points as Glendale, Beverly Hills, Alhambra, Culver City, Montebello and South Pasadena was cut to 15 cents.

Perhaps a more important aspect of the 1948 fare revision was that it equalized PE and LATL fares within the Los Angeles local zone. PE's traditionally lower inner-zone fare was raised to 10 cents by merging the two innermost zones, and in fact LATL briefly offered a lower fare (three tokens for a quarter). An important benefit to riders was the institution of free universal transfer privileges between PE, LATL and LAMC routes. This provided a strong argument in favor of dissolving Los Angeles Motor Coach, which was accomplished in the following year.

Commission Findings. In the same decision that granted increased fares, the Railroad Commission prescribed a new program of property rehabilitation directed primarily toward improvement of rail facilities. The recommendations were quite specific, key items being acquisition of 50 PCC cars for Hollywood service and construction of suitable facilities for buses at Van Nuys and Ocean Park. The program was directed toward providing a foundation on which a future rapid transit system could be built. Talk of rapid transit was already common in Los Angeles at that time. For example, the Commission urged that provisions for the rail line be made in planning extension of the Hollywood Freeway into the San Fernando Valley.

Pacific Electric reviewed the Commission's recommendations and contemplated the heavy expenditures involved, weighed against the continuing adverse revenue trend, which persisted despite fare increases. Its conclusion was that an independent study of the system was needed to determine the prospects for profitable operation, and the

PE 3000-3024 were among the very last White 798 buses made, delivered in May and July 1948. All of the hydrotorque-equipped Whites survived into LAMTA days, though not all were in active service for that long. *White*

Railroad Commission was persuaded to grant an extension of the effective dates of compliance with the various provisions of its order.

In order to obtain a survey based on familiarity with the system's problems, PE hired Arthur C. Jenkins, author of the Railroad Commission's own 1939 report. Jenkins had left the Commission to become vice president and general manager of the Gray Line of San Francisco, was thereafter transportation manager at Key System, and in 1948 had his own consulting engineering office.

PE's Rebuttal. The conclusions of the Jenkins study were embodied in an application filed with the Commission in February 1949. The proposal was for a "modernization" that would bring PE's passenger service up to current industry standards (which meant bus substitution) in order to restore profitability in the face of increasing costs and inability to attract new patronage. It was different from the prewar "rehabilitation" program that was intended to bring the rail plant up to acceptable standards, and it was estimated to cost $7 million as compared to an $11 million outlay required to implement the Commission's own program.

At that stage, PE planned to end all rail passenger service on the Northern District and to maintain only the Glendale–Burbank and Hollywood Blvd. lines of the Western District and the Watts, Long Beach and San Pedro lines in the south. Two hundred new buses would be purchased to replace the abandoned rail lines, and extensive expansion of motor coach operating and maintenance facilities would be undertaken.

EFFECTIVE JULY 1, 1949

TIME TABLE 8

PACIFIC ELECTRIC

RAIL LINES MOTOR COACH

RAIL AND MOTOR COACH

LOS ANGELES TERMINAL
Main St. Station, 610 So. Main St.

LOS ANGELES-
EL MONTE-
BALDWIN PARK
RAIL LINE

LOS ANGELES-
POMONA VIA COVINA
MOTOR COACH LINE

LOS ANGELES-BALDWIN PARK-
COVINA-SAN DIMAS-
LA VERNE-POMONA

Subject to change without Notice

Schedule 8-29

H. O. MARLER
Passenger Traffic Manager
Los Angeles

For many years PE timetable covers were adorned with cuts of both cars and buses. *G. L. Squier Collection*

Los Angeles Motor Coach Is Disbanded. On May 1, 1949, Pacific Electric received 128 buses along with the 82–Wilshire Express and Limited, 83–Sunset and 89–Fairfax lines as its share of the Los Angeles Motor Coach Co., dissolved on that day. The Wilshire services were operated from the Ocean Park carhouse and the other two lines from West Hollywood. All three ex-LAMC routes retained their traditional numbers (which had been shown on the buses), as PE's own 82–North Hollywood and 83–Canoga Park lines (whose numbers were not generally known) were renumbered 88 and 90. The former Motor Coach buses were gradually renumbered, repainted and assimilated into the PE fleet. They included exactly 100 Yellow and GM diesels plus 28 White 798s.

All the buses went to their owners except for 13 LATL White 798s; along with cash, these were LATL's payment for PE's half interest in the Virgil Avenue garage and its store of spare parts. Virgil became LATL's operating Division 7, while Vineyard, located on PE property and leased to LATL for 25 years, became Division 8. Using these facilities, LATL took over operation of Rts. 80–Talmadge–Hyperion, 82–Wilshire (local runs to Fairfax Avenue only), 84–Western, 85–Crenshaw–Vine–La Brea, 86–Vermont–Los Feliz, 87–Silver Lake–Riverside Drive and 90–Olympic.

It was during this period that PE began to actively use line numbers. They appeared in timetables and on the cardboard dash signs that had begun to appear in the side windows and behind curbside windshields of PE buses before the war.

PE immediately integrated its new routes into its existing bus system, but LATL continued operation of the ex-LAMC lines as its "Los Angeles Motor Coach Division" for about a year. The prewar diesels were transferred to the LATL fleet and replaced at Vineyard by postwar TDH-4507s, modified by the addition of a red belt stripe to their NCL yellow, green and white color scheme. Other routes besides the former Motor Coach Lines were based at Virgil Avenue, and when LATL buses assigned there were operated on the "Motor Coach Division" they had special nameplates affixed over their LATL decals. Before long, however, the operations had been merged completely.

Modernization Resumes. Arthur Jenkins' studies had included not only methods to improve operations but also

Twin 2127 was photographed at 6th and Main while discharging passengers from the 75 line, where these buses were often used. The winged emblems date the photo to 1950 or later. *Motor Bus Society*

Right: A comparison of old and new uniforms for drivers on the Wilshire Express service. Los Angeles Motor Coach assets were divided between its corporate owners on May 1, 1949. LAMC 4510 would soon be repainted into PE colors and become 2628. *SCRTD Collection*

After repainting, the LAMC GMs looked like 2602 (ex-4536) snapped between tripper runs at North Hollywood. *Gerald L. Squier*

The GM diesels taken over with Los Angeles Motor Coach were transit buses and as such mostly stayed on the busy urban routes formerly served by LAMC. In Metro days, however, with new TDH-4801s on Wilshire-Sunset, the 2600s were seen on such routes as Ventura Blvd., Studio City, North Hollywood, Riverside Drive, Los Angeles-Temple City, Pasadena-Pomona and Riverside-Arlington. *Both: SCRTD Collection*

LAMC 3357 has been handed over to PE and given a new emblem, but retains its yellow and white colors with a red belt stripe in this view at North Hollywood Station. It would soon become PE 2421.
Western Transit Society

an evaluation of the option to dispose of all or part of PE's passenger service. Sale of Western District local lines to LATL and of the San Fernando Valley operations to Asbury Rapid Transit was seriously considered. In preliminary talks Asbury balked at PE's proposal to include a fleet of Whites with the San Fernando Valley routes. It was the expectation of improved profitability through bus substitution on lighter rail routes and one-man car operation of heavy lines that kept these options from being pursued more vigorously.

Announcements of proposed bus substitutions and other service changes were not greeted with the tacit concurrence afforded the prewar improvement program. PE's public relations had, in the meantime, sunk considerably. Riders and public officeholders were becoming sensitized by the cycle of antiquated and poorly maintained rail equipment, service cuts, fare increases and an ever-increasing emphasis on freight operations at the expense of passenger service. It turned out that historical restrictions in PE's bonds and franchises provided temporary impediments to bus conversions, and over two years of public hearings, with most testimony being hostile to the company, were necessary before the modernization program was approved essentially as Jenkins had proposed it.

Details of the Program. System modernization at a cost of $7 million was carried out during an 18-month period in 1950–1951. It included purchase of 200 new buses for rail service replacements and construction of several new garages and terminals. Dieselization of freight operations and construction of new freight trackage connecting the Baldwin Park line with the outer part of the Glendora line at Azusa were other projects accomplished during this period.

The equipment policy for the modernization plan was determined early in 1950, when an evaluation was completed of two sample buses: 2150, the first king-size Twin Coach 52-S2, and 2700, a 102-inch-wide, 35-foot GM TDH-4510 which was the only bus of its kind built after the 1948 delivery of 500 to Brooklyn. The Twin was to be PE's last gas bus, and GM diesels became the new system standard. An order for 124 additional GM's placed at the time 2700 was purchased did not specify 4510s, however, because in the meantime GM had announced the 40-foot TDH-5103. It is interesting to note that the Motor Transit influence on bus specifications had not dissipated, as the 5103s had a nonstandard interior plan including 48 high-backed seats. These became part of all future PE (and its successor, Metro) bus orders.

The rail equipment had not been neglected either, and in July of 1949, rebuilding of the Hollywood suburban cars for one-man operation had begun. These cars, built during the 1920s and modernized in 1939–1940, were completely refurbished inside and out, and received new treadle-operated folding doors replacing the old sliding variety. The first of the 132 rebuilt cars went into service on the Glendale–Burbank line in the summer of 1949 supplementing the PCC cars. They were renumbered into the 5050 series behind the PCCs (which were 5000–5029). The remainder of the cars were refurbished the next year for the Hollywood and Valley lines.

The first step in the postwar conversion program was taken on July 1, 1950, when eight PDA-4101s replaced interurban cars on Newport Beach line 55 (for the second time); on July 2 the Santa Ana line was cut back to Bellflower, with express bus service instituted as part of line 58 to serve the abandoned portion of the line. At the other end of the system, the outer branches of the Ventura Blvd. bus line were once again cut back from Northridge and Woodland Hills to Reseda Blvd. due to poor patronage.

That summer also saw the arrival of PE's first order of TDH-5103s, resplendent in a new red and silver color scheme, which provided sufficient equipment to accelerate the conversion program. The next step was taken on September 17, 1950, when rail service was discontinued on the Venice Short Line between Los Angeles and Santa Monica.

Posed at the entrance to Macy Yard in 1950 is the Twin 52-S2 that was tested in the spring of that year as a possible replacement for interurban cars. The windshield sign places the bus on the LA-Alhambra-Temple City line. *SCRTD Collection*

Left: The second bus in the 1950 evaluation was this GM TDH-4510, seen here painted as 2150 probably was initially, all red with an aluminum roof. Emery Park was 2700's most frequent assignment in later years. *General Motors*

Long Beach garage, at the throat of Fairbanks Yard, frames three postwar White 798s. These units were built as city buses, with 44 standard seats and hydrotorque transmissions. *SCRTD Collection*

The replacement bus line (75V) ran limited to Virginia Road and was through-routed at its outer end with the Santa Monica via Beverly Hills line, which was accordingly redesignated 75S. On October 1, 1950, the Echo Park Avenue local car line in Los Angeles and the inner (Sunset Blvd.) part of the Hollywood Blvd. rail service were replaced by a new bus line (91) which ran down Hill Street and out Venice Blvd. to provide local service as far as Crenshaw Blvd. Service on San Vicente Blvd. between Venice and Olympic Blvds. was not replaced and all remaining Hollywood Blvd. rail service was routed via the subway.

The TDH-5103s were the first PE buses to have two-piece front destination signs—all previous equipment had one-piece curtains. The split was about two-thirds/one-third with the curbside (long) sign replacing the existing indication—typically a city name. The new short sign was intended to replace the cardboard dash signs and the first 24 buses were accordingly delivered without dash sign racks. It did not take long to discover that the two-piece signs could not cover all the required indications and dash sign racks were added to all the new buses. This layout became standard and all of the new GM's (except for the parlor PDA-4101s) were ordered with the new array.

During the next two weeks buses were substituted for interurban cars on the Pasadena via Oak Knoll (70), Sierra Madre (67) and Baldwin Park lines of the Northern District. The Baldwin Park car line was replaced by two bus routes, the new Hellman Avenue line (69) covering the inner portion and diversion of some Garvey Avenue buses to Baldwin Park taking care of the remainder.

During 1951 the final step in the modernization program was forced when the state condemned Aliso Street, the Northern District entrance into Los Angeles, for construction of the Ramona (now San Bernardino), Santa Ana and Hollywood Freeways. As soon as 65 more TDH-5103s could be obtained, rail service ended on the Northern District. The Monrovia–Glendora (68), Pasadena via Short Line (71) and Sierra Vista (92) routes were replaced by buses on September 30, 1951.

At that point most of the principal routes forming the Pacific Electric system were being operated by new diesel buses although half of the roster (337 buses) still consisted of gasoline Whites. The antique wooden interurban cars and the steel interurbans of the 1915–1924 era had been withdrawn and only the refurbished "Hollywood" cars serving the Western District and the Watts local line, and the second-hand "blimps" of the Southern District remained of PE's standard equipment. Only the 30 Glendale PCCs could be said to have had substantial useful life remaining, while the expanding freeway network meant that bus service to and from downtown Los Angeles could begin to compete with the electric lines in terms of speed as well as comfort and convenience. Neither, of course, came close to matching the private automobile in popularity.

Eight PDA-4101 parlor coaches were put into service on the Newport line in 1950 and were soon serving some San Bernardino Express runs as well. PE's only postwar parlor buses, they became favorites for charter service and other special assignments.
SCRTD Collection

New Facilities. Two new downtown terminal facilities were opened to accommodate the additional bus traffic resulting from the modernization program. By far the most important was the Los Angeles Street Motor Coach Terminal, opened on October 8, 1950, for the newly converted Northern District interurban routes. It consisted of four island platforms underneath the bus deck behind Main Street station, as well as a bus maintenance area under the viaduct which occupied space formerly used for a box-motor freight terminal. It was arranged so that buses could enter from Maple Avenue, next to the bus deck ramp, and exit onto Los Angeles Street.

Buses were stored in the yard behind the terminal between Los Angeles and Maple Streets, and in a new yard east of Maple St. just south of the viaduct. The terminal was not used after 7 P.M. or on Sundays, Main St. station being able to handle the traffic during these times.

The pressure on the Subway Terminal bus deck had been relieved on September 11 with the opening of a new terminal at 5th and Olive Streets. The new facility, across from the bus deck on the west side of Olive Street, provided a storage yard and loading area for Western District lines 51, 86 and later 76.

There were also two important garage projects carried out as part of the modernization. Ocean Park Carhouse was renovated for use as a garage at a cost of $315,000, the work including a facelift for the building as well as new washing and fueling facilities. This garage also replaced a former Los Angeles Motor Coach storage lot just to the north. A more significant change was total conversion of the Macy Street Yard to a bus storage and shop location after abandonment of the last Northern District rail lines. Macy Street had been used by buses probably as early as 1941, but in 1951 all tracks were removed and the yard was paved over.

Fare Changes. The third revision to the PE fare structure since 1946 was made effective December 10, 1950, affecting only the Los Angeles local service. Fare zones were restructured by reducing the size of the inner zone to a four-mile radius from six miles and setting the boundaries of the outlying zones at two-mile intervals. While the fare per zone was not changed, addition of an extra zone increased the average fare. A ride from Hollywood to downtown Los Angeles, previously 10 cents, was now 15 cents. From that time on, all changes in local zones applied jointly to PE and LATL.

By 1952, the transformation of the Pacific Electric system was all but complete. The 1,100 miles of trackage operated during the mid-1920s had shrunk to 750—mostly used for freight service only. Total mileage of motor coach route operated conversely had grown from 646 in 1945 to 1,021 in April of 1952. The number of railcars had meanwhile shrunk from 476 to 203 and the number of buses had grown from 340 to 660 in the same period. Similarly, rail movements had dropped from 2,733 to 1,161 while motor coach movements had grown from 2,578 to 4,698. Initially, the conversion of parts of the system to bus operation had diminished the $1.76 million loss of 1947 to $61,000 in 1951. The 1952 figures, however, again showed a substantial loss ($1.12 million) and it was evident to Southern Pacific management that PE's days of profitability as a passenger carrier were over.

On January 24, 1952, inner zone fares were increased to 15 cents cash, with tokens (not used by PE since 1948) sold at two for 25 cents. At the same time, interurban fares were in effect increased by abolishing round-trip and most commutation discounts. The price of tokens was raised to three for 40 cents on November 3, 1952, shortly after PE had applied for a temporary fare increase of 5 cents per ride on the interurban lines pending study of a new fare

The PE placed the very first order for TDH-5103s, GM's first 40-foot, 102-inch "king size" bus. With 48 high-backed and mostly forward-facing seats, these buses were used to replace electric cars on eight suburban and interurban routes during 1950 and 1951. The bright red and silver "teardrop" livery and winged-front emblem were introduced to PE with these coaches.
Motor Bus Society

Older buses were slowly painted red and silver after 1950, and the scheme is seen here on 2269 at Macy Street. *Andrew Harrison*

Left: The "teardrop" livery applied to a TD-4505, shown at Macy Street Yard.
Gerald L. Squier

The TDH-4801s were put into service with a flourish—a motorcycle escort through the Cahuenga Pass ensured their arrival in time to be greeted by dignitaries at their destination. *SCRTD Collection; National Motor Museum*

structure. The increase was granted and went into effect on April 27, 1953.

In an effort to improve the appearance and operation of its equipment, PE initiated a planned program of maintenance including repainting and body repair. Beginning on July 1, 1952, the 95 Whites of the 2200 and 3000 series and the 30 PCC cars started through the Torrance Shops at a scheduled rate of 10 buses and five railcars per month. The PCCs received new floors and doors in addition to fresh paint inside and out. The buses were treated to general body repairs and were repainted into the new red and silver teardrop color scheme. In addition, seven suburban buses per month (five 2050 series Whites and two 2500 series Yellows) were scheduled for overhaul.

Buses to Hollywood. When a plan was announced to extend the Hollywood Freeway through Cahuenga Pass, PE worried that it would have to pay to relocate trackage to provide access to the Van Nuys line right-of-way and so filed an application to replace the cars with buses. At the same time the West Hollywood local line, which shared tracks on Santa Monica Blvd. with the Van Nuys line, was proposed for conversion to buses because of track renewal requirements in connection with scheduled road work. PE estimated the cost of track work on both lines at $612,000.

Replacement of both rail lines was authorized by the PUC on August 31, 1952, and the San Fernando Valley line was motorized on December 28 as line 93. The new bus route used the Hollywood Freeway between downtown and Santa Monica Blvd. on weekdays and the local route via Sunset Blvd. evenings and weekends. On the same day, buses of the Santa Monica via Venice line (75V) started making local stops between downtown and Crenshaw Blvd. (except in rush hours) and the 91 line was accordingly cut back to 15th and Hill. Sunset Blvd. buses were also rerouted via the Hollywood Freeway between Grand St. and Vermont Ave. on February 1, 1953. Conversion of the West Hollywood rail line had to await the arrival of new buses.

By that time GM was accepting orders for air-suspension buses, scheduled to go into production early in 1953. The TDH-5103, preferred by PE, was to be superseded by the TDH-5105, which was slightly heavier. Buses exceeding 35 feet in length or 96 inches in width were operated at that time in California by special permission of the PUC, which declined to authorize the 5105 based on pre-production specifications. GM accordingly produced the TDH-4801, a lighter bus on a shorter wheelbase, and Pacific Electric received the first 35 of these buses in April 1953 (2900–2934); they were the first air-ride GM transits made of any model. The planned changeover of the Subway–Santa Monica Blvd.–West Hollywood line was carried out on June 1, 1953, using the 4801s. The replacement bus line was numbered 94 and absorbed the Echo Park Avenue branch of line 91, the balance of which was discontinued at that time. Local service on Venice Blvd. had already been taken over by the 75V, and service between Sunset Blvd. and Hill Street was provided by the new 94.

Here is the diesel-fueling station, built in 1950 as part of the Ocean Park Carhouse renovation project, with four TDH-5103s assigned to the 75 line. *SCRTD Collection*

This panoramic view of Macy Yard, in addition to the usual Whites and 5103s, shows the big Twin 2150, the TDH-4510, and various uncommon types. *SCRTD Collection*

PE received a group of TDH-5103s early enough in 1951 that there was snow on the ground in Birmingham, Mich., when the GM photographer took this official view.
Interurban Press

ROSTER OF BUSES

Pacific Electric Railway
(1940–1953 only)

Numbers	Make	Model	Seats	Built	Notes
315-317	Twin	30-G	31	1940	
1685-1694	Yellow	PG-3701	41	1940	Suburban seats, 6-71 diesel engines 1951
1910-1924	Twin	35-RL	37	1940	Suburban seats
2000-2023	White	788-6	41	1940	Suburban seats
2100-2124	Twin	41-G	41	1940	Suburban seats
220	Yellow	PG-2505	14	1941	Combo
2050-2094	White	798-6	45	1941	Suburban seats
2500-2534	Yellow	TD-4505	42	1941	Suburban seats
2025-2049	White	798-6	45	1942	Suburban seats
2200-2219	White	798	45	1942	Renumbered 2300-2319 on 1/22/47
2320-2324	White	798	44	1943	ODT allocated
2325-2379	White	798	44	1944	ODT allocated
2380-2394	White	798	44	1945	
2125-2129	Twin	44-D	44	1946	
2220-2234	White	798	44	1946	Hydrotorque
2235-2289	White	798	44	1947	Hydrotorque
3000-3024	White	798	44	1948	Hydrotorque
2395-2409	White	798	44	1944	(1949) Los Angeles Motor Coach Co. 3311-3325
2410-2422	White	798	44	1945	(1949) LAMC 3361, 3366, 3369, 3372, 3376, 3377, 3379, 3380, 3383, 3386, 3356, 3357, 3387
2600-2618	GM	TDH-4507	45	1947	(1949) LAMC 4534-4538, 4533 down to 4520
2619-2638	GM	TD-4507	45	1946	(1949) LAMC 4519 down to 4500
2639-2677	Yellow	TD-4502	45	1940	(1949) LAMC 4301-4314, 4316-4340
2678-2699	GM	TD-4506	45	1945	(1949) LAMC 4341-4362
225-232	GM	PDA-4101	45	1950	
2150	Twin	52-S2	52	1950	(1950) Sample
2700	GM	TDH-4510	39	1949	(1950) Sample
2701-2824	GM	TDH-5103	48	1950	
2825-2889	GM	TDH-5103	48	1951	
2900-2934	GM	TDH-4801	48	1953	

Buses sold with Glendale and Pasadena routes 1/41: 100-102, 130-131, 250-252, 254-261, 262-273, 274, 275, 277-279, 287, 289-294, 296-298, 350-352, 354-372 and 500-502 (68 buses).
Buses turned over to Metropolitan Coach Lines 10/1/53: 225-232, 1686-1694, 2000-2023, 2025-2049, 2050-2094, 2125-2129, 2150, 2220-2289, 2300-2319, 2320-2324, 2325-2379, 2380-2394, 2395-2422, 2500-2534, 2600-2699, 2700, 2701-2889, 2900-2934 and 3000-3024 (695 buses).

The first TDH-4801 rides the transfer table at PE's Torrance Shops while being fitted for service in May 1953. Within a year the old car shop had been closed and replaced by a much smaller bus overhaul shop at Macy Street. The 2900s ran on the Van Nuys Line after the summer of 1954.
Interurban Press

PE timetables continued to carry updated cuts reflecting the buses and cars. The buses got newer, the cars didn't.
G. L. Squier Collection

CHAPTER SIX

ASBURY RAPID TRANSIT 1913-1954

Vying for the Valley; orange top for service

Hollywood was an important junction point for the Asbury system as well as for Pacific Electric. Here, an Asbury Mack CQ bound for Pasadena via Glendale meets a Pacific Electric San Fernando Valley car at Hollywood Blvd. and Highland. The bus, the car and the hotel are no longer part of the Hollywood scene. *SCRTD Collection*

FOR MANY YEARS, independent bus companies tried to carve a niche between the local streetcar lines of the Los Angeles Railway and the suburban and interurban rail lines of Pacific Electric. It was in order to counter the competition of the independent operators that both railway companies started operating their own buses and in addition joined forces to start the Los Angeles Motor Bus Co. linking their operating areas.

The innovative expansion plans of the independents, as well as their rapid action to fill potential service needs, kept the managements and legal representatives of both railways constantly on the alert. Over the years the rail carriers found themselves continually starting new bus lines and improving rail service in response to the creative proposals of the independents.

The largest of the independent bus companies to endure, Asbury Rapid Transit, was a consolidation of suburban and interurban lines operating primarily in the

All ready to climb Mt. Wilson on the toll road, this chain-drive Mack provides a backdrop for its well-dressed passengers. The gravity-fed gas tank and weighted tailgate helped to assure power and traction on the heavy grades. The date is July 30, 1914, and the attractions of the Mt. Wilson Hotel await the travelers at the end of the line.
Pasadena Historical Society

At the summit, passengers could mail a card at the Mt. Wilson Post Office to commemorate completion of the arduous trip. The $50 fine for smoking indicates that forest fires were as difficult a problem in those days as they are now.
Pasadena Historical Society

San Fernando Valley, northwest of Los Angeles. Several of these lines date back prior to the beginning of state regulation in 1917, and the backbone of the Asbury system was formed by one such route. This was the aptly named Original Stage Line, which ran from downtown Los Angeles to San Fernando. Other routes connected such far-flung points as Mount Wilson and Ocean Park with Los Angeles and Pasadena. Many of the lines still exist, but their interurban nature has been submerged by urban sprawl.

Mount Wilson Stage Line. Motor stage service from Pasadena to the Mount Wilson Hotel was operating as early as 1914, and by 1917 had been extended into Los Angeles, later using the Union Stage Depot as a terminal. One trip a day was made on the Toll Road, up the mountain in the morning and back down in the evening. The 27-mile run from Los Angeles culminated in nine miles of winding road from the Toll Gate to the mile-high summit. The final leg of the trip from Pasadena to Mount Wilson at first took two hours to complete. Improvements in equipment reduced this to an hour and 40 minutes during the twenties.

The attraction which enticed passengers to endure the trip was, of course, the 100-inch reflecting telescope, whose 4½-ton mirror and 11-ton base had been hauled up the mountain by truck during 1915 and 1916. Hotel traffic soon caused a trip to be added going up the mountain on Friday evenings and returning on Saturday mornings.

In 1919, the operator of the Mount Wilson line, N.A. Webb, started another route, the Arroyo Seco Stage Line, connecting Pasadena with Switzer's Relay, a resort nine miles back in the Sierra Madre Mountains. By the mid-twenties, the line had been extended a fraction of a mile further to Oak Wilde. Weekend service was operated year-round with four trips scheduled Saturdays and six on Sundays. During the vacation season (June to September) a daily morning trip was also operated. By 1925, eight stages were being operated on the two lines. Webb went into partnership with F.S. Hendricks in 1921, and they in turn sold out to T.C. Gillespie in April 1926.

Original Stage Line. W.C. Dunlap entered the jitney business at its height in 1916, at the age of 21, driving a Studebaker financed by his cousin, a local tire distributor. He ran the stretched touring car with its locally built bus body in downtown Los Angeles for three months before admitting that he was barely covering his operating expenses. Discouraged and ready to turn in his vehicle to the dealer who sold it to him, he was referred to a gentleman named Claggett in San Fernando who wanted to buy a new bus.

When the first PE interurban cars reached San Fernando via Van Nuys in March of 1913, Claggett (and others) were already running their rebuilt touring cars along a more direct route (San Fernando Road) to Los Angeles. Dunlap inquired his way to San Fernando and Claggett soon persuaded him to run his new bus alongside Claggett's two older Studebakers, on the long interurban line.

Dunlap found the new route to his liking and by the end of 1916, he had bought out Claggett as well as the five remaining competitors. He soon added four new Studebakers and started the first scheduled bus service to the San Fernando Valley. Before long, the farmers along the route were setting their watches by the Original Stage Line buses.

By 1922, there were 14 buses in service and a trip to Los Angeles left every 45 minutes. In May 1923, Dunlap incorporated the Original Stage Line with himself as president, E.A. Shipsey as vice-president, and F.W. Morgan as secretary. During the next year, two short routes were added radiating from San Fernando. One line replaced a private bus which had run to the Olive View Sanitarium north of town, and the second served the new Veterans Hospital just being completed in Sylmar.

By the fall of 1927, the interurban route had 15-minute service in the mornings and evenings, and half-hour ser-

To San Fernando Valley Points

Take Original Stage Line at Sixth and Los Angeles Streets. We are serving the towns of West Glendale, Burbank, Moreland Automobile Factory, Dundee, Roscoe, Pacoima and San Fernando.

Our service is every 45 minutes week days, one-half hour service Saturdays, Sundays and Holidays. Our fare to Burbank is 25 cents one way, 49c round trip. Our fare to San Fernando is 54 cents one way and 97 cents round trip.

vice throughout the day. The Olive View and Veterans Hospital lines each had six trips a day. The fare from Los Angeles to Burbank was 25 cents and one could ride all the way to San Fernando for 50 cents. Nineteen twenty-seven also saw the completion of a new depot and shop building which occupied an entire block in San Fernando. The equipment at that time totaled 25 buses.

Attractions such as the hiking trails in Pacoima Canyon, the new Mulholland Aqueduct and the San Fernando Mission were advertised as likely points of interest for a Sunday sightseeing ride. Even though the route of the Original Stage Line passed the factory of the Moreland Motor Co. in Burbank, none of the local products was operated. By this time, Studebaker had deemphasized its commercial vehicle line and Dunlap had switched his allegiance to Mack and White.

Pasadena-Ocean Park Stage Line. As a result of a 1919 strike against the Pacific Electric Railway, interurban jitney service flourished between inland cities and the beaches, particularly to Santa Monica, Ocean Park and Venice. At the end of the strike in September, Harry A. Wilson, one operator of such a service, approached the commissioners of Santa Monica regarding a permanent

Mt. Wilson Stage

The ride from Los Angeles through luxurious Pasadena and up nine miles of winding road to Mount Wilson, a mile high in the Sierra Madre Mountains, is one of the most fascinating offered the pleasure seeker and the tourist. The panorama that is unfolded at every turn of the road is an ever-changing one, which makes the trip one of incomparable charm.

The world's greatest telescope, with a 100-inch reflector, occupying a special constructed dome and with a glass mirror weighing about four and one half tons, is the wonder of the astronomic world.

MT. WILSON HOTEL AND CABINS

The hotel is open every day in the year, offering comfortable cabins at $1.50 per day and up. Excellent meals are served at the following prices: Breakfast, $1.00; luncheon, $1.25; dinner, $1.25, with special weekly rates.

STRAIN'S CAMP

The most delightful place in Southern California for a camping vacation for those who like the mountain heights.

Strain's Camp is under the Mt. Wilson Hotel management and is situated just 300 feet below the summit and only a short distance from the hotel and cottages.

DAILY TIME TABLE OF AUTO STAGE

Leave Union Stage Depot, Fifth and Los Angeles Streets	9:00 A.M.
Leave Pasadena, 51 So. Fair Oaks	10:00 A.M.
Arrive Mt. Wilson Hotel, at the summit	12:00 Noon
Leave Mt. Wilson Hotel on return trip	3:00 P.M.
Arrive Pasadena	4:45 P.M.
Arrive Los Angeles	5:30 P.M.

The printed illustrations are reproduced from a 1921 brochure. One shows Original Stage Line No. 2, a White chassis with a body built by the Motor Transit Co., itself a successful line operator. Original Stage Line would soon move its Los Angeles terminal to the Union Stage Depot—built and operated by Motor Transit Co.

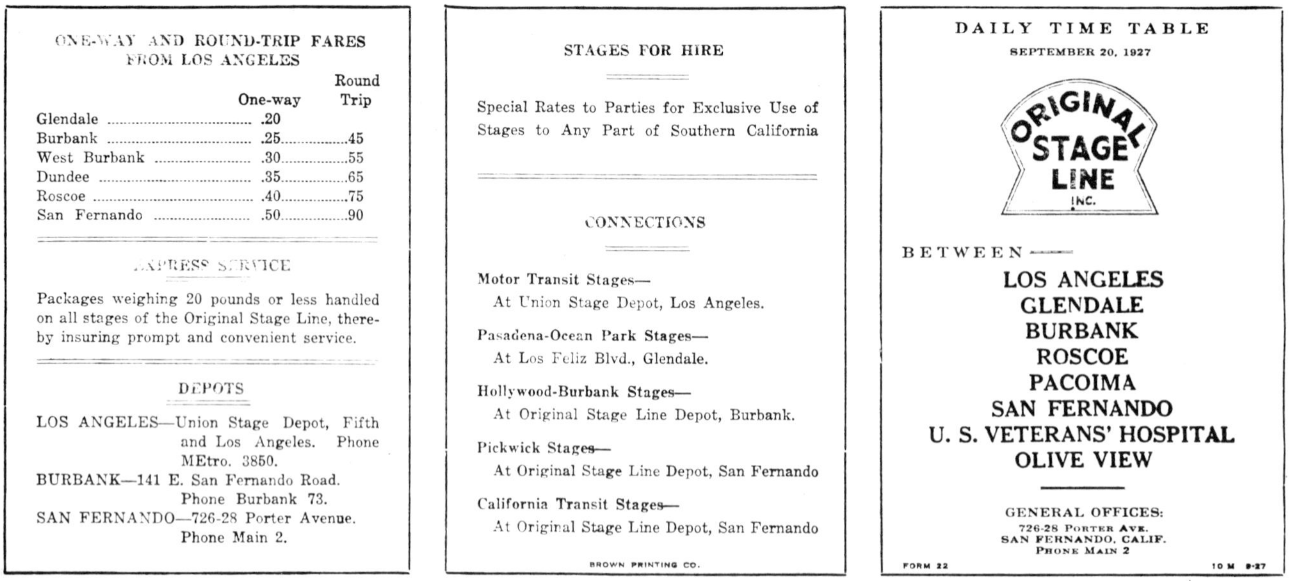

ONE-WAY AND ROUND-TRIP FARES FROM LOS ANGELES

	One-way	Round Trip
Glendale	.20	
Burbank	.25	.45
West Burbank	.30	.55
Dundee	.35	.65
Roscoe	.40	.75
San Fernando	.50	.90

EXPRESS SERVICE

Packages weighing 20 pounds or less handled on all stages of the Original Stage Line, thereby insuring prompt and convenient service.

DEPOTS

LOS ANGELES—Union Stage Depot, Fifth and Los Angeles. Phone MEtro. 3850.
BURBANK—141 E. San Fernando Road. Phone Burbank 73.
SAN FERNANDO—726-28 Porter Avenue. Phone Main 2.

STAGES FOR HIRE

Special Rates to Parties for Exclusive Use of Stages to Any Part of Southern California

CONNECTIONS

Motor Transit Stages—
At Union Stage Depot, Los Angeles.

Pasadena-Ocean Park Stages—
At Los Feliz Blvd., Glendale.

Hollywood-Burbank Stages—
At Original Stage Line Depot, Burbank.

Pickwick Stages—
At Original Stage Line Depot, San Fernando

California Transit Stages—
At Original Stage Line Depot, San Fernando

BROWN PRINTING CO.

DAILY TIME TABLE
SEPTEMBER 20, 1927

ORIGINAL STAGE LINE INC.

BETWEEN—

LOS ANGELES
GLENDALE
BURBANK
ROSCOE
PACOIMA
SAN FERNANDO
U. S. VETERANS' HOSPITAL
OLIVE VIEW

GENERAL OFFICES:
726-28 PORTER AVE.
SAN FERNANDO, CALIF.
PHONE MAIN 2

FORM 22 10 M 9-27

The front panels from a 1927 Original Stage Line timetable. *Author's Collection*

Mount Wilson Stage Line No. 3 was a 14-passenger side-door stage on a White light truck chassis. Six such cars, some of 18-passenger capacity, were used in the 1920s on this line and on the Arroyo Seco route to Switzer's Relay. *Motor Bus Society*

An early Original Stage Line coach is pictured in this 1923 builder's photo. The 25-passenger body is by the Crown Motor Carriage Co. (as it was then known) and the chassis was a standard Mack AB. OSL took delivery of at least three more AB chassis during 1925 and 1926. *Crown Coach*

A standard Mack BCA-2 city service body on a 225-inch wheelbase AB chassis characterizes this Pasadena-Ocean Park bus. The use of a stock eastern vehicle without modification was unusual for early California stage lines. P-OPSL took delivery of four ABs in 1925 and two more in 1926; all were 29-passenger buses.
Pasadena Historical Society

Pasadena-Ocean Park Stage Line operated at least six buses built up on Reo Speed Wagon chassis. They ranged from 17- to 21-passenger capacity and were typified by this side-door stage design. All were passed on to the new corporation (Pasadena-Ocean Park Stage Line Inc.) in 1926.
Motor Bus Society

route. The commissioners and the Railroad Commission reacted favorably, and the Pasadena-Ocean Park Stage Line was formally approved in December.

The bus line provided a one-seat, 28-mile ride from Pasadena to the beaches of Santa Monica and Ocean Park. It ran by way of Eagle Rock, Glendale, Hollywood, Beverly Hills and Sawtelle, but local passengers could not be carried west of Hollywood where the line duplicated PE rail service.

The original equipment comprised two 12-passenger Studebaker tourers, but new 25-passenger buses were promised. Initially service was offered at two-hour intervals, with the first trip of the day leaving at 7 A.M. By 1922 there was hourly service using 10 buses at a terminal-to-terminal fare of 51 cents. PE's fare was higher, and the rail ride involved a change of cars requiring a walking transfer in downtown Los Angeles.

Harry Wilson sold the Pasadena-Ocean Park Stage Line to a partnership of N.A. Webb, F.S. Hendricks and D.E. Hamilton (late of the Pasadena-Pomona Stage Line) in August 1921 for $25,000. The price included the rights, the buses, and the Pasadena Union Bus Depot at 55 S. Fair Oaks. In May 1925 the partnership sold the line along with 19 buses and the depot to T.C. Gillespie.

Studio Stage Line. A certificate was granted to T.C. Gillespie in June 1926 for a line connecting Universal City, Hollywood and Culver City using three White buses. Previous attempts by other operators to run both legs of the line had been unsuccessful. The Universal City part of the line was first authorized in 1920, when Harry Wilson, encountering no protests from PE, started operating as Universal City Stage Line. He sold out in the same year and apparently the line was operated sporadically until Universal City was annexed by Los Angeles in February 1924.

Subsequently the Los Angeles Board of Public Utilities and Transportation authorized operation of the route by George A. Mason, who sold the rights to Gillespie. The Hollywood-Culver City Transit Co. was started by John W. Martin in 1923. The line ran mainly on unpaved streets through sparsely populated territory and was abandoned in 1924.

The impetus for reinstituting bus service and linking the two routes was a change in the operating methods of the motion picture industry. The key event was the establishment of the Central Casting Corp. in Hollywood as a clearing house for the extra personnel used in movie production. While many of the studios were within easy reach of

Another P-OPSL Mack—this one with a low-slung parlor body. P-OPSL did a significant amount of tour and charter business and this bus seems eminently suited for such service. The body resembles those built by Lang for model AB chassis, although we are not able to positively identify it as such.
Motor Bus Society

Representative of P-OPSL equipment during the mid-twenties, six of these 25-passenger Whites were used in service to the beach. The body is typical of those built locally by Crown Coach and Motor Transit on commercial chassis. *Motor Bus Society*

An all-metal 29-passenger aluminum body, perhaps by Braun, is the distinctive feature of this Mack of the late twenties. The chassis is still the ubiquitous AB —constantly modified and improved by the manufacturer during these years. P-OPSL bought at least eight ABs during this period.
Pasadena Historical Society

Central Casting, the three large Culver City studios (MGM, De Mille and Hal Roach) were put at a disadvantage, since the travel time by existing public transportation was about an hour and a half and required transfers. Central Casting provided 21,700 extras to these three studios in the first three months of its existence.

Studio Stage Line promised a one-seat, half-hour ride, and would also serve the studio employees who lived in the Hollywood area. Despite protests from PE and LARy, primarily over local rights, testimony from representatives of the three movie studios prevailed. The award of the route to Gillespie included contested local rights between Hollywood and Wilshire Blvd.

Consolidation. T.C. Gillespie merged his interests by incorporating as Pasadena–Ocean Park Stage Line, Inc., on January 15, 1926, and applying to the Railroad Commission to combine his holdings into the new corporation. Minority interests were held by Elmer P. Bromley and V.L. Ferguson. On October 29, 1926, the corporation was authorized to issue stock and acquire four routes: Pasadena–Ocean Park, Mount Wilson, Arroyo Seco, and Studio

Stage Lines. Operating headquarters were at the Pasadena Union Stage Depot on Fair Oaks Avenue.

The predecessors contributed a total of 35 vehicles to the corporation, ranging in capacity from seven passengers to 29. The Mount Wilson and Arroyo Seco routes together turned over six Whites (three 14-passenger and three 18-passenger stages) and a Mack truck used for freight service, while Studio Stage Line added a 17-passenger Graham and two autos, a Nash and a Chandler. The largest and most diverse stable of equipment had been operated by the Pasadena–Ocean Park Stage Line. The newest buses were six 29-passenger AB Macks purchased by Gillespie since his acquisition of the line. The next newest group consisted of six 25-passenger Whites with locally built bodies. Reo was represented by six Speed Wagon chassis with capacities ranging from 17 to 21 passengers. The remainder of the roster consisted of an older White, a Moreland and a Stewart (all 21-passenger), three Bethlehems and a Tower (all 18-passenger), and an eight-passenger Cadillac car.

Local Rights to Ocean Park. Apparently encouraged by the award of local rights between Hollywood and Culver City on the Studio line, Gillespie applied for similar operating authority between Hollywood and Ocean Park on the Pasadena–Ocean Park route. He proposed to reroute his line from Santa Monica Blvd. (served by PE) to Wilshire Blvd. (unserved by public transit between Beverly Hills and Sawtelle) west of Beverly Hills, and to provide local service beyond Hollywood except on the Sawtelle–Santa Monica segment, already being served by Bay Cities Transit Co.

The proposal to compete with one of PE's oldest and strongest rail routes brought the expected response from the railway: an offer to increase and upgrade its own service. This would normally have allowed the Railroad Commission to deny the competing application provided that PE made good on its offer. In this case the decision was not to be so simple.

Hearings were held in the spring of 1927, and in addition to the usual testimony from employers and the Chamber of Commerce, Gillespie produced an unprecedented parade of 195 witnesses to testify in favor of the proposed local authority. Not until December 1928 did the Commission reach a decision in favor of Pacific Electric, one commissioner remaining unconvinced and writing a dissenting opinion.

The decision required that, in recognition of the expressed public sentiment for bus service, PE produce a plan to provide such service and implement it within a reasonable period of time. The result was the Hollywood–University–Ocean Park bus line, which was started in September 1929 when the UCLA campus opened. Recognizing the futility of further competition, Gillespie cut his service back from Ocean Park to Marshfield and La Brea except for one trip a day to hold the rights in order to serve the Rose Parade on New Year's Day.

At the same time Gillespie instituted joint rates with Pacific Electric so that passengers could transfer to the interurbans in Hollywood to complete their trips to the beach. The western portion of the PE bus line was later transferred to the Los Angeles Motor Coach Co. and operated as an extension of its Wilshire Blvd. service.

Auld Brothers. Development of the territory between Burbank and Lankershim (now North Hollywood) began in 1923 when Earl L. White started selling home sites in a new development which he called Magnolia Park. The first bus route into the area ran to the south of the new tract. This was the Hollywood–Burbank Auto Line, started by the Community Investment Co. in January 1924. The buses ran between Hollywood and Burbank via Dark Canyon (now Barham Blvd.) and Olive Avenue.

There was no direct route to Cahuenga Pass and Hollywood from Magnolia Park, and when the City of Burbank refused to build a road, White funded construction of the new street himself and called it Hollywood Way. In May 1924, White's application to start a bus line into his own development was approved. The new line connected Burbank to the east with PE's Lankershim station to the west via Magnolia Avenue and Lankershim Blvd. Once the real estate venture was well established, PE was persuaded to take over the bus line and started operating it in July 1925.

The growing film industry came to Burbank in January 1926, when First National Studios bought 78 acres of wild alfalfa and onion patches along Olive Avenue for $1.5 million. Construction of a studio began in March and 72 days later the facility was complete, including eight stages and six paved streets. Hoping to grow with the industry, John B. Auld bought the rights and equipment of the Hollywood–Burbank Auto Line for $5,000. Then in August he and his brother Clarence bought the Magnolia Park line from PE for $1 and added a spur along Hollywood Way to the gates of the First National Studios on Olive Avenue.

First National was soon purchased by the Warner Brothers, and in October 1927 released the first all-talking motion picture, *The Jazz Singer.* While the studio prospered the Auld Brothers did not fare as well. They encountered financial difficulties on the Magnolia Park line and abandoned it in the fall of 1927. As their financial situation worsened and their equipment was repossessed, the Aulds attempted to maintain service on the Dark Canyon line with a single bus, an AB Mack. When this too was repossessed, they declared bankruptcy. The receiver immediately recovered the Mack and restored service on the Dark Canyon line in order to maintain the value of the franchise.

W.C. Dunlap of Original Stage Line took advantage of these difficulties and in September 1927 started a new route between Burbank and the First National Studios via Magnolia Avenue and Hollywood Way, replacing part of the line abandoned by the Auld brothers. Dunlap also began negotiating with the receiver to buy the Hollywood route, as did T.C. Gillespie.

Decision and Merger. Both Original Stage Line and Pasadena–Ocean Park Stage Line applied to the Railroad Commission to serve Auld brothers territory, Dunlap by operating between Hollywood and Burbank via Dark Canyon, the First National Studios and either Olive Avenue or Hollywood Way and Magnolia Avenue, and Gillespie by

Original Stage Line turned to model 40 Twin Coaches fitted out as parlor buses for the long San Fernando interurban line in 1928. Five are posed here at San Fernando Rd. and Chatsworth Dr. to show off the curtained windows and plush seats that made the hour-long trip into Los Angeles more comfortable. *Whittington Collection*

extension of his Hollywood–Universal City line into Burbank. The municipalities of Glendale and Burbank both favored the Original Stage Line proposal, and in February 1928 the Railroad Commission authorized the receiver to sell the Dark Canyon line to Dunlap. The Commission awarded rights on Magnolia Blvd. to Original Stage Line after determining that the Aulds had abandoned their service without authority.

Starting in May of 1931, six of these 33-passenger Mack 6-BC-3S buses provided base service on the Original Stage Line route between Los Angeles and San Fernando. Several were still operating into the late 1940s. *Motor Bus Society*

Late in 1928, Original Stage Line purchased seven new parlor-type Twin Coaches for the San Fernando line, bringing the total number of buses in use to 30. Apparently paying for the Twins and operating the new routes entailed a greater expense than the company could manage, especially when the economy slowed down after the stock market crash, for in May 1930 the Original Stage Line was taken over by the Pasadena–Ocean Park Stage Line, though each company continued as a separate entity. The Twins disappeared soon after.

Don L. Campbell, vice president of POPSL, also became general manager of OSL, and the headquarters of the combined operation were moved to the new Hollywood Union Bus Depot (formerly the central fire station) on Cahuenga Blvd. The Arroyo Seco line was discontinued in March 1931, and in the following month the Hollywood–Universal City segment of the POPSL Studio line was replaced by some rerouted trips of the OSL Hollywood–Burbank line via Magnolia Blvd. In May 1931 six new Mack BC's arrived to take the place of the departed Twins as first-line equipment on the San Fernando line.

Few changes of significance were made in the operation of either company during the period of their joint ownership by T.C. Gillespie. The opening of a new county highway to Mount Wilson via La Canada in 1935 prompted an application for its use as an alternate route. The new "high-gear road," now a portion of the Angeles Crest

The Asbury brothers bought 10 Mack 6-CQ-3S buses for their newly acquired operation in July of 1935. The buses are shown here in front of the trucking company headquarters after completion of one of the longest driveaway shipments attempted up to that time. The buses made the transcontinental run from Allentown, Pa., in eight days and 12 hours. *Mack*

Asbury's first rear-engined buses, now painted, numbered 32-41, and with headsigns installed, pose in front of Pasadena's City Hall before going into service. All good stories have an unsolved mystery—a careful count will show 11 buses, not 10. Could the eleventh (with the hood in front) be the elusive number 42? *Mack*

Coach 32 was one of a group of 10 Mack CQs which brought Asbury into the modern era of rear-engined buses in 1935. Here, it loads at the Pasadena Union Bus Depot shortly after going into service. *Mack*

Below: Asbury bought 3 CTs originally for P-OPSL including unit 46 pictured here. The "V" dash sign identified the alternate route to San Fernando via Riverside Drive and Victory Blvd. *Gerald L. Squier*

Asbury management bought small buses for use on the light routes of both affiliates. Two of these Mack CGs were bought in 1936 for OSL, presumably for the San Fernando feeder lines. The third, shown here, was consigned to P-OPSL; it was specially geared for Mt. Wilson service. *Motor Bus Society*

Highway, was wider, better paved, and well graded. The old Mount Wilson Toll Road, which ascended from the end of Lake Avenue in Pasadena, was essentially a single-lane affair with turnouts, and it incorporated 10 percent grades and hairpin switchbacks. Little use was made of it after the application to use the new road was approved on March 26, 1935. Passenger service over the Toll Road was discontinued in August 1936, and freight service followed in December.

Asbury Ownership. Brothers J.T. and F.H. Asbury had started the Asbury Trucking Company early in the century, and expansion had pushed the routes of the commodity hauler south to the Mexican border and north into Oregon. A second and newer concern, Asbury Transportation Co., was a fast-growing carrier of bulk petroleum products. Steady Mack customers, the Asbury brothers purchased Pasadena–Ocean Park Stage Line and Original Stage Line from T.C. Gillespie in the fall of 1935 and bought 10 new model CQs to replace older equipment.

At the request of the city of Burbank, Original Stage Line started a trial service in May 1936. The new line ran from 10th Street through downtown Burbank on Olive Avenue, then via Lake and Alameda Avenues to the First National Studios, where it met the through bus via Magnolia Park.

With recovery from the Depression came renewed residential development in North Hollywood and Van Nuys, and a natural consequence was a demand for better public transportation. The Valley line of Pacific Electric and its wooden cars were suffering from deferred maintenance, and PE started exploring the possibility of bus substitution with the Board of Public Utilities and Transportation.

At that time there were three highway routes between Los Angeles and the San Fernando Valley. The most direct was through Cahuenga Pass north of Hollywood, which was also the route of the Valley interurban rail line. PE's existing Ventura Blvd. and North Hollywood bus lines also went that way. The second route was San Fernando Road through Glendale and Burbank, traversed by Original Stage Line, and the third was Riverside Drive. This recently completed highway was a logical candidate for transit service, but flooding had washed out a bridge over the Los Angeles River. The approach to the replacement structure involved a tight turn, difficult for any vehicle larger than an automobile to negotiate.

Informal meetings started in February 1936, between PE and the Board of Public Utilities and Transportation came to the attention of Don Campbell, manager of Original Stage Line. As a result, after deducing PE's intentions, OSL applied for an alternate route between Los Angeles and San Fernando via Riverside Drive. The new line would have been 35 miles long and required an hour and a half each way, whereas the existing route was 22½ miles long and the scheduled running time was one hour, but the proposed route would have tapped the most populous sections of North Hollywood and Van Nuys.

If such a bus route had been established by Original Stage Line, it would have preempted Pacific Electric's plan to replace the Valley interurbans with buses. PE's counterproposal was to abandon the interurban and substitute bus service over two alternate routes, one paralleling the rail line through Cahuenga Pass and the other via Riverside Drive. A few days later, PE supplemented its application to add two feeder lines in OSL territory: North Hollywood–Roscoe–Sunland and North Hollywood–Burbank–Glendale.

Not to be outdone, Original Stage Line answered with its own proposal for a line between Burbank and North Hollywood using the less direct trial route via Lake Avenue, which passed the various motion picture studios. A second application followed a day later and specified a line from Hollywood along Ventura Blvd., dividing to serve San Fernando via Reseda and Canoga Park via Girard; this route would have completely duplicated PE service.

Valley Routes Resolved. The population of the San Fernando Valley had grown from 52,000 in 1930 to an estimated 95,000 six years later, and the contending proposals caused considerable controversy in the region. Subsequent public hearings polarized the residents, with North Hollywood being the most vocal for the OSL plan and San Fernando against. Public testimony and the conclusions of the regulatory commission were strongly in favor of retaining the PE rail line, so all applications for parallel bus routes were turned down in April 1937. The Railroad Commission recognized the need for better service between Burbank and North Hollywood, and Original Stage Line was awarded a new route, consolidating its hold on the area. The new line traversed a large loop serving Studio City via Moorpark Avenue, Colfax Avenue, and Ventura Blvd., then turned north and east through North Hollywood via Laurel Canyon Blvd. and Magnolia Avenue, and finally returned to Riverside Drive via Lankershim, Burbank and Cahuenga Blvds.

PE's proposed Sunland line was denied because of the small likelihood of any return but a portion of the proposed alternate route along Van Owen Street and Van Nuys Blvd. between North Hollywood and Ventura Blvd. was authorized by the Commission. PE chose not to start the service, since it would only have diverted potential passengers from the rail line.

Original Stage Line routes radiating from Burbank were changed in August 1937, when service into Hollywood was reorganized into two alternate routes, the first via Olive and Moorpark Avenues and the second via Magnolia Blvd., Hollywood Way and Barham Blvd. Service to the Studio City–North Hollywood area was also changed, with the large loop served clockwise via Lake and Alameda Avenues and counterclockwise via Magnolia Blvd. and Hollywood Way.

At the same time a new line was started from Burbank to the Union Air Terminal (later Lockheed Air Terminal) via Burbank Blvd., Victory Blvd., Hollywood Way and Empire Avenue. The line was discontinued in November 1938 because of sparse patronage, but service to the airport would later be restored over a different route.

During 1938 the Pasadena–Ocean Park Stage Line added seasonal race track extensions to two of its regular routes. The Studio line was extended from Culver City to the Hollywood Turf Club in Inglewood, and the Ocean Park line was extended from Pasadena to the Santa Anita race track in Arcadia. Service to Santa Anita had first been run during the 1935–1936 racing season using rights of Motor Transit Co. via Foothill Blvd.

ROSTER OF BUSES

Original Stage Line
Pasadena–Ocean Park Stage Line
(1931–1938 only)

Operator	Numbers	Make	Model	Seats	Built	Notes
O	70-75	Mack	6-BC-3S	33	1931	
P	32-41	Mack	6-CQ-3S	31	1935	
O	76-77	Mack	6-CG-3S	20	1936	
P	78	Mack	6-CG-3S	21	1937	
O	79-80	Mack	6-CQ-3S	31	1937	
P	43-44	Mack	6-CW-3S	25	1937	
O	81	Mack	6-CW-3S	25	1937	
P	45	Mack	6-CT-3S	35	1937	(1938) Demo
P	46-47	Mack	CT-3G	35	1938	

Painted in a new, more intricate livery and lettered for its new owner, CQ number 39 relaxes between runs at the Hollywood terminal. These buses were used mainly on the suburban routes (rather than the interurban route to San Fernando) because of their rear doors.

Gerald L. Squier

Below: One of the original P-OPSL CQs (32) waits alongside the PE elevated structure in the days when San Fernando runs ended at Main St. Station. The bus is signed for a Burbank short turn.

Interurban Press

Asbury Rapid Transit Formed. Since the acquisition from T.C. Gillespie, stock of Original Stage Line and Pasadena–Ocean Park Stage Line had been held jointly by the two Asbury brothers and their wives. Merger of the companies was carried out in two phases. The name of Original Stage Line was changed to Asbury Rapid Transit System on August 31, 1939, and the equipment and rights of Pasadena–Ocean Park Stage Line were transferred to Asbury on September 19.

Both of Asbury's predecessors had been faithful Mack customers, and the consolidated property continued to buy Macks, including six CM's delivered in November 1939 as new buses but actually used for a short time on special routes to the New York World's Fair. Asbury would operate 13 gas CM's in all.

In February 1939, service was again changed in the North Hollywood–Studio City area as the long and sparsely patronized loop route was abandoned in favor of direct service from Burbank to the North Hollywood PE station via Magnolia Avenue. Service between North Hollywood and Warner Brothers was retained on a smaller "Studio Loop."

Expansion Attempts Frustrated. During 1939 Asbury continued to try to expand its Los Angeles suburban operations. Acquisition of off-street terminal property near Olympic and Hill prompted attempts to change the terminal of the San Fernando and Mount Wilson routes to the new location. A new route to Beverly Hills via Olympic Blvd. was sought. The Board of Public Utilities and Transportation denied the requests for the terminal change and for the new line, fearing increased downtown traffic.

When Pacific Electric announced that the Redondo Beach via Gardena interurban rail line and its Torrance feeder would be abandoned without replacement on Janu-

Reconditioned after being used briefly in service to the New York World's Fair, Asbury's first CM-3Gs arrived late in 1939. Bus 52 travels along Brand Blvd. in Glendale en route from Hollywood to Pasadena. The CMs were the mainstay of Asbury service during the war years.

Motor Bus Society

Asbury received 18 gas-electrics for the new Highland Park line in December of 1939; they were the only model CM-4Gs produced by Mack. Beverly Glen Blvd. was the western terminal of the proposed Olympic Blvd. line which was never operated by Asbury. *Mack*

ary 14, 1940, the city of Torrance decided to start its own replacement bus service. Since action could not be taken immediately, the city contracted with Asbury to provide interim free transportation. Asbury started the line on January 15, operating from Lomita to its new terminal at 945 S. Hill, and on the same day the company applied to make the route permanent.

The City of Torrance started its own service on January 25, extending the line south to Walteria, and Asbury revised its application to conform. The City of Gardena, also left without access to Los Angeles, started its own municipal bus line on January 15, connecting with LARy's 7 car line at 116th and Athens Way. Neither municipality was interested in continuing to operate bus service, and Torrance endorsed Asbury's application for the new line. Gardena similarly supported a proposal by Landier Transit Co. for a new route between that city and Huntington Park, connecting with several LARy lines en route as well as with PE's Long Beach interurbans.

The Railroad Commission decided to consolidate both applications for hearings, in the belief that the territory would support only one operator. After hearing from all interested parties, and noting that the Board of Public Utilities and Transportation was continuing to deny applications for new bus lines into Los Angeles because of already congested downtown streets, the Commission offered a compromise decision. In June 1940, Asbury was awarded rights for a new bus line connecting Walteria, Lomita, Torrance and Gardena with LARy cars at 116th and Vermont.

The decision satisfied no one, least of all Asbury Rapid Transit. The City of Gardena thought that the line should have been awarded to Landier, while Torrance wanted through service to Los Angeles, and both municipalities continued to operate their own buses. The City of Gardena tried to gain a rehearing but failed, and Asbury, not wanting to compete with two municipal systems, refused the certificate without ever operating the new line. Gardena extended its own service into Los Angeles in 1949, and both municipal operations still thrive.

Service to Highland Park. In one instance, Asbury Rapid Transit did succeed in starting a new Los Angeles line, but it too was not to endure. Never at a loss for an innovative proposal, Asbury applied for local rights over the Los Angeles–Pasadena portion of the Mount Wilson line. Needless to say, PE was not overjoyed by the prospect of additional competition, and neither was the Los Angeles Railway, whose busy W car line would be paralleled for most of its length by the new route. Applications were submitted early in 1939 requesting the enlarged rights as well as an alternate route via the Arroyo Seco Parkway (Pasadena Freeway), then under construction.

Asbury's belief was that residents of Garvanza, just inside the Los Angeles city limits adjacent to South Pasadena, would patronize such a line. In fact, they once had; Pacific Electric had abandoned its South Pasadena rail line some four years earlier without replacing its through service to Los Angeles. While awaiting word from the Railroad Commission, Asbury applied to the Los Angeles Board of Public Utilities and Transportation for the local rights within the city limits.

The Board authorized a permit to be issued during July, and Asbury promptly ordered 18 CM buses from Mack; gas-electric drive was specified because of the steep grades to be encountered on the line. The permit was actually issued in October, and when the buses arrived, Asbury decided to start service on the portion of the line within Los Angeles even though the Railroad Commission had not yet acted.

Service began on December 10, 1939, and the original

This wartime photo of downtown Los Angeles shows the Trailways Depot as well as an Asbury Mack just leaving Pacific Electric's Main Street Station. Behind the bus a PE Watts–Sierra Vista car approaches the loading zone. *SCRTD Collection*

timetable called for 126 trips a day, which was reduced to 114 trips in April 1940, even though patronage increased from 122,000 in January to 143,500 in March. The line ran from Asbury's new terminus at Olympic and Hill via Figueroa Street and Pasadena Avenue (now York Blvd.) through Highland Park to San Pascual Avenue and Hough Street in Garvanza. The gas-electrics were used exclusively on the new line except on New Year's Day, when some of them were borrowed for Rose Parade service between Hollywood and Pasadena.

PE and LARy immediately complained to the Railroad Commission about Asbury's operation of the uncertificated route. The bus company argued that no certificate was needed because the service was being operated entirely within a single municipality, while lawyers for the railways said that the route was part of a larger operation that did cross municipal boundaries. Their contention prevailed, the Railroad Commission on September 10, 1940, ordering Asbury to cease operation of the Highland Park route within 90 days.

The vote of the Commission was 3 to 2, and Asbury chose to appeal the decision, encouraged by the dissenters. Meanwhile, the well-patronized buses continued to roll. It took an additional nine months, until June 1941, for the original decision to be affirmed, and service was finally discontinued on July 12. On the next day, LARy increased service on the W line to accommodate the former Asbury patrons, and indeed bought 16 of the gas-electric Macks for use on its own lines.

Asbury and the Aircraft Industry. Just as Asbury's predecessors had answered the needs of the growing motion picture business in earlier days, Asbury responded to the phenomenal growth of the region's aviation industry in the late 1930s. As early as 1937, Vega Airplane Co. had been formed in Burbank to build Hudson bombers for Britain. The signing of a contract for 250 of these aircraft in the summer of 1938 was, at the time, the largest aircraft order ever placed.

The Union Air Terminal was the primary commercial airport for the Los Angeles area in 1939, and Vega was in the process of completing a factory adjacent to the airport at Empire Avenue and Hollywood Way which would enclose 25 acres under one roof and house 10,000 employees. Traffic tie-ups at shift change times were already so bad in 1939 that the Railroad Commission recommended introduction of public transportation. Meanwhile, employment at the Lockheed Aircraft Co. had grown from 6,500 to 13,000 within a year, and its facilities at Empire Avenue and San Fernando Road would soon house twice that number.

This growth, coupled with increased residential development west of the Southern Pacific main line between Los Angeles and Burbank, caused the Railroad Commission to grant Asbury's perennial request for a new route along Riverside Drive. This thoroughfare was authorized to be used as part of an alternate route to San Fernando via the Union Air Terminal in December 1940, but no local service was permitted within the Los Angeles city limits.

Similar expansion at the southern end of the system took place in February 1941, when extension of the Culver City line to Mines Field in Inglewood was authorized. The extension served plants of Douglas Aircraft, North American Aircraft, and Interstate Aircraft, as well as the area's second commercial airfield, later to become Los Angeles International Airport.

Direct service between Hollywood and the Vega plant and Union Air Terminal was started in April 1941. The new line began at the Hollywood terminal on Cahuenga Avenue and followed the route of the Dark Canyon line to Hollywood Way, which it used to the airport. Union Air Terminal was the only commercial landing field in the Los Angeles metropolitan area during World War II; it was not until 1946 that the major airlines moved across town to an expanded Mines Field.

Asbury in Wartime. Like other transit operators in the area, Asbury Rapid Transit started new routes and increased service on existing lines to bring workers to local defense plants. The focus of the company's attention continued to be the complex of Lockheed and Vega plants. Early in March 1942 a temporary wartime service was started to connect Van Nuys, North Hollywood, and western Burbank with a new Lockheed plant at Empire Avenue and Victory Place.

In April 1942, 40 daily San Fernando trips were diverted through the airport at Lockheed's request to serve the Vega plants there. Lockheed merged its subsidiary, Vega, into the parent corporation in 1943, and employment at the combined facilities peaked at more than 94,000 by the end of World War II. During the summer of 1942, service to Arcadia was made permanent when Santa Anita race track was turned into a staging area for the transport of Japanese-Americans to internment camps.

Original Stage Line and Mount Wilson Stage Line had been tenants at the Union Stage Depot at 5th and Los Angeles Streets since the 1920s. When PE closed the old terminal in favor of a modernized Main Street Station, Asbury followed right along. The new station was opened on September 27, 1942, after which Asbury's San Fernando

Hard pressed for equipment to serve the aircraft plants, Asbury turned to Crown in 1944 for three large capacity buses. They finished out their days in racetrack service to Santa Anita and Hollywood Park; 63 was caught here between runs by the camera of Ira L. Swett. *Interurban Press*

White 788 number 66 was one of two acquired from the City of Santa Monica in 1946 to help carry wartime traffic. Santa Monica found itself able to cope adequately using newer and larger equipment.
Motor Bus Society

Below: Asbury returned to Mack for its large postwar equipment order and 10 single-door C-41-GTs arrived in June of 1947. The buses were transferred to Metropolitan Coach Lines with the sale of Asbury, but were not kept long; Jesse Haugh sold them off quickly along with other nonstandard equipment.
Motor Bus Society

In addition to the Macks, Asbury received six Twin Coach 41-S buses in 1947. Like the Macks, they were muzzle-loaders, continuing the tradition of single-door gas buses. The first group was joined the next year by four more 41-Ss and from then on, all new Asbury buses would be Twins. The scene is at the Hollywood terminal. *Motor Bus Society*

When presented with the task of taking over the local lines of Burbank City Lines in 1949, Asbury once again turned to Crown Coach for help. Crown, West Coast distributor of Ford buses, came to the rescue with a dozen reconditioned transits. Units 301-312 pose for a family portrait in front of the NBC radio studios at Sunset and Vine before going into service. *Crown Coach*

runs loaded next to PE buses in the former interurban train concourse.

In response to an ODT request that bus mileage be reduced, Asbury suspended its one remaining daily trip between Hollywood and Ocean Park in October 1942. The Mount Wilson Observatory was closed to the public in February 1943, and bus service was accordingly suspended in March.

Postwar Expansion. When the war ended and equipment needs eased, Asbury Rapid Transit reacted to the continued growth of the San Fernando Valley by extending bus service into new areas. June 1946 brought authorization for a new line from North Hollywood to Roscoe (now Sun Valley), though the idea was not a new one and the line had first been proposed by Pacific Electric in 1936, when it had been turned down by the Railroad Commission. The population of the surrounding area had grown in the meantime from 1,000 to more than 15,000.

As dense residential development spread northward along the main line to San Fernando, Asbury sought to use Glenoaks Blvd. (parallel to San Fernando Road and separated from it by SP tracks) as an alternate route. An application was submitted in March 1946, but in April, Burbank City Lines started a new local route on Glenoaks from downtown to the city limits. Moreover, Burbank City Lines protested Asbury's application and requested restrictions against local passengers on the proposed line. As a result the new routing, started in January 1947, was via Hollywood Way, Glenoaks Blvd. and Osborne Street to San Fernando.

Postwar growth in Pacoima and Panorama City prompted Asbury to apply for a route between Hollywood and San Fernando via Laurel Canyon Blvd. in 1946. The application was denied, but a rehearing was requested and granted; this disclosed substantial public sentiment in favor of the line. Objections came from PE, worried about competition with its San Fernando Valley rail line. A compromise solution allowed Asbury to start its service in May 1947. Instead of running into Hollywood, Asbury's route terminated at PE's North Hollywood station. Another request by Asbury to extend the line into Hollywood was denied in June 1947, affirming the stand of the Commission on preserving patronage on the rail lines.

The return to peacetime conditions was reflected in permission to resume seasonal race track services, but Asbury had to defer these for a year because of a lack of equipment. A 10-year fight for a route to Van Nuys via Riverside Drive ended in June 1947, when the PUC denied Asbury's applications and gave the rights to PE. Asbury ended its use of PE's Main Street Station on September 27, 1947, in favor of a temporary stand on Los Angeles Street between 6th and 7th. In December, property was leased for a new off-street terminal at 8th Street and Maple Avenue, and routings were changed accordingly to use Los Angeles Street inbound and Spring Street outbound.

Ford 309 is snapped in Burbank during December 1951. Note that the bus has been repainted into the same scheme as the prewar Macks.
Motor Bus Society

The new North Hollywood–Roscoe line was extended to Sunland in April 1948, but a request for a southward extension to Studio City was rejected in favor of a new PE line from North Hollywood to Sherman Oaks via Studio City. General Motors opened a new auto assembly plant on Van Nuys Blvd. north of Roscoe Blvd., and in May 1948 Asbury started service there from San Fernando. Service to Ocean Park was discontinued permanently in August, after a brief resumption following wartime suspension, and the Inglewood extension of the Culver City line was discontinued in June 1949. Staggering of work shifts at aircraft plants served by the line, and increased availability of private autos, were the reasons cited.

Burbank City Lines. Local bus service in Burbank was provided during the early 1940s by Carl Eckles, whose Burbank Bus Service was modeled after similar small operations in Whittier and Santa Ana which he had started and made profitable. With the increase in local employment caused by the growing defense industry, Eckles was hard pressed to keep drivers on the job and to find enough buses to maintain adequate service. He kept the operation going through the war in spite of these handicaps.

Pacific City Lines acquired the routes and equipment during 1944 and operated them for a time as Burbank City Lines before selling out in turn to former National City Lines employees A.W. Howe and T.W. Burke in December 1946. After several years of marginal operation led to a protracted labor dispute, Burbank City Lines informed the City Council that service would be discontinued on July 16, 1949.

At the request of the city, the company agreed to continue service for three months while an effort was made to find a new operator. The Chamber of Commerce recommended that Asbury Rapid Transit be invited to provide replacement service, and Asbury agreed to do so for a nine-month trial period effective October 15. Temporary rights were awarded by the city on September 29, and approvals from the Board of Public Utilities and Transportation and the PUC followed promptly. City Lines operated three routes centered on downtown Burbank: 1—Victory Blvd; 2—Glenoaks Blvd.-Verdugo Ave.; 3—Burbank Blvd.-Alameda Ave. The Burbank Blvd. local line, running to the west from downtown Burbank, was extended along Olive Avenue between San Fernando Road and Victory Blvd. to become a branch of Asbury's Riverside Drive route. The Glenoaks Blvd.-Verdugo Ave. through route was combined with Asbury's Hollywood–Burbank Short Line via Fairview Avenue. The remainder of this line, a loop through Magnolia Park, was abandoned, but the Hollywood–Burbank Long Line was revised to provide some service to the area. The Victory Blvd. and Alameda Avenue lines were combined in a U-shaped through route. Asbury bought 12 second-hand Ford Transits from Crown Coach, the local distributor, to operate the Burbank local lines.

Cost Reduction. An effort to economize as a result of the postwar traffic decline led Asbury Rapid Transit to conclude that operating costs as well as unprofitable route mileage had to be cut. Following the experience of some large California truck operators, Asbury decided to try liquefied petroleum fuel and six new king-size Twin Coach buses delivered in June 1950 were propane-powered. By that time the Asbury brothers had retired from the business and sold it to A.J. Eyraud, Jr.

Service from San Fernando to the GM plant in Van Nuys and from Los Angeles to Mount Wilson ended in the fall of 1950 because of poor patronage. The last vestige of Asbury's temporary wartime service was given up in December when the line from North Hollywood (Colfax and Riverside Drive) to Lockheed Plant B-1 was discontinued. The line had been cut back from Van Nuys earlier in the year.

In November 1951 the Sunland line was cut back again to Sun Valley, the outer loop of the Veterans Hospital–Olive View Sanitarium line was discontinued, and the Warner Brothers Studio loop route between North Hollywood and Burbank was abandoned. Local lines in Burbank

The 41-S Twins were repainted into the new postwar colors. Bus 62, one of the last order of CMs, shows the rounded sash characteristic of late production batches of wartime Macks. *SCRTD Collection*

Left: All dressed up in the new postwar paint scheme, CM 56 poses at the Glendale garage. The dark areas were Pullman green, the stripe was silver and the roof, maintaining the tradition of many years, was orange. The cardboard dash sign is for the former Studio route between Hollywood and Culver City. *Motor Bus Society*

were rearranged soon afterward, service on Alameda Avenue being cut back to St. Joseph's Hospital and through-routed with the Burbank Blvd. line. Victory Blvd. became a separate route, and all Riverside Drive trips operated through the airport.

In spite of minor reroutings during 1952 and 1953, Asbury Rapid Transit's route structure remained essentially static. Patronage fell, and attempts to make up operating deficits by increasing fares (February and September 1952 and again in September 1953) were not successful. As might be expected, Asbury management began to search for a buyer to take over the operation.

The quest was without success until Jesse Haugh's Metropolitan Coach Lines acquired the passenger operations of the Pacific Electric Railway in 1953. Asbury provided Metro's only competition in the San Fernando Valley and West Los Angeles areas. Haugh believed that the potential operating and maintenance economies made possible by consolidation would bring the Asbury lines into the black.

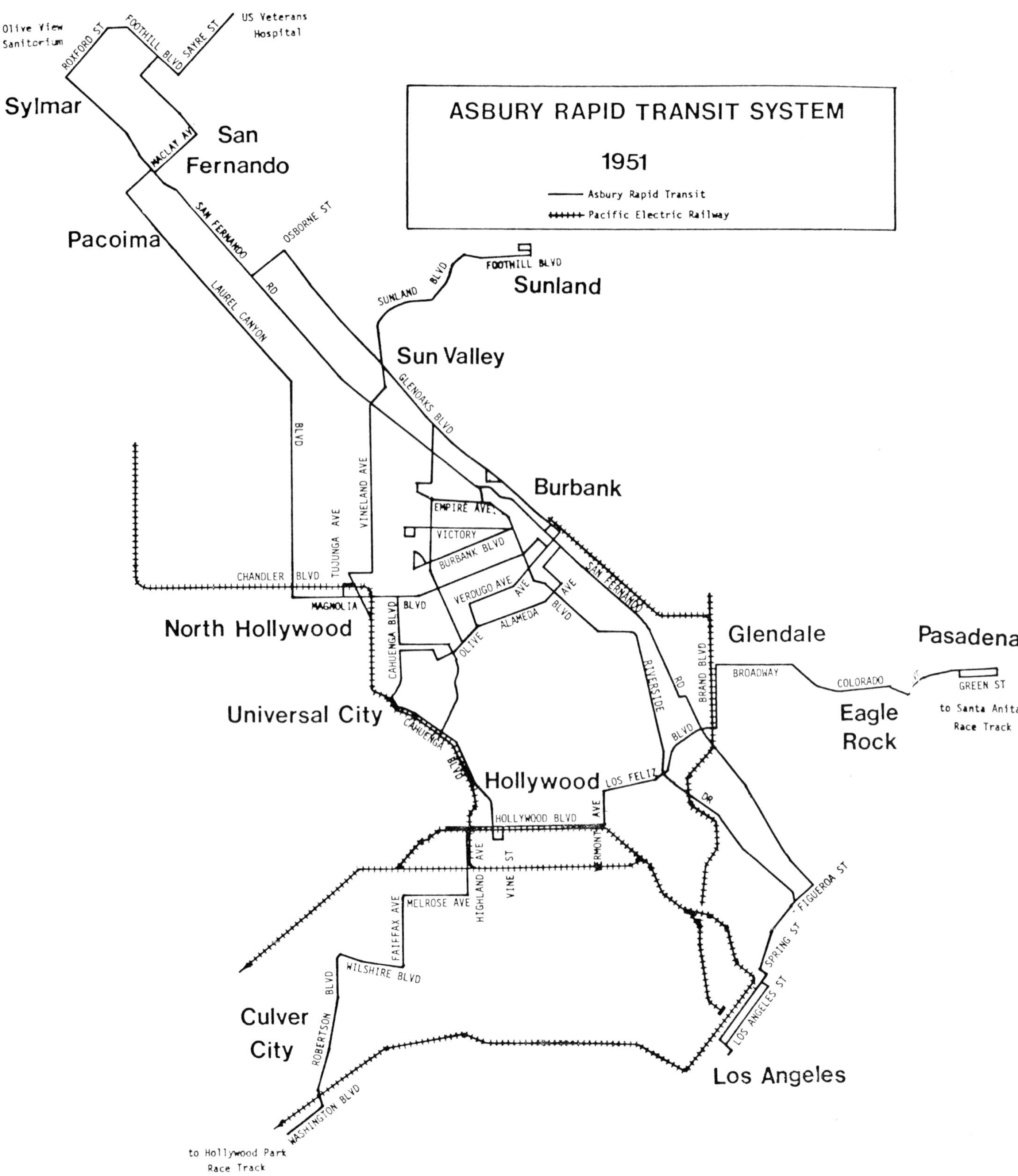

This was the Asbury system in 1951. The short local lines in Burbank contrasted with the long runs characteristic of the balance of the system.

Eli Bail

Unable to purchase large buses from General Motors in the 1950s, Asbury turned to Twin Coach for equipment. Examples of the last two orders of propane-powered buses are compared at the offstreet terminal at 8th and Maple. Differences in detail between king-size buses produced before and after acquisition of Twin Coach by Flxible are evident.
Interurban Press

Below: King-size Twin 113 waits between runs to San Fernando at the downtown terminal. The advertisement bids passengers to visit the Los Angeles County Fair.
Andrew R. Harrison

Flxible-Twin 135 was the last bus of Asbury's final order. Later repainted into Metro two-tone green, these buses operated for LAMTA as well after sale of the Metro system to that agency. *Flxible*

ROSTER OF BUSES

Asbury Rapid Transit System (1939-1954)

Numbers	Make	Model	Seats	Built	Notes
50-55	Mack	CM-3G	41	1939	(1939) World's Fair Transportation Co.
100-117	Mack	CM-4G	41	1939	
56-58	Mack	CM-3G	37	1941	
59-62	Mack	CM-3G	45	1942	
63-65	Crown	H-5	53	1944	
200-201	Mack	?	?	?	
202-204	Ford	?	27	1946	
66-67	White	788-1	41	1940	(1946) Santa Monica Municipal Bus Lines 503, 505
205-208	Ford	?	27	1947	
82-91	Mack	C-41-GT	53	1947	
100-105	Twin	41-S	42	1947	
106-109	Twin	41-S	42	1948	
301-312	Ford	?	29	?	(1949) Crown Coach (distributor)
110-115	Twin	52-S2P	54	1950	
116-125	Twin	52-S2P	54	1951	
126-135	Flxible	FT2P-40	54	1954	

Buses sold to Metropolitan Coach Lines 8/3/54: 32-41 except one, 43-47, 50-67, 77, 82-91, 100-135, 202-208 and 301-312 (98 buses).

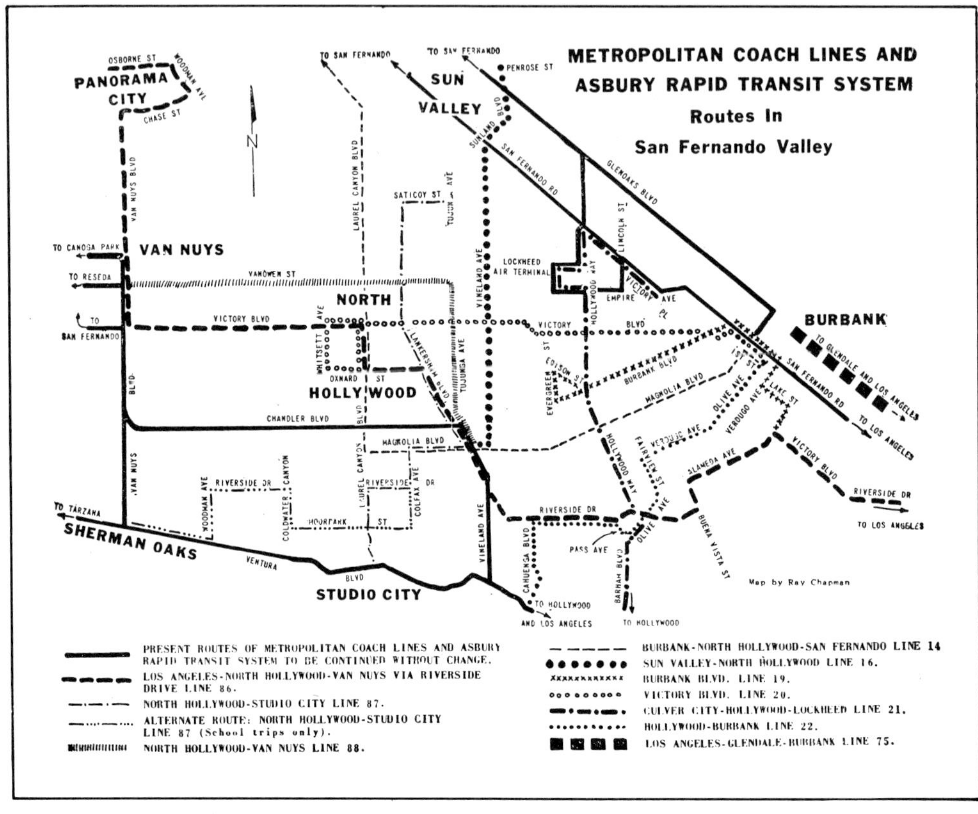

The Asbury lines would soon be integrated with those of Metropolitan Coach Lines as shown on this map.
Author's Collection

CHAPTER SEVEN

METROPOLITAN COACH LINES 1953-1958

Metro to the rescue; red to green

The changing of the guard: O.A. Smith hands over the reins of Pacific Electric passenger service to Jesse Haugh. Both presidents, resplendent in their bow ties, are surrounded by PE, parent Southern Pacific and Metro company officers as well as officials of the Bank of America. Clockwise from left: SP General Counsel George Buland; Metro Secretary-Treasurer Richard Haugh; PE attorneys Fred Lindley and E.D. Yeoman; Smith and Haugh; Bank of America officials John Kerfoot, H.M. Schuppert, C.J. Medberry and John Walter; PE Assistant to the Vice President Donald Lewis, and SP officials Henry McCleer and Harry J. Walker. *SCRTD Collection*

TYPICAL OF TRANSIT SYSTEMS in the postwar years, Pacific Electric's operating costs rose faster than its revenue in spite of frequent fare increases. Economies gained by the modernization program of 1950–1951 and tax savings achieved by selling rights-of-way were not enough to offset a decrease in passenger volume as the freeways grew and employment decentralized. Even though continuing emphasis on freight traffic had increased revenue from that source, PE's financial problems were still not solved.

Considering the Southern Pacific's historic attitude, one evident answer was to find a buyer for PE's passenger service. On March 3, 1953, PE announced an agreement to sell its passenger operations, both rail and bus, to Jesse Haugh. A former Pacific City Lines executive, Haugh had formed Western Transit Systems as a holding company in 1947 and subsequently acquired the San Diego Transit System as well.

Metropolitan Coach Lines was incorporated in California on May 18, 1953; it was capitalized by Haugh at $8.5 million, $7.2 million of which was to cover the purchase price of the Pacific Electric assets and the remainder was for organizational expenses and working capital. The sale was completed on October 1, 1953, with all of PE's passenger operating rights and all facilities and property related to the bus lines being turned over to Metro. These included

Hollywood Blvd. after the streetcars came off. An ex-LAMC TDH-4507 is westbound on the 89 line with the Hollywood First National Building in the background. *SCRTD Collection*

the Pasadena, Ocean Park and West Hollywood garages, Macy Street shops, servicing and storage locations at Van Nuys, Sunland, Long Beach (Morgan Avenue) and Echo Park Avenue, stations at Pomona, Riverside and Whittier, and 695 buses.

The situation of the rail lines was somewhat more unusual. As part of the sale agreement, Pacific Electric provided Metro with rent-free use of facilities (cars, tracks, overhead and stations) for a period of two years, with an option to rent the property on a month-to-month basis beyond that time. Included in this category were the Main Street Station and offices, the Los Angeles Street Motor Coach Terminal, the Subway Terminal and the stations at San Bernardino and Long Beach as well as all other passenger facilities throughout the system.

The eventuality of ever having to exercise the rental option seemed remote when Haugh stated his intention to abandon all rail service within six months or request substantial fare increases. At that time only the Hollywood Blvd. and Glendale–Burbank rail lines remained in the Western District and the Watts, Bellflower, San Pedro and Long Beach lines in the Southern District. Haugh promptly applied to abandon them all.

New Metro Buses. During hearings on the acquisition, Haugh testified that Metro planned to buy 100 new buses a year to replace the interurban cars and PE Whites. Plans were also disclosed at that time to modify existing installa-

Coach 1692 at 6th and Main in PE silver and red but with Metropolitan Coach Lines within the PE winged herald. It would soon be repainted into Metro green. *Both: Motor Bus Society*

tions and construct new servicing and storage bases so that system operation could be reorganized on a regional basis. As a follow-up to purchase of the initial 35 by PE, the TDH-4801 became Metro's standard, with 100 placed on order as promised soon after the takeover. Key System had ordered 30 similar buses in the meantime, but because of a lengthy strike they had not been shipped, and these were sold to Metro in December 1953.

The buses arrived in Key System paint inside and out and wore Key numbers 2100–2129. They had never reached Oakland and were shipped from GM with their Metro-peculiar features not completely installed. The delivery paperwork noted that extra markers, stanchions and adapters, new two-piece roll signs and platforms for the seats ahead of the wheel housings should be added and that the heating system should be changed. The work not completed at the factory was performed at Torrance. As if to explain the reason for the existence of the TDH-4801, the final note on the GM delivery record cautioned that "These coaches, when completed, must not exceed 16,500 lbs. on the rear axle with seated load, including full complement of fuel, water and oil."

A Christmas present for riders on the Wilshire Blvd. line, these buses appeared in a new paint scheme of dark green around the windows, light green below and a white roof. This was introduced concurrently in San Diego and on Western Transit Systems properties; its colors were supposedly particularly resistant to smog. They were numbered 301–330 starting a new roster sequence.

The 100 TDH-4801s (400 series) of Metro's first order started to arrive in the spring of 1954, with 30 of them replacing older diesels on the Sunset Blvd. line (83, ex-LAMC) on June 16. A second group replaced the 2900s in base service on the Santa Monica Blvd. line (94) shortly thereafter. The equipment policy was never in question as the TDH-4801 became the standard of the system. Metro operated the first 165 built (including the initial PE order) and eventually 268 of the 547 produced.

Asbury Acquired. On August 3, 1954, Metro acquired control of its largest competitor, the Asbury Rapid Transit System. As had been the case with PE's purchase of the Motor Transit Co. a quarter century earlier, Asbury became a wholly-owned subsidiary and was separately operated.

The Asbury rights to operate the Burbank local lines were still temporary and had been renewed seven times in five years, principally to avoid franchise tax payments; permanent rights were secured on April 20, 1954. On July 22, the PUC approved the sale of Asbury Rapid Transit to Metropolitan Coach Lines for $150,000. The transfer of assets took place on August 3 and included Asbury's routes, 98 buses, the Glendale garage at Los Feliz Blvd. and Central Avenue, and terminals at San Fernando and Hollywood.

At that time much of the company's older equipment was not being operated and had served only to inflate Asbury's book value. By September Metro had disposed of all 19 remaining Fords, 11 old Macks, the two second-hand Whites, and one of the Crowns. The other buses were sufficient to run the operation, and they continued to cover the Asbury routes in the Asbury colors. Asbury's 140 miles of route covered an area to the north and west of Los Angeles, and there were two seasonal race track services. Metro numbered the Asbury routes from 12 to 26, after the Bellflower car line, which was officially line 11. In the former PE scheme they should have taken numbers upward from 95. The list was as follows:

12	Los Angeles–San Fernando
13	Los Angeles–Burbank via Riverside Drive
14	North Hollywood–San Fernando
15	San Fernando–Olive View VA Hospital
16	North Hollywood–Sun Valley
17	Hollywood–Pasadena
18	North Hollywood–Burbank
19	St. Joseph's Hospital–Burbank Blvd.
20	Victory Blvd. Local
21	Hollywood–Culver City
22	Hollywood–Burbank (Short Line)
23	Hollywood–Burbank (Long Line)
24	Hollywood–Lockheed
25	Hollywood–Hollywood Park Race Track
26	Hollywood–Santa Anita Race Track

This was the first time visible line numbers appeared on Asbury buses with certain alternate routings receiving

Newly repainted TDH-4801 318 posed at Torrance Shops adorned in a bright red ribbon for this December 1953 photo, while against the wall another member of the class may be seen still in Key System colors. *SCRTD Collection*

Below (two photos): Metro buses of 1955. One of 17 TDM-4515s for the Los Angeles-San Bernardino run, and one of the 83 TDH-4801s.
266: SCRTD Collection
531: Gerald L. Squier

common numbers for ease of identification. The appearance of Metro-style timetable folders and a map showing both Metro and Asbury routes in the San Fernando Valley were other manifestations of the new ownership. The Asbury buses stayed in their former paint scheme of silver and dark green with an orange roof for some time, as route consolidations were made gradually and the operations of the two systems cautiously merged.

The New Look. Jesse Haugh was extremely conscious of the Metro image and took every available opportunity to improve it. The most visible asset of the new company was, of course, its equipment and one of the first programs that Haugh instituted was to repaint the red PE equipment into Metro green. By the time that Metro reached its first anniversary, more than 200 of the newer GM's had gone through the shops and the program continued at the rate of one a day. All the remaining GM's and Yellow Coaches followed through the shops as well as the newer Whites.

Dents were knocked out and new panels installed prior to painting; in the interior, the driver's area was repainted dark green for eye comfort and a safety stanchion was added near the farebox. The prewar diesels also received new bumpers and turn signals which gave them a more modern look. Metro initially replaced the lettering in the winged PE herald on the older equipment with "Metropolitan Coach Lines." At first glance, the change was difficult to detect. Along with the new green paint scheme, however, came a new herald, a variation of the one used by Haugh on his other properties. Emblazoned over a winged shield was the word "Metropolitan" and across the wings, "Coach Lines" on the shield itself was a motto like one used in the past by PE, "Safety, Courtesy, Service."

Revisions in Hollywood. Almost a year after applying to abandon the Subway–Hollywood Blvd. car line, Metro

An excellent night photo at the Hollywood Bowl showing 4801s ready to take concertgoers home over various routes. *SCRTD Collection*

New Year's is always a big bus day in Pasadena. The Rose Parade and the Rose Bowl football game cause an incredible traffic crunch which lures thousands onto buses for transportation to these events. Three Asbury Twins wait patiently to go into service on New Year's Day, 1955. *SCRTD Collection*

This page and opposite: Metro's two-tone green livery was about as complete a change from PE red as possible, and it took some time before the last red buses were repainted. Many Whites of course never wore Metro green. These views depict the various types of Yellow Coach, GM and White buses inherited by Metro as they appeared in the new paint scheme, which was later to be adopted by the Metropolitan Transit Authority as well and thus used on the Yellow Cars and buses taken over from Los Angeles Transit Lines.

All: SCRTD Collection except 3017: P. Allen Copeland

ROSTER OF BUSES

Metropolitan Coach Lines
Purchased from Pacific Electric Railway 10/1/53
(695 Buses)

Numbers	Make	Model	Seats	Built	Notes
225-232	GM	PDA-4101	45	1950	
1686-1694	Yellow	PG-3701	41	1940	6-71 diesel engines
2000-2023	White	788-6	41	1940	Suburban
2025-2049	White	798-6	45	1942	Suburban
2050-2094	White	798-6	45	1941	Suburban
2125-2129	Twin	44-D	44	1946	
2150	Twin	52-S2	52	1950	
2220-2234	White	798	44	1946	Hydrotorque
2235-2289	White	798	44	1947	Hydrotorque
2300-2319	White	798	45	1942	
2320-2324	White	798	44	1943	
2325-2379	White	798	44	1944	
2380-2394	White	798	44	1945	
2395-2409	White	798	44	1944	
2410-2422	White	798	44	1945	
2500-2534	Yellow	TD-4505	42	1941	Suburban
2600-2618	GM	TDH-4507	45	1947	
2619-2638	GM	TD-4507	45	1946	
2639-2677	Yellow	TD-4502	45	1940	
2678-2699	GM	TD-4506	45	1945	
2700	GM	TDH-4510	39	1949	
2701-2824	GM	TDH-5103	48	1950	
2825-2889	GM	TDH-5103	48	1951	
2900-2934	GM	TDH-4801	48	1953	
3000-3024	White	798	44	1948	Hydrotorque

TDH-4801 411 on the 91 line. The most famous movie theater in Hollywood provides the background. *SCRTD Collection*

received permission and substituted the second bus line 91 for the rail service on September 26, 1954. The new line was extended over the Hollywood–Beverly Hills–University line (77), and the equipment used was the last group of 400-series TDH-4801s, which had been in storage at West Hollywood since their delivery during the summer.

The rail replacement route (via Santa Monica Blvd.) was designated 91W and the Sunset Blvd. branch (an extension of the Gardner Jct. short turns on the car line) was designated 91S. Rush-hour use of the Hollywood Freeway was increased at this time as certain line 91 trips continued on the Freeway beyond Santa Monica Blvd. to the San Fernando Valley bypassing Hollywood.

Hollywood bus service was rearranged to alleviate traffic congestion by through-routing lines to avoid turning movements in areas of heavy traffic. Two short lines were grafted onto a single longer one, saving buses and platforms hours as well. The Western and Franklin line (78) and the Hollywoodland portion of the Hollywood–Beverly Hills–University line were appended to the Fairfax Avenue line (89, ex-LAMC), so that the busy intersection of Hollywood and Vine ceased to be a regular terminus. Moreover, the former LAMC Wilshire and Sunset lines were through-routed in downtown Los Angeles to reduce the number of buses terminating there; the Wilshire line became 83W and the Sunset service 83S. There was, however, more service on Wilshire than Sunset, so that there were still some Wilshire buses that terminated downtown.

In the Eastern District, Metro revised San Bernardino service effective in November 1954 by creating a new Rt. 60 between Los Angeles, San Bernardino and Redlands. All trips on line 63 beyond Pomona were transferred to the new line, which had two routings at first: Los Angeles–Pomona–San Bernardino–Redlands via Foothill Blvd. (60G) and Los Angeles–Pomona–Riverside–San Bernardino–Redlands via Valley Blvd. (60V). The Garvey Local (63G), Valley Local (63V), Brooklyn Avenue (63B), Baldwin Park and Pomona via Covina services stayed as Rt. 63. The Riverside–Arlington route (62), extended to San Bernardino and Redlands in 1947, was once again cut back to

A night view of El Monte Division in March of 1955. The Whites have not been repainted and the only evidence of new ownership are the words "Metropolitan Coach Lines" on the old PE herald. *SCRTD Collection*

end at Riverside. A little later, an alternate route via Arrow Highway was added to line 60.

Meanwhile, at the other end of the system, routes in the San Fernando Valley were rearranged and extended to serve new residential areas. On November 29, 1954, the Birmingham Hospital line (85) was extended to Reseda and cut back to Van Nuys, exchanging terminals with the Van Nuys–Canoga Park line (90) which was extended to Sherman Oaks in its place. Some Ventura Blvd. trips were rerouted at the western end of that line to serve the newly developed Encino Park area.

Divisional Operation. One of the major changes promised by Metro management was a revision of the operating structure of the system along the lines of a transit property, with semi-autonomous divisions, rather than a centralized interurban or intercity type of operation. This was accomplished by assigning certain administrative functions to newly established operating divisions, based in existing garages at Pasadena, Riverside, Long Beach, Ocean Park and Macy Street, plus new facilities at Van Nuys, El Monte and West Hollywood.

Centralization of maintenance was achieved in February 1954, when the capability to perform major body and engine work was transferred from Torrance Shops to Macy Street. By April, construction was in progress on new buildings and other improvements at the old Van Nuys storage lot, and this was reopened on June 30, 1954, as Metro's first new operating division. Van Nuys had a capacity of 66 buses and had cost $315,000 to rebuild.

Construction of the second new division began in August on two and a half acres of newly acquired land off Hoyt (now Santa Anita) Avenue, El Monte. This division was to relieve overcrowding at Macy Street by taking care of 127 buses assigned to San Gabriel Valley and San Bernardino services. Built at a cost of $350,000, it opened on January 1, 1955. On that day, too, Fairbanks garage, Long Beach, was changed over to the divisional mode of operation.

The second fleet of 100 new buses arrived in February 1955. Included were 83 TDH-4801s (501–583), largely

A Summer Day in San Bernardino

THE DEPOT ON 3rd Street between E and F, originally built by the Southern Pacific, was taken over by PE in 1914 when the interurban line from Los Angeles reached San Bernardino. A second story was soon added to accommodate PE's Eastern District offices. The mission-style station served PE trains as well as the connecting buses of the Mountain Auto Line and Motor Transit Co. for many years, eventually becoming an all-bus depot when rail passenger service ended. It served as a terminal for PE buses and later, those of successor Metropolitan Coach Lines. Later sold to Greyhound, it continued in use until it fell victim to the plague of urban renewal.

The date is June 13, 1955, and through the camera of Ira Swett, we record the comings and goings on the working side of the depot. Three generations of equipment parade by to fill the Los Angeles schedule. First we see 253, a brand-new MCL TDM-4515; next, a Limited run is covered by 229, an ex-PE PDA-4101 of 1950; and last, waiting to go into service is 2085, a 1941 White model 798-6 suburban.

All three buses had 45 forward-facing seats and underfloor loaders but varied widely in the origin of their designs. The White was basically a city bus built without the rear door and with luggage racks and high-back seats. 229, however, as evidenced by its drumhead tail sign, was a parlor bus, but with an added row of seats. The TDM-4515 was one of GM's first dedicated model purpose-built suburban buses continuing the line of the TD-4505 and TDM-4509. They were greatly favored by eastern operators, but a decided curiosity on the West Coast.

used to replace older equipment on the Whittier and Santa Ana lines (58W and 58S) and the Garvey and Valley Blvd. routes (63G and 63V). The other 17 new buses were suburban TDM-4515s (251–267), assigned to the San Bernardino and Riverside lines (60) because of their significant freeway mileage; the longest—70 miles.

New green and white "Metro Coach Lines" signs appeared on the terminal building at 6th and Main Streets on March 8, 1955, in place of the red "Pacific Electric" sign which had been a landmark since 1937. Service to a new Southern California attraction began on April 2, 1955, as new line 58D started carrying employees to a still unfinished Disneyland in Anaheim. Soon after the amusement park opened on July 18, doubles and even triples became commonplace on morning express runs.

Another area attraction received bus service for the first time a year later. Starting on July 23, 1956, certain line 58S trips were diverted via Buena Park and Stanton to serve Knott's Berry Farm.

Southern District Rail Lines. No fewer than 18 public hearings had been held on Metro's application to replace the four Southern District rail lines with buses during 1954, and the PUC's decision was finally announced on February 15, 1955. Metro's primary reason for wanting to substitute buses for the car lines was that the two-year period of rent-free operation would come to an end on October 1, and with PE completing its planned dieselization of freight operations, Metro would be obliged to pay the entire operating and maintenance costs of the electrical distribution system.

Opposition to bus substitution was vocal and well organized. Municipalities along the proposed route argued that buses would have to run over streets that were inadequate to accommodate them. Metro's planned use of the incomplete Long Beach Freeway aroused similar objections because of its choice of an interim alternate routing. Additional objections came from independent bus operators in San Pedro and Compton, and along Avalon Blvd., whose

Walt Disney dedicated his "new concept in family entertainment" on July 17, 1955. Starting in November, Disneyland saw special trips arrive direct from 6th and Main by this specially painted and decorated TDH-4801, 530. It is shown here on Disneyland's 1890s main street, not its usual venue. *SCRTD Collection*

Left: Specially painted by the Walt Disney Studios, TDH-4801 530 and a double are about to leave on the 9:45 a.m. express schedule. The almost impossible photograph was taken inside the Los Angeles Street Motor Coach Terminal in downtown Los Angeles. *SCRTD Collection*

business would be harmed by the change. Metro, meanwhile, had issued folders detailing the changeover of service and listing the line numbers assigned to the new bus routes:

72	Los Angeles–Long Beach
73	Los Angeles–San Pedro
74	Los Angeles–Bellflower
95	Watts

They were never to be used.

The preponderance of testimony was against Metro, and the Commission ruled accordingly despite its recognition that operating expenses would indeed increase because of expected equipment rental charges, and would later increase again when Metro took over maintenance of the overhead and substations. The argument was that a recently approved fare increase would still provide a sufficient return on Metro's investment. The company made its position clear on April 7 when it applied for a 22 percent interurban fare increase.

Since taking over PE's passenger service, Metro had benefited from two local fare increases, both joint with Los Angeles Transit Lines. The first had taken effect on November 30, 1953, when token prices were increased from three for 40 cents to seven for $1 without changing the 15-cent, first-zone cash fare or the 5-cent zone fare. Cash fares went up to 17 cents in the first zone and 6 cents in subsequent zones on March 7, 1955.

The PUC held hearings on Metro's new application to raise interurban fares (its first) during June and July 1955. An increase averaging about 19 percent was approved in September, and went into effect on October 17. The proposed equipment rental agreement had been submitted to the Commission in the meantime and had been approved at $50,000 annually: $32,000 for taxes and $18,000 for 78 rail cars.

Almost forgotten, a fifth Southern District rail line came to the attention of the PUC in the fall of 1955. In September, authorization was received by Metro to use buses on the Catalina Dock line (second route 53) during the winter or at other times when traffic did not warrant an interurban train. This was to be Metro's only success (albeit a seasonal one) in changing over a Southern District rail line. The first bus service was offered on November 31 and was operated sporadically thereafter.

Promotions. In order to counter the adverse criticism that it had inherited along with PE's transportation plant, Metro attempted to establish a new image—that of a friendly but harassed tax-paying corporate citizen. The office of Director of Public Relations was established and feelers were put out in an attempt to change the traveling public's attitude toward its transportation system.

Tours of Metro offices and facilities were arranged for community leaders, teachers and students. Service improvements and new equipment were introduced with great fanfare and much publicity. Chambers of Commerce and other community groups were courted to gain grassroots support throughout the service area. A program of free return fares for shoppers was instituted with some success in Huntington Park and later in Van Nuys. A particularly bright spot resulted when a Christmas promotion for the Wilshire Miracle Mile shopping district produced a vividly painted TDH-4801 complete with snowmen.

Haugh's public relations ventures were successful and resulted in some changed attitudes, but unfortunately the stigma left by PE's latter-day, public-be-damned attitude was difficult to overcome. One area that was constantly pressed to the public was that of countering rail rapid transit plans with the concept that the freeways were Los Angeles' real rapid transit system. Some schedule times were indeed shortened as more freeways were completed and additional lines rerouted to use them. The problem was that increasing traffic density defeated these gains as they were made. It was not until the opening of the El Monte Busway by the Southern California Rapid Transit District that freeway routes could show measurably better performance than those on neighboring streets.

The promotions did, however, prove that it was possible to communicate with the public and that favorable results could be gained. These efforts would become widely imitated and become the model for such efforts throughout the industry.

Buses Return to Glendale. As in the Southern District, a tortuous path was followed to abandonment of the Glendale–Burbank rail line. The Los Angeles Board of Public Utilities and Transportation had turned down the first conversion proposal after PUC approval. Reapplying to the PUC, Metro again received permission to abandon the rail line. The decision ignored protests of the Glendale City Council, and the Los Angeles Board continued to withhold its approval. When the 1.8-mile private right-of-way on Glendale Blvd. and Allesandro Street (valued at $100,000) was offered to the city for one dollar, the Los Angeles City Council intervened in favor of Metro, causing the resignation of the president of the Board.

The changeover finally took place on June 19, 1955. The 30 multiple-unit PCC cars judged unsuitable for use on the Southern District, went into storage in the now unused subway, replaced by 40 new 500-series TDH-4801s which had been held at Torrance Shops since February. The bus line (75B) was operated as part of Rt. 75, through-routed with trips to Santa Monica via either Beverly Hills or Venice Blvd.

In an attempt to accommodate one of the objections to the replacement of Glendale rail service, Metro had offered to institute a short feeder line through a hilly area adjacent to the rail right-of-way in the Silver Lake district. The proposed 96–Lake View Heights route would have operated on narrow, hilly streets, and Metro, lacking suitable equipment had offered to obtain "a 23-passenger, 30-foot, gasoline-powered bus" especially for this line. The PUC declined the proposal, citing the inhospitable geography and the predicted sparse patronage as reasons.

Asbury Routes Consolidated. Between August 1954 and the fall of 1955, the operations of Metropolitan Coach Lines and Asbury Rapid Transit had for all practical purposes come under a single management. Some facilities had been integrated, and a common labor contract had

Free Rides

For Shoppers In Huntington Park

SAVE MONEY by taking advantage of the fare refund plan now available to people who buy in Huntington Park.

Fare refund checks are issued on all streetcar and bus lines leading to the excellent downtown Huntington Park shopping center. Ask your operator for a refund check for 17c, 23c, or 30c when you pay your fare.

After making a purchase of $2 or more at your favorite store, present the refund coupon on the date punched, and you'll receive free return fare.

The coupons are issued Monday through Saturday between 9 a.m. and 5 p.m., and on Mondays and Fridays from 9 a.m. to 8 p.m.

Co-operating in this money-saving plan are the progressive Huntington Park merchants listed elsewhere in this bulletin.

RIDE HOME FREE

After Buying at These Huntington Park Stores:

BARCUS PHOTO SERVICE
2662 E. Florence Ave.

BOND'S
6421 Pacific Blvd.

BONELLI'S, INC.
2621 E. Gage Ave.

CO-ED SMART SHOPPE
6525 Pacific Blvd.

COMAR'S CHILDREN'S FINE SHOES
6358 Pacific Blvd.

DAYTON'S JEWELRY
2676 E. Florence Ave.

DEARDEN'S
6315 Pacific Blvd.

EDDY'S MEN'S WEAR
7009 Pacific Blvd.

JAY ELAM & SONS
6328 Pacific Blvd.

W. T. GRANT CO.
6409 Pacific Blvd.

HARGRAVES STATIONERS
6310 Pacific Blvd.

HUNTER'S INC.
6831 Pacific Blvd.

HUNTINGTON PARK TUX SHOP
2610 Saturn Ave.

JAY'S LUGGAGE SHOP
6532 Pacific Blvd.

JOYCE SHOP
6704 Pacific Blvd.

KEMP'S KIDDY SHOP
6900 Pacific Blvd.

KIRK JEWELRY CO.
6619 Pacific Blvd.

LEONA'S
6712 Pacific Blvd.

LEVENSON'S
6509 Pacific Blvd.

LLOYD'S
6815 A Pacific Blvd.

MARSH'S
6609 Pacific Blvd.

MODERN WOMAN
6915 Pacific Blvd.

MAYOR JEWELRY CO.
6507 Pacific Blvd.

MORRIS'
6623 Pacific Blvd.

PACIFIC TELEVISION & APPLIANCE CO.
6332 Pacific Blvd.

PUNCH & JUDY KIDDIE WEAR
6815 Pacific Blvd.

RALEIGH LTD.
6620 Pacific Blvd.

George Allen
RED CROSS SHOES
6708 Pacific Blvd.

TATE'S
6523 Pacific Blvd.

VARON'S JEWELRY
6502 Pacific Blvd.

FREE RIDES FOR HUNTINGTON PARK SHOPPERS

HUNTINGTON PARK

RETURN TRIP FREE

WITH $2.00 PURCHASE AT HUNTINGTON PARK STORES
(LISTED ON BACK)

ON
- LOS ANGELES TRANSIT LINES
- METROPOLITAN COACH LINES
- SOUTHERN CITIES TRANSIT, INC.
- ATKINSON TRANSPORTATION CO.

A cash fare refund promotion was started in June of 1955 with the Huntington Park Chamber of Commerce and Merchants Association. The Metro public relations department also advertised the bargain fares using radio spots and newspaper ads. A "take one" leaflet is reproduced here.
Both: SCRTD Collection

Coach 328 was painted Chinese red with white snowmen and placed in service on Western District lines December 5, 1955, to promote the Wilshire Miracle Mile shopping district. It was returned to its normal green and white after the Christmas season. *SCRTD Collection*

been negotiated with employees of both companies. Studies of common fares and fare zones as well as a joint transfer arrangement were completed and presented to the PUC, along with a proposal for route revisions.

Metro moved toward consolidating Asbury with its own operations on August 7, 1955, when Metro's Sunland storage lot was closed and part of Metro (once Motor Transit) line 56 was moved into Asbury's Glendale garage. Since there were no diesel fueling facilities at Glendale, Metro leased 13 propane Twins from Asbury to operate the service. Also Asbury closed its San Fernando lot and leased 15 GM diesels from Metro to operate its lines 14 and 15 plus part of line 12 from the Van Nuys division. Asbury line 21 was operated from Metro's West Hollywood division using 2600-series diesels.

In order to reduce confusion, all Asbury buses were repainted into Metro colors, but they continued to carry the Asbury Rapid Transit name. The leased buses were relettered for their new operators, so that the Asbury name appeared for the first time on a diesel bus.

The proposed route changes were put into effect on August 29, 1955. Metro Rt. 86 on Riverside Drive was revised and extended to replace Asbury Rt. 13 and the St. Joseph's Hospital leg of 19. Use of the Hollywood terminal was discontinued, with the Culver City and Lockheed lines through-routed and combined into new Rt. 22 from Hollywood and La Brea to Burbank via Universal City and Olive Avenue. A new Rt. 14–Burbank–North Hollywood–San Fernando was created by through-routing the 14 and 18 lines at North Hollywood, and the Victory Blvd. line (20) was extended to a new shopping center in Van Nuys. Former PE lines were also revised: the North Hollywood–Studio City–Sherman Oaks line (87) was cut back to Studio City except for school trips, and the North Hollywood line (88) was extended to Van Nuys via Van Owen Street.

Asbury's San Fernando terminal was given up a year later, on August 20, 1956, and the lines terminating there were rerouted accordingly. The Van Nuys–Reseda line (85) was extended to San Fernando, Northridge, L.A. State College and Granada Hills to offer an alternate routing to the direct line along Sepulveda Blvd. (84).

West Hollywood Division. Construction was started on the largest of the three proposed new operating bases on October 17, 1955. The design was similar to Van Nuys and El Monte, and the location was 4½ acres bought from the Southern Pacific along San Vicente Blvd., West Hollywood, adjacent to PE's old Sherman Carhouse. The 132-bus garage was opened on July 16, 1956, and cost $515,000. At Macy Street, new light towers were erected and modern paint spray booths installed during 1956.

Equipment purchases in 1956 consisted of 23 (not 100) buses. Three TDM-4515s (200–202) with 41 reclining seats were assigned to the San Bernardino line, while 20 TDH-4801s (600–619) came earmarked for replacement of the Bellflower rail service. When it became plain that this hope was not to be realized, and new buses were placed in operation on the experimental "Park-Ride Flyer" route between the Hollywood Bowl parking lot and downtown Los Angeles, started with 400-series 4801s on November 26, 1956. After averaging 40 to 100 autos a day over its contemplated 90-day trial period, the park-ride line was given the benefit of continued operation and expanded publicity in an attempt to bring traffic up to the breakeven point of about 2,000 riders per week. It was doomed to failure since, like so many such services, it picked up its riders at the end of the bottleneck (Cahuenga Pass in this case) rather than at the beginning. Traffic leveled off at 100 passengers per week, and the service was discontinued on May 24, 1957.

A TDH-5103 is snapped under the canopy of the Subway Terminal bus deck. Once an automobile parking area, it was reconstructed to provide offstreet loading for the Western District interurban bus lines.
Interurban Press

Below: The Olive Street loading area was on the west side of the street between 4th and 5th streets. It relieved the pressure on the Subway Terminal bus deck by providing offstreet loading for lines 51, 76 and 86. *SCRTD Collection*

Headsigns. Metro changed the headsign layout of its buses to a more common configuration in 1956. All the postwar GM's (except 2700) which had been delivered with the two-piece PE signs were converted to the new one-quarter (curbside) and three-quarter (street side) layout. The short sign displayed the route/branch designation (like 94 or 58W) and the long sign the destination—a town name or a street.

At this time, the 2700, 2800, 2900, 251, 300, 400 and 500 series were changed over to the new signs and shortly thereafter, the prewar Yellows and GM's (2500s and 2600s) were also converted. The Whites, whose limited life was recognized, and the 225 and 1685 series parlor coaches (which had half-size signs) were not converted. The 600 and 200 series coaches which arrived in that year were delivered with the new layout.

Rail Ownership. With no hope in sight of being able to substitute buses for the remaining rail lines, Metro decided to buy the equipment and facilities needed to continue their operation. The PUC approved sale of 78 interurban cars, seven pieces of work equipment, the substations and

This view of Glendale Division in MCL days shows the results of a general cleanup as well as the Asbury equipment repainted into Metro green.
SCRTD Collection

the overhead by Pacific Electric to Metropolitan Coach lines on December 23, 1956. Metro put $15,000 down toward the $525,000 purchase price, rationalizing the transaction by the fact that the company would now be paying less in interest charges than it previously had in rental fees.

The decision was spurred by the end of PE electric freight service on December 11, 1956, with the sole exception of night switching at West Hollywood, which was to last until January 1958.

Out in the San Fernando Valley, Asbury's Burbank Blvd. line (19) was extended into North Hollywood and the Riverside Drive line (86) was extended to Pacoima in 1957. The Brentwood Branch of the Santa Monica via Beverly Hills line was again appended to the Wilshire route and designated 83B. All San Bernardino and Riverside trips as well as peak-hour Pomona via Covina runs were routed via the San Bernardino Freeway on June 3, 1957. At this time Metro and Asbury together owned 762 buses, including 36 propane Twins, 95 gasoline Whites and one gas Twin (2150). Metro had replaced more than 200 inherited Whites, and in fact about 60 of the remaining 95 were spares or were in storage at Macy Street. The remaining buses were, of course, all GM diesels.

Race Track Service. Metro inherited the Hollywood–Santa Anita and Hollywood–Hollywood Park lines from the Asbury Rapid Transit System and the Los Angeles–Santa Anita service as part of PE's route 68. Metro continued to expand these services as new rights from Los Angeles to Los Alamitos Race Track were received in February of 1955 and additional rights to Santa Anita from Santa Ana, Riverside and San Bernardino were received in July of 1957. The race track services (grouped as route 57)

Van Nuys Division. Most of the buses are 400s, but emerging from the wash rack is 2689 lettered "Asbury" on the front panels.
National Motor Museum

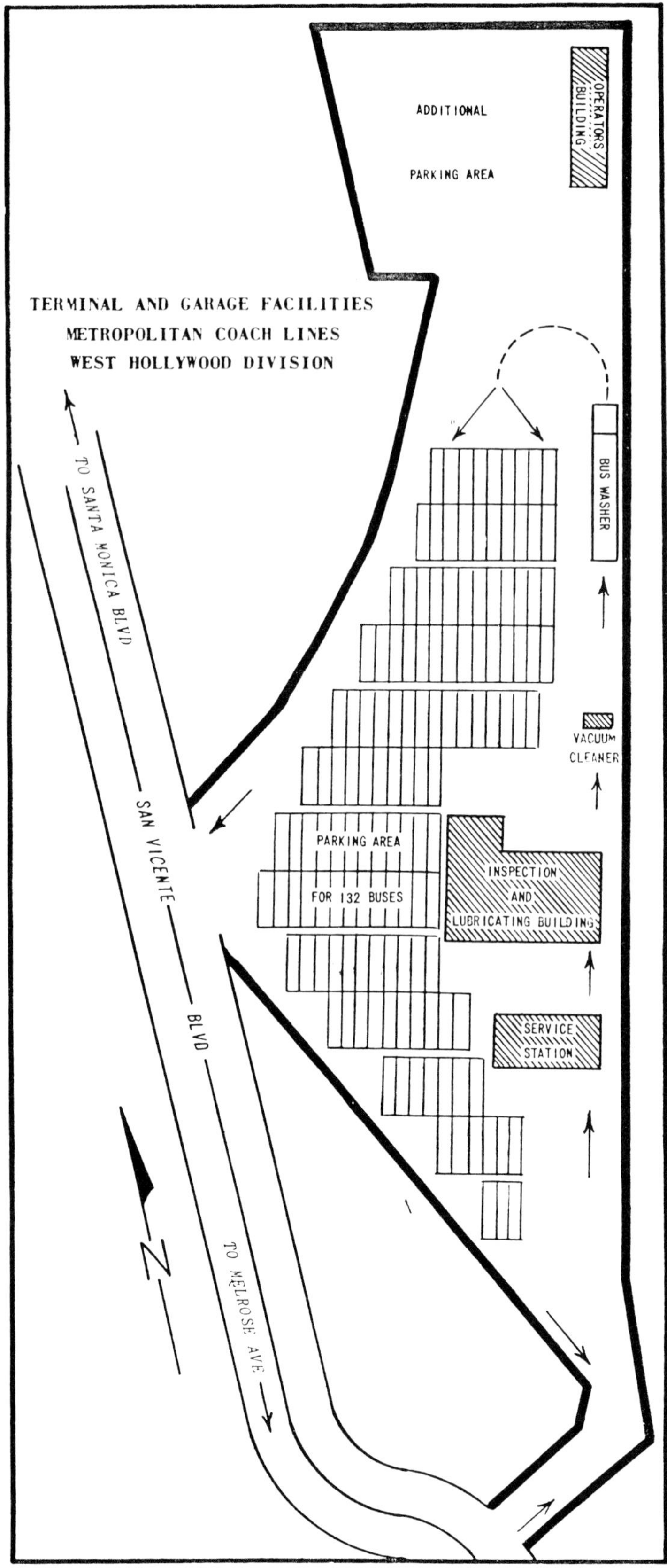

Grading began October 17, 1955, on the 4¾-acre site of the new West Hollywood Division. This plot plan shows the layout for the efficient flow of operations as buses pulled in from their runs. The new facility housed coaches for lines 21, 83S, 83W, 88, 91 and 94. *Author's Collection*

ROSTER OF BUSES

Metropolitan Coach Lines New Equipment (1953–1958)

Numbers	Make	Model	Seats	Built	Notes
301-330	GM	TDH-4801	48	1953	Built for Key System
400-499	GM	TDH-4801	48	1954	
251-267	GM	TDM-4515	45	1955	Suburban
501-583	GM	TDH-4801	48	1955	
200-202	GM	TDM-4515	41	1956	Suburban
600-619	GM	TDH-4801	48	1956	

Buses turned over to Los Angeles Metropolitan Transit Authority 3/3/58: 200-202, 225-232, 251-267, 301-330, 400-499, 501-583, 600-619, 1686-1694, 2150, 2220-2289, 2500-2534, 2600-2699, 2700, 2701-2889, 2900-2934, 3000-3024 (726 buses).

were well patronized and primarily used suburban equipment drawn from the spares at each operating division.

Bellflower. The PUC finally permitted conversion of the Bellflower rail line in March 1957; the first application had been filed on December 12, 1955. The decision included an employee compensation clause to which Metro objected; the case went to the California Supreme Court and the PUC was upheld, but Metro refused to change the line to buses until a more equitable labor agreement could be reached. The company asked for an extension of the time limit for acceptance of the new certificate, expecting to settle the issue as part of negotiations for a new labor contract though the stated reason was a shortage of buses.

As it turned out, contract talks broke down as the old agreement expired on December 1, 1957, and the Metro system ground to a halt. The only previous labor dispute that had affected these routes was the nationwide rail strike of 1946. The walkout lasted 54 days, and the vote to accept a 21-cent wage increase and a five-day week was 511 to 490. The strike lent impetus to a growing movement for legislative action to allow unified ownership and operation of the region's transportation systems, thought necessary to provide more effective transit planning.

As of June 1, 1957, Metro and Asbury operated 53 bus lines totaling 1,315 route miles and four rail lines totaling 68 route miles.

LAMTA. The Los Angeles Metropolitan Transit Authority already existed, having been created by the legislature in 1951 to study the feasibility of a monorail system in the Los Angeles area. After years of study with no tangible results, a bill was passed and signed in 1957 to enable the Authority to own and operate any form of transit system.

Only Metropolitan Coach Lines, with its subsidiary Asbury Rapid Transit, and Los Angeles Transit Lines then remained as major local transit entities in the area. LAMTA

The new West Hollywood Division on July 16, 1956, with Sherman Carhouse in the distance on the right. Two buses have barely visible "Asbury" lettering.
SCRTD Collection

Right: "Bald-headed" TDH-4801 No. 315 gets squeaky clean at West Hollywood Division in July of 1956. Washers installed at the new divisions helped Metro establish a better image for its passengers.
SCRTD Collection

was given options to buy these properties for $33 million, and the underwriting of a $40 million bond issue was secured to accomplish the purchase On March 3, 1958, Metro bought out Asbury as a matter of administrative and legal convenience, and on the same day all three systems passed to the Authority. The purchase price of the Metro and Asbury operations was $13.6 million.

Despite his continued efforts, Jesse Haugh never succeeded in his quest for an all-bus Metro system. When negotiations to sell were completed, all four Southern District rail lines were still operating, and 73 interurban cars went to LAMTA along with 822 buses, 60 of which were just being delivered. The order consisted of 10 additional 41-passenger reclining seat TDM-4515s (203–212) and 50 more TDH-4801s (620–669). When Metro's operating rights were formally revoked by the PUC on August 26, 1958, the Pacific Electric bus story was brought to an end.

In 1956 the layout of the front route and destination signs was changed to the arrangement used until recently in Los Angeles. Note the "74" route sign in this view, the proposed route number for the Bellflower line for which the 600s were intended.
SCRTD Collection

A close view of 201, posed in Griffith Park when new in 1956. Metro 200-202 became LAMTA 2400-2402, and, along with 10 similar buses ordered by Metro but not delivered until after the takeover, they were sold fairly early because of their lower seating capacity.
SCRTD Collection

After eliminating the last Western Division rail line (to Glendale and Burbank) in 1955, MCL was still left with the interurban lines to Long Beach, San Pedro and Bellflower. This operation, which MCL repeatedly tried to rid itself of, was typified by this vignette of "Blimp" 314 northbound at Slauson Tower. But the rail lines actually outlived the private company and were inherited by its successor, Los Angeles Metropolitan Transit Authority which finally retired them in 1961. *Interurban Press*

The PDA-4101s of the 225-232 series were most often found on the San Bernardino line in Metro days, occasionally on the Newport Beach service, and were frequently called upon for charter duties.
SCRTD Collection

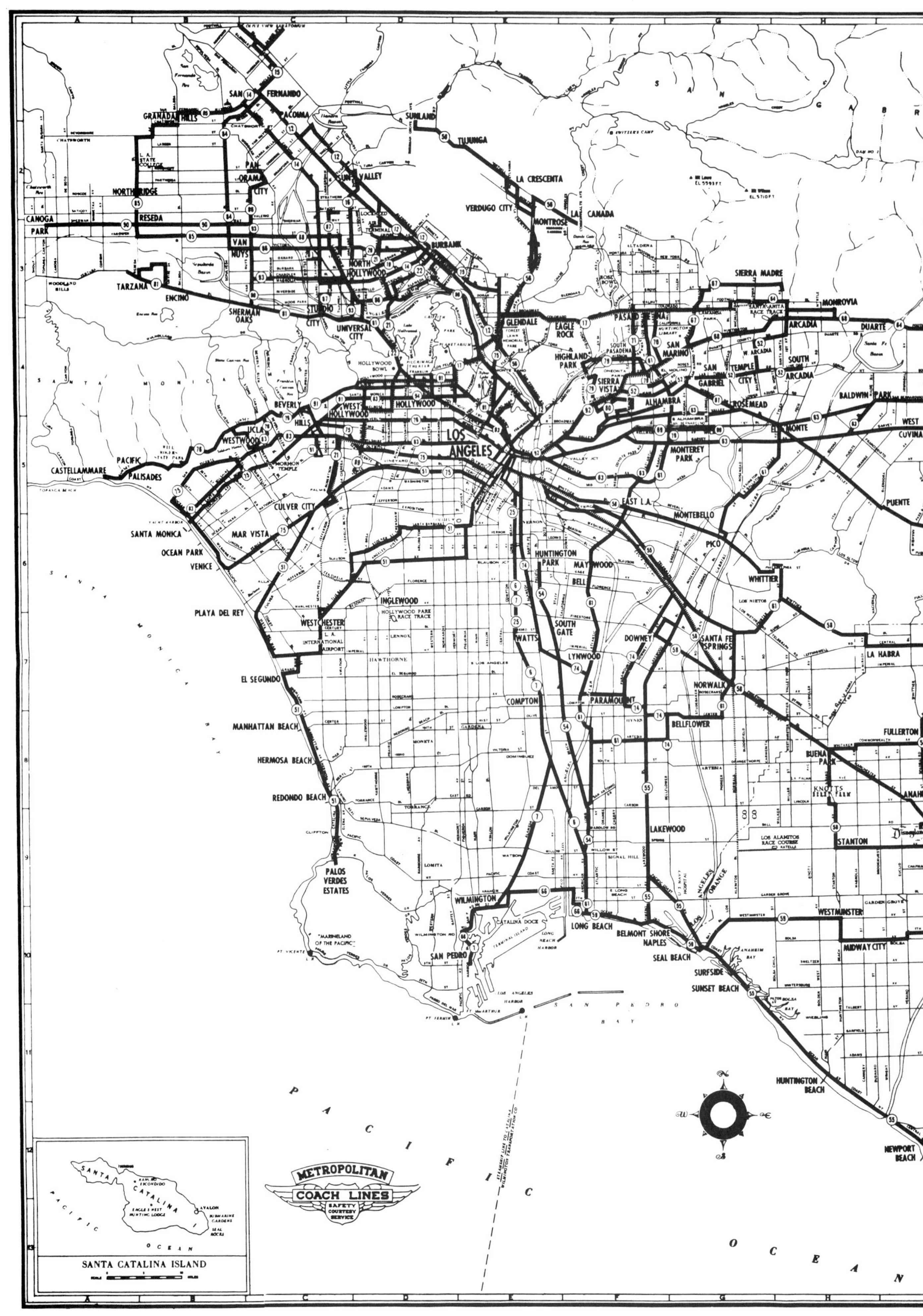
METROPOLITAN
COACH LINES
SAFETY
COURTESY
SERVICE
SANTA CATALINA ISLAND
LOS ANGELES
HOLLYWOOD
PASADENA
GLENDALE
BURBANK
LONG BEACH
SAN PEDRO
WILMINGTON
SANTA MONICA
VENICE
REDONDO BEACH
HERMOSA BEACH
MANHATTAN BEACH
EL SEGUNDO
INGLEWOOD
COMPTON
WHITTIER
NORWALK
DOWNEY
FULLERTON
HUNTINGTON BEACH
NEWPORT BEACH
SEAL BEACH
SAN FERNANDO
VAN NUYS
NORTH HOLLYWOOD
PACIFIC OCEAN

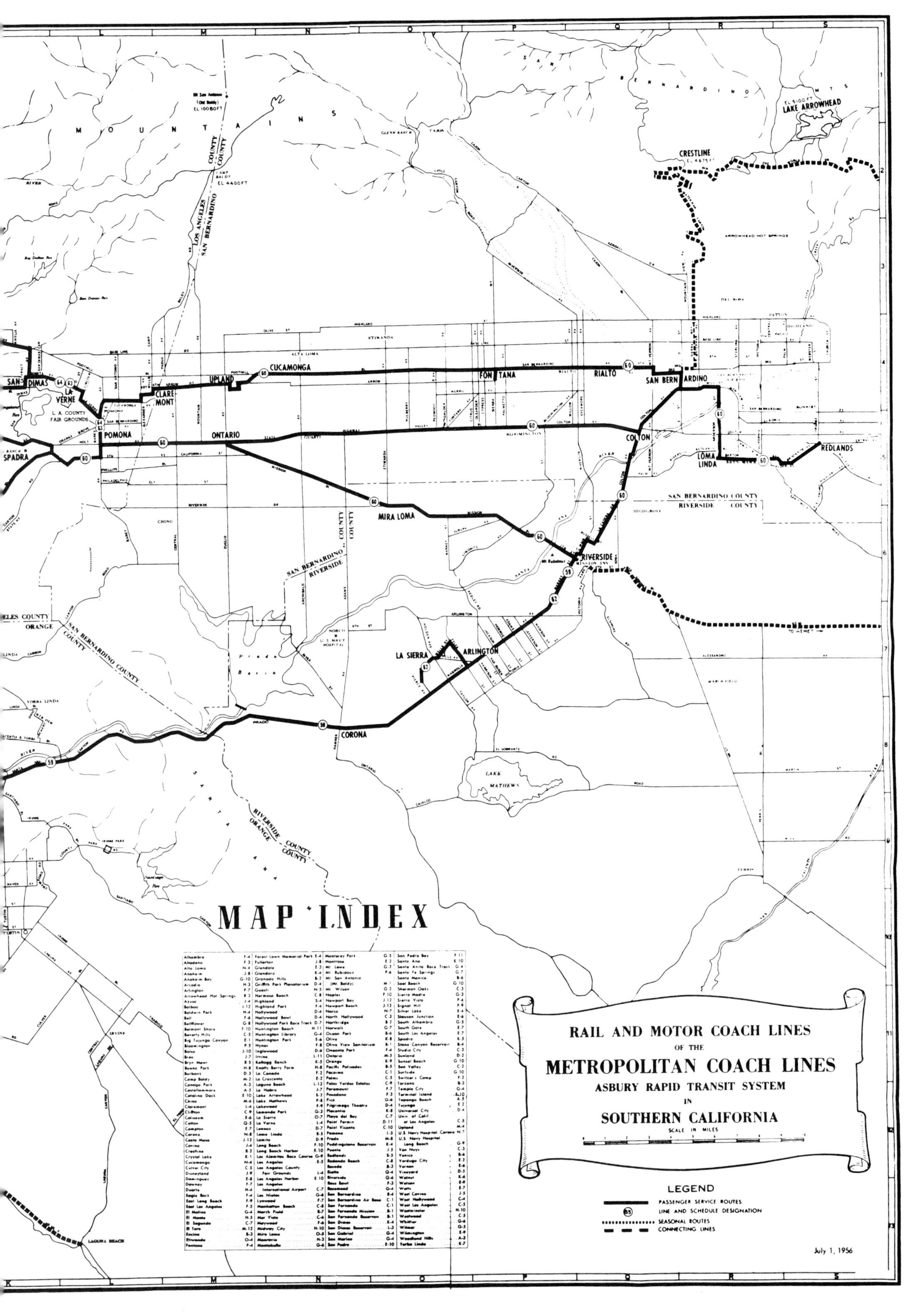

MOUNTAINS
SAN BERNARDINO MTS
Mt San Antonio (Old Baldy) EL 10080 FT
Camp Baldy EL 4400 FT
LAKE ARROWHEAD EL 5100 FT
CRESTLINE EL 4675 FT
ARROWHEAD HOT SPRINGS
LOS ANGELES COUNTY
SAN BERNARDINO COUNTY
SAN DIMAS
LA VERNE
L. A. COUNTY FAIR GROUNDS
CLAREMONT
POMONA
SPADRA
UPLAND
CUCAMONGA
ONTARIO
FONTANA
RIALTO
SAN BERNARDINO
COLTON
LOMA LINDA
REDLANDS
SAN BERNARDINO COUNTY
RIVERSIDE COUNTY
MIRA LOMA
RIVERSIDE
MISSION INN
LA SIERRA
ARLINGTON
CORONA
LAKE MATHEWS
CHINO
ETIWANDA
TO HEMET
SAN BERNARDINO COUNTY
ORANGE COUNTY
RIVERSIDE COUNTY
ORANGE COUNTY
MAP INDEX
Alhambra F-4
Altadena F-3
Alta Loma N-4
Anaheim J-8
Anaheim Bay G-10
Arcadia H-3
Arlington P-7
Arrowhead Hot Springs R-3
Azusa J-4
Balboa J-12
Baldwin Park H-4
Bell F-6
Bellflower G-8
Belmont Shore F-10
Beverly Hills C-5
Big Tujunga Canyon E-1
Bloomington P-5
Bolsa J-10
Brea J-7
Bryn Mawr R-5
Buena Park H-8
Burbank D-3
Camp Baldy M-2
Canoga Park A-3
Castellammare A-5
Catalina Dock E-10
Chino M-6
Claremont L-4
Clifton C-9
Coliseum E-6
Colton Q-5
Compton E-7
Corona N-8
Costa Mesa J-12
Covina J-4
Crestline R-2
Crystal Lake K-1
Cucamonga N-4
Culver City C-5
Disneyland J-9
Dominguez E-8
Downey F-7
Duarte H-4
Eagle Rock F-4
East Long Beach F-9
East Los Angeles F-5
El Molino G-4
El Monte H-5
El Segundo C-7
El Toro M-12
Encino B-3
Etiwanda O-4
Fontana P-4
Forest Lawn Memorial Park E-4
Fullerton J-8
Glendale E-3
Glendora K-4
Granada Hills B-2
Griffith Park Planetarium D-4
Guasti N-5
Hermosa Beach C-8
Highland S-4
Highland Park F-4
Hollywood D-4
Hollywood Bowl D-4
Hollywood Park Race Track D-7
Huntington Beach H-11
Huntington Library G-4
Huntington Park E-6
Hynes F-8
Inglewood D-6
Irvine L-11
Kellogg Ranch K-5
Knotts Berry Farm H-8
La Canada F-2
La Crescenta E-2
Laguna Beach L-13
La Habra J-7
Lake Arrowhead S-2
Lake Mathews P-8
Lakewood F-9
Lamanda Park G-3
La Sierra O-7
La Verne L-4
Lennox D-7
Loma Linda R-5
Lomita D-9
Long Beach F-10
Long Beach Harbor E-10
Los Alamitos Race Course G-9
Los Angeles E-5
Los Angeles County Fair Grounds L-4
Los Angeles Harbor E-10
Los Angeles International Airport C-7
Los Nietos G-6
Lynwood F-7
Manhattan Beach C-8
March Field R-7
Mar Vista C-6
Maywood F-6
Midway City H-10
Mira Loma O-5
Monrovia H-3
Montebello G-6
Monterey Park G-5
Montrose E-2
Mt. Lowe G-2
Mt. Rubidoux P-6
Mt. San Antonio (Mt. Baldy) M-1
Mt. Wilson G-2
Naples F-10
Newport Bay J-12
Newport Beach J-12
Norco N-7
North Hollywood C-3
Northridge B-2
Norwalk G-7
Ocean Park B-6
Olive K-8
Olive View Sanitorium B-1
Oneonta Park F-4
Ontario M-5
Orange K-9
Pacific Palisades B-5
Pacoima C-1
Palms C-5
Palos Verdes Estates C-9
Paramount F-7
Pasadena F-3
Pico G-6
Pilgrimage Theatre D-4
Placentia K-8
Playa del Rey C-7
Point Fermin D-11
Point Vicente C-10
Pomona L-5
Prado M-8
Puddingstone Reservoir K-4
Puente J-5
Redlands S-5
Redondo Beach C-8
Reseda B-3
Rialto Q-4
Riverside Q-6
Rose Bowl F-3
Rosemead G-4
San Bernardino R-4
San Bernardino Air Base C-1
San Fernando C-1
San Fernando Mission B-1
San Fernando Reservoir B-1
San Dimas K-4
San Dimas Reservoir L-3
San Gabriel G-4
San Marino G-4
San Pedro E-10
San Pedro Bay F-11
Santa Ana K-10
Santa Anita Race Track G-4
Santa Fe Springs G-7
Santa Monica B-6
Seal Beach G-10
Sherman Oaks C-3
Sierra Madre G-3
Sierra Vista F-4
Signal Hill F-9
Silver Lake E-4
Slauson Junction E-6
South Alhambra G-5
South Gate E-7
South Los Angeles E-7
Spadra K-5
Stone Canyon Reservoir B-4
Studio City C-3
Sunland D-2
Sunset Beach G-10
Sun Valley C-2
Surfside G-10
Switzer's Camp F-2
Tarzana B-3
Temple City G-4
Terminal Island E-10
Topanga Beach A-5
Tujunga E-2
Universal City D-4
Univ. of Calif. at Los Angeles C-5
Upland M-4
U.S. Navy Hospital, Corona N-7
U.S. Navy Hospital, Long Beach G-9
Van Nuys C-3
Venice B-6
Verdugo City E-2
Vernon E-6
Vineyard D-5
Walnut K-6
Watson E-9
Watts E-7
West Covina J-5
West Hollywood C-4
West Los Angeles C-5
Westminster H-10
Westwood C-5
Whittier G-6
Wilmar G-5
Wilmington E-9
Woodland Hills A-3
Yorba Linda K-7
RAIL AND MOTOR COACH LINES
OF THE
METROPOLITAN COACH LINES
ASBURY RAPID TRANSIT SYSTEM
IN
SOUTHERN CALIFORNIA
SCALE IN MILES
LEGEND
PASSENGER SERVICE ROUTES
LINE AND SCHEDULE DESIGNATION
SEASONAL ROUTES
CONNECTING LINES
July 1, 1956

SUNLAND

MOTOR COACH LINE 56

Los Angeles-Glendale-
Montrose-Verdugo City-
La Canada-Tujunga-
Sunland

No Passengers will be handled locally between any two points both of which are South or East of Verdugo and San Fernando Roads.

Subject to Change Without Notice

Schedule 56-7

610 SOUTH MAIN STREET
LOS ANGELES 14, CALIFORNIA

MCL adapted the earlier Pacific Electric timetable designs to reflect its new image. Shown is the cover of a line 56 schedule in 1955. *G. L. Squier Collection*

Better Transit

Over Metro-Asbury Lines

in the

San Fernando Valley

Begins

August 29, 1955

METROPOLITAN COACH LINES
610 S. Main St.
Los Angeles 14, Calif.

TRinity 2792

●

ASBURY RAPID TRANSIT SYSTEM
319 W. Los Feliz Road
Glendale 4, Calif.

CItrus 2-8845

Integration of Metro and Asbury lines in the San Fernando Valley was announced with this brochure in August of 1955. *G. L. Squier Collection*

EPILOGUE

Did the Newport line get posher buses because Pacific Electric President Oscar A. Smith was a commuter? In rail days, he treated himself (and fellow passengers) to the club car "Commodore." Could be—but at any rate here is a PG-3701 of the 1685 class whipping down the Pacific Coast Highway on the way to Newport and Balboa, circa 1952. The buses had been rebuilt with 6-71 diesel engines and repainted into the teardrop livery. The abandoned interurban tracks can be seen just behind the bus in the dunes along the shore. *Interurban Press*

SO MANY WORDS have been said about Pacific Electric's destruction by the bus manufacturing, oil and rubber interests, but the truth lies much closer to home. It was the Southern Pacific as owner, the Public Utilities Commission as regulator and the City of Los Angeles as an apathetic bystander that forced PE's passenger traffic from rail to bus.

Remembering always that PE's parent was in the transportation business (not necessarily *rail* transportation) the events described become quite understandable. Realizing that PE's real worth to SP was as an originator of freight, not as a passenger carrier, make the results of these events inevitable. There was never any question of PE's place in the scheme of things as far as SP was concerned and postwar happenings forced the public and the press to recognize the same facts.

It is an interesting sidelight to this history that the trunk lines of the Motor Transit system, at first submerged into a subsidiary role to PE's interurbans, eventually returned as strong bus routes when the rail plant wore down. Pacific Electric kept Motor Transit ready just as parent Southern Pacific had used its subsidiary Southern Pacific Motor Transport during the twenties.

When it became clear in the postwar years that there was no quick fix for a rundown rail plant operated by obsolete methods with antiquated equipment, PE looked for a more economical solution and found it. A straightforward evaluation was made at that time between gasoline and diesel buses, and as on every other large transit property in the country (Chicago's preoccupation with propane excepted) the same conclusion was reached. World War II had brought the technology of the diesel engine coupled with the hydraulic transmission to new heights of efficiency and reliability, and it was time to apply these advances.

The fact that General Motors had a better engineered product to sell and had, like a good many enterprising businesses, set up favorable financing arrangements, have somehow come to be held as "unfair advantages." Whatever happened to free enterprise, anyhow? If there was any favoritism in PE's equipment evaluation, it was in the substitution of eight parlor buses in lieu of more mundane equipment by the irrepressible PE President O.A. Smith for his beloved Newport Beach line.

The battle between the Southern Pacific and the PUC regarding the complicated financial relationships which SP had developed with its subsidiary was becoming more heated and SP found an expedient solution. The rental agreements, leases, mortgages and bonds related to equipment, tracks and real estate were all becoming more costly to maintain in an area of postwar inflation and increasing labor costs. The results of the financial evaluation were obvious and both parties, agreeing to disagree on methods of restoring the rail plant to viability, chose a different and less expensive solution: bus substitution.

PE waited, in vain, for the formulation of a local transportation policy. On the state level, commitment to the growing freeway system was clear, and instead of fostering more dedicated, grade-separated right-of-way (as through Cahuenga Pass) the City of Los Angeles remained mute. While the politicians debated and the newspapers lamented, no coherent plan, much less one dollar of financing, came forth. Meanwhile, the increase in the number of automobiles and miles of freeway made any plans other than those for bus substitution academic.

If there was any influence on the course of events by the oil and rubber interests, it was to promote at the local and state levels the trend that was already in full swing, toward the freeway and the automobile. Nowhere was this change as evident as it was in Southern California. The voices promoting rail transit were weak and the initial capital expenditure was high. Once again, the circumstances which had spurred the growth of the motor coach industry in the twenties were prevalent and again, the industry responded.

The appearance of Jesse Haugh allowed the SP to return to what it knew best to be profitable, hauling freight. Haugh applied hard-won business sense to the operation of the former PE transportation plant. An organization was adopted which allowed someone other than the President to make a day-to-day operating decision and self-contained regional operating units were instituted. New forays in the field of public relations were attempted but came to naught as Haugh became the focal point for the public abuse brought on by years of SP neglect.

Inevitably, private ownership could not maintain profitable operation and the Los Angeles Metropolitan Transit Authority was reconstituted from a planning agency to assume operation of the regional transportation system. The operations of LAMTA and its successor, the Southern California Rapid Transit District, are certainly a prime subject for future discussion, but some interesting aspects of their growth deserve mention here.

First, the basic Pacific Electric/Motor Transit/Asbury interurban and suburban route structure remained recognizable through innumerable reidentifications, changes, combinations and recombinations. Secondly, local operations in Glendale, Alhambra, Pasadena, Pomona and (for a time) Riverside were reunited with the larger system from which they had been separated. Other local operations in the area to the southeast of Los Angeles and in Inglewood and San Pedro were also acquired and incorporated into the regional system.

The passenger terminals of bygone years have mainly been replaced, but an occasional building, spared by urban renewal, can still be recognized. Operating facilities have generally endured, but modernization has obliterated some well-remembered landmarks as well as providing some new ones. Certain operating methods, equipment peculiarities and tariff restrictions can still be traced to the earliest origins of the pioneer bus operators. Old customs die hard and with serious rail planning becoming a reality and double-deckers seen again on Wilshire Blvd., who can tell what other revolutionary ideas will bring us once again, full circle, to the heyday of those pioneer transportation operators.

Index

Bold face numbers denote illustrations.

S

T

U

V

W

Y